# DOUBLE TAKE

# ACT TWO

## *JOHN BADDELEY*

*With*
*Illustrations by MAC*

# Contents

## Act Two

## *END*

# Act Two

## 33

## BRASS MONKEYS

It doesn't always rain in Manchester but the winter of '68 was hellish cold, so presumably it had frozen over. 'Flu was sweeping the country almost as badly as the Asian outbreak of '57 and I had it. Another call from Granada took me back for an episode of a series with the overall title of *City '68*. The title for this particular story could have been *Over My Dead Body* – if it wasn't, it should have been. The plot centred on the problem of a town council that was desperate to find space for a new housing development. The only area of any size was the cemetery. So it became an argument about the needs of the living against maintaining respect for the dead. There was disharmony between the practical and the spiritual and as the holy ground covered two boroughs it allowed for friction all round. It could have been *Swizzlewick* all over again.

There was drama on the home front too. By the previous Christmas it became fairly obvious that number three was in the pipeline. Having found a reasonable priced and more importantly warm, private hotel in Hulme, I was anxious to hear news from home about the outcome of Penny's visit to Hannington of Child Deliveries Inc. She, having been given the affirmative and as a concerned mother-to-be, raised the issue as to how were we going to manage in our bijou residence adjacent to the Thames. I found myself saying:
'Don't worry, when I get back, we'll get a larger house.'
As I put down the phone, I regarded myself in the hall mirror and uttered with a cry of desperation:
'But how?'

Not only the nation's but my 'flu raged, which was not helped by location filming taking place on a snowbound and bitterly cold day in one of Manchester's largest cemeteries. For the sake of the drama, the name of this well-known burial ground was changed at the entrance gates, causing genuine funeral parties, bowed with grief, considerable confusion. Because of the dramatic increase in fatality numbers at that time due to the prevailing conditions, there was a constant stream of hearses and mourner's cars disrupting our filming – the director, crew and cast found it most inconsiderate. There was one particular moment, when I was having a duologue with another member of the town council, that I became aware of a cortege approaching, which was about to pass on the roadway that lay between us and the camera. I paused as it crossed our 'shot' and then continued as it cleared camera right. I expected to be required to do another 'take' without the distraction of the black limousines but no, the director said that it was perfect and the fact that I was seen respectfully replacing my trilby before continuing 'was so natural'. I had the vision of the grieving family watching it on the 'telly' at home some weeks later, saying:

'Look, there's us!'

Exciting for Dad's final moment to be seen by the nation on TV, but did he get a fee?

In breaks in the filming that day, feeling feverish and wondering whether there might be no point in my leaving the place, I jogged round this vast home for the departed in an attempt to keep my circulation going. Watching from a suitably concealed vantage point, I watched a gravedigger filling in a previous customer's resting place. Although he wasn't actually singing, he was humming a merry ditty, and he did have a 'fag' in the corner of his mouth. I watched transfixed and thought he's not going to ...... but of course, he did. As he reached the end of his musical performance, he also reached the end of his Woodbine and duly chucked the stub into the open grave and carried on shovelling. All good material for when I was to play the 1$^{st}$ 'you know who' in *Hamlet* at a later date.

Returning home, we immediately set about seeking the larger residence I had foolhardily promised. Having set myself a price limit that I felt within the possibilities of being able to 'con' a mortgage out of Abbey National B.S., I soon realised that I was pitching well under the market values. Having been rejected or out bid for several mansions, desperation was beginning to set in and I was despondent when Mr Barnes, the house agent, phoned to say that the owner of a property we were about to view that day had already accepted an offer. I went through the 'Props for Sale' in the *Richmond & Twickenham Times,* which had come out that very morning, for anything suitable. I saw a 'family house' in Teddington, for which they were asking 20% above my top.
'Can't afford it and where the hell's Teddington?'
I phoned back Mr Barnes and made an appointment to view the property within the hour.

Coming from our haven by Richmond Bridge, albeit on the more unfashionable side, I found Teddington somewhat dull, especially the end we were visiting. I remembered that Noël Coward had been born there and that he too had found it somewhat uninspiring and could only remember the green roof of the parish church. However, the six bed-roomed, Edwardian corner villa with large garden, garage and car-port, seemed ideal. Although somewhat in need of TLC, with only sisal matting on the floors (apart from a sitting room), with rooms to furnish, and not having a penny in the Bank, I made an immediate offer. As we were the first to view, they said they would come back to us. I was so convinced that they would get their asking price, that I phoned that same day around mid-night, awakening them from their slumbers, offering the full whack, if they would leave their new sitting-room carpet – agreed. Now, to raise the funds. To my concern but not complete surprise, ANBS rather baulked at the idea, even though I had never lapsed in paying my monthly dues on my first mortgage.

'Why do you need such a large house?' they enquired, suspecting that I might wish to rent out rooms to members of our far-flung Empire. Believing that attack is the better part of defence, I pointed out that with my family and career prospects, I was not sure it was large enough. It worked and we were to dwell there for the next 31 years, even managing to pay off the mortgage. It was the soundest financial investment I ever made.

With number three imminent and the need to soothe brows at the nervous Building Society, I felt I should seek out some form of remuneration. Would the dear old 'Beeb' take me back? Who should I approach that might put in a word? I had worked in Belfast for their Head of Radio Drama, Ronald Mason, who seemed to have taken a fancy to my work and indeed, I was to wonder if it was also to me. He was over in London on attachment, so I contacted him and asked if I could see him, stating that I wished to ask something of him. He invited me round to the house he was renting on Strand-on-the-Green, for a drink the following Sunday evening. I arrived to find him well imbibed with another exile from the Emerald Isle, a well-known actor whose initials were DD. They were so full of Irish whiskey and 'the craic' that I was uncertain if my journey had been really necessary. I hardly said a word and that was a record. The main item on the agenda was D bemoaning the fact that he and Mrs D were unable to conceive. This took me back to a similar conversation Penny and I had had over a dinner table some years earlier, with another celebrated theatrical couple, whose initials I will not give, to whom we recommended our golf playing, tin-soldier collecting, gynaecologist from Wimbledon. His expertise had done the trick, for in a short time a child was born who grew up to become another distinguished thespian. So, through the 40% proof haze, I suggested a similar course for DD and promised to let him have the details of our fertility man. I would add that this scenario was again successful. What I do for the profession.

Delighted though I was to be of service, my own problem was not touched upon until DD headed at speed upstairs to relieve

4

himself. Ronald, in a state of total inebriation, remembered I had come on a mission and asked what it was I wanted to ask. As I heard the flush of the ceramic upstairs, I knew I had precisely ten seconds, without pausē, repetition or hesitation, to deliver my soliloquy.

'D may have problems producing, we do not and are due to go into Act 3 in July, so I need financial input. Is there a possibility of my coming back on 'the Rep?' His immediate response:

'Leave it to me – ah, D, feeling better?'

A fortnight later a call came from the BBC Drama Repertory office with an offer to join the Company in September – would I be free. I considered the offer for at least three seconds and accepted.

Buoyed by the knowledge of an income coming in, we waited for the arrival of the third in line. Whereas Mark had been a fortnight late (he always found it difficult to be punctual), Tessa had been held up for only 24 hours, so we were on standby for the next from the moment of conception. We had invited guests to dine with us round our soapbox dining table, in order to show off our recent bricks and mortar purchase. The starter had been avocado with vinaigrette and unbeknown to the master of the house, the chef consumed an additional half of the A&V (there being an odd number at table), prior to bringing in the main course. Whether an odd number is lucky or no, consumption of the extra oil (presumably not virgin) led to our daughter, Louise Katherine, deciding that the time had come to stand on her own feet. We went with all convenient speed to St Theresa's in Wimbledon (Mr Hannington by now having a bed there) for the arrival of another family member and a further strain on the pursestrings – and most welcome too. Of course, it was another perfect Sunday child.

--------0--------

Prior to rejoining dear old 'Auntie', I had the chance to work in the TV studios of my new hometown – something that sod's law usually denies. The director was Ronnie Baxter who was of a similar stature to Ronnie Corbett – indeed, he could have teamed up with them and become one of the 'Three Ronnies'. This production was part of a series called *Never Mind the Quality, Feel the Width'* featuring John Bluthal and Joe Lynch – I guess it was all Jewish and Irish 'gags'- subtle combination. The most amusing aspect to come out of it for me, was that at a later date Ronnie asked me to be in an episode of a series with Jimmy Clitheroe, who was even smaller than Ronnie himself. It was the first time that I had come across the phenomena of both physical and vocal development ceasing before puberty. *The Clitheroe Kid* featured Jimmy as the naughty schoolboy and indeed, he behaved like a school kid. In rehearsal lunch-breaks he would insist on us playing football, exactly like the lunch-breaks at school. Newcomers like myself had to address him as Mr Clitheroe – it took time before you could be on 'Jimmy' terms. He had a large Mercedes, indeed, so large that he was frequently stopped by the police in the belief that they had seen a child at the wheel, or even worse, nobody. His death was extraordinary and sad. Following his mother's funeral, the mourners returned to the house for the Wake and after a time he excused himself, saying he wanted to lie down. As he hadn't come down after an hour or so, a friend went to see how he was, to discover him dead on his bed – from natural causes.

Perhaps the most famous theatrical personality of small stature (I hope that is politically correct enough) was Wee Georgie Wood. In his latter years, he wished to be addressed as George Wood. When touring, he liked to stay at his favourite 'digs' and his Manager would contact the landlady with the request that she refrain from calling him 'Georgie' and to use the prefix 'Mr'. She was also asked to make no reference to size.

"There was a landlady of Leeds, who in respect would go down on her knees" – she was, indeed, respectful and full of decorum for the whole week. On his departure on Sunday morning, she expressed the pleasure she'd had in caring for him during his visit.

'It's been so good to see you again, Mr Wood. I hope you'll stay with us again soon.'

He thanked her for the service he had received.

'Oh, Mr Wood, the pleasure was all mine,' she beamed.

As he turned for the door, she quickly reminded him: 'Don't forget your little coat.'

## BH REVISITED

It's always reassuring to return to familiar territory, as long as you enjoyed the previous experience and that it has not changed for the worse. The BBC Drama Repertory Company was always a pleasure, even though I knew it was not a career-builder but it did pay the ANBS. Life could not have been more blissful that Christmas, spent in our new house and with the new member.

It was another round of plays, readings of literature, letters and poetry, also doing silly voices in comedy shows. Meeting newcomers to me like Miriam Margolyes, Geoffrey Matthews, Jo Manning Wilson, Anthony Jackson (Jacko)* as well as golden oldies; Carleton Hobbs, Norman Shelley, James McKechnie, Godfrey Kenton, Marjorie Westbury and the husky toned Mary Wimbush, was sheer bliss. Hours were spent in the BBC Club, where I would observe and listen to senior actors reminisce, one being William Fox, a man of eloquence and elegance, who always seemed to be surrounded by beautiful young women. I told him I wanted to be like him when I grew up. He simply said: 'In that case, don't grow up!'
Bill lived another another forty years and died aged ninety-seven.
Jacko and I spent thirty immature years in the Club until his premature death at the age of sixty-two.

It was in this period that I just appeared in *Hitch Hikers Guide to the Galaxy*. I mention this simply because it made me a bit of a cult, although I don't remember a thing about it. Happily engaged though I was, I was feeling restless, in that I wanted to tread the boards again. I had been in a 'try-out' of a musical written by two old mates from both Bristol and the BBC Rep – David King and Anthony Hall. They put on their work for two performances at the Questor's Theatre, with the title *The King's Men* based on Will

Shakespeare & Co., when James VI of Scotland became James I of England in 1603. I played James with a broad north of the border brogue, studied at the Andrew Cruikshank school of realism. I had just one number, dealing with James' aversion to tobacco. As we were all gainfully employed at the 'Beeb' and received no remuneration for our comradely efforts, I was only able to give a cursory nod towards rehearsals – two in fact. I was somewhat taken aback to find that we played to full houses, nearly every seat being occupied by representatives of West End managements – I had imagined it would be just a few of the authors' friends, neighbours and relatives. Thank God I'd worked on my song with my singing teacher, Ms 'Whatsername'. It gave me a taste for musicals and the theatre again. I just needed someone who was putting on a musical that had a character that would suit me.

Interrupting my second helping of pesto pasta, the phone rang. It was Peter Dews.
'How about doing a musical for me in Brum?' (that was quick).
'Are you doing anything?'
'Yes, I'm on the BBC Rep.'
'Again? Why not come up 'ere and play the lead.'
'But I'm working Peter – regular money – I've got five mouths to feed - to say nothing of the dog.'
'We'll pay you our top whack, full pay from day one no silly rehearsal money, we'll try and work round broadcasts and furthermore, you can stay as long as it suits you.'
How could I refuse, he was almost begging.
'It's right up your street, luvvy; a bombastic Brummie 'airdresser. Go and meet the composer, Monty Norman and the lyricist, Julian More – they'll luv ye.'
'Who's written the book?'
'David Turner, he knows you of old.'
'What's it about?'
'Ballroom dancin' – and hair'
'Called?'
'You'll never guess – *Quick, Quick, Slow.*'

'And what made you think of me?'
'It were that 'Tobacco' number you did at Questors.'
I'd never have guessed.

Having suitably hoodwinked Norman and More, I was accepted and agreed to do it. They had done several musicals in town and I remembered seeing Paul Scofield in *'Expresso Bongo'*, so realised they obviously liked having class actors in their casts. I now had to find a way of extricating myself from my BBC contract. The 'Beeb' had been good enough to take me on when I needed them, so I did not wish to slap them in the face by simply resigning after nine months – who knows I might well need them again. I wanted my leave-taking to seemingly come from another direction, so I devised a wicked plot. I asked to see the Head of Radio Drama, Martin Esslin.
'Martin, I want your advice.'
'John, I vill be delighted if I can be of serwice.'
I felt I was in old Vienna with every cadence.
'Martin, I love being on the Rep. The work is stimulating, the Corporation caring and those I work with a delight. However, I feel that I should develop my skills by being in the theatre, for I believe it will enhance, not only my work in the theatre, but also in radio drama. An opportunity has arisen to do just that and I am seeking your opinion. The Birmingham Repertory Theatre has offered me a season with a range of challenging parts, starting with a musical. Should I take this option?'
'John, for yourself and indeed, for us, you must return to ze zeatre. Furthermore, venever you vish to return to us, you only have to ask.'
I was so moved that I almost changed my mind. However, I movingly said:
'Martin, your comments and guidance I will always treasure, you have persuaded me, thank you.'
So that was it – Birmingham prepare yourself.

--------0--------

10

I was late for the first rehearsal. This is not my habit – remember, 'good time keeper', but there was an understandable, if not acceptable reason. What's more, I was not the only one. We were due to meet at 11am on 21 July 1969, which apart from being Louise's first birthday, (the celebrations of which I would not be able to attend), was also the day that man first stepped onto the surface of the moon. The world, west of Dubai, watched that historic moment in the middle of the night – so getting to bed around 6am meant virtually everyone overslept. My declamatory entry into the rehearsal room of:

'A small step for Baddeley, but a giant leap for Birmingham,' went down only moderately well with the bleary-eyed cast.

*Quick, Quick, Slow,* was an everyday story of the Bradshaw family. There was Arthur, the father, a self-made, vulgar and domineering owner of a string of hairdressing salons; his cock-pecked wife, Betty; and their beautiful, if intellectually challenged daughter, Linda. The child's outstanding, nay only talent was ballroom dancing. However, to achieve the accolades that Dad required (for he could see business opportunities presenting themselves), Linda needed to have an outstanding dancing partner. So her sub-standard present one is ditched and Dad 'buys' the best lad going, Norman, who is not much brighter than Linda. A well-known dancing instructor is brought in to help achieve Dad's aim. Arthur wants 'class', or as he puts it, he is looking for "top shelf not bottom drawer." Of course, it's love at first 'over-sway' and the two lovebirds eventually drive off on Norman's Harley Davidson (no small feat on a stage the size of the Station Street theatre) into the sunset, leaving Arthur's dreams shattered and a Night Club (Linda's Place) to dispose of.

With numbers like: 'One Step Ahead', 'Going Round in Circles', 'Gang Bang', 'Inside Knowledge', 'Arthur's Beautiful Moment' and 'Ballroom' it was an undoubted success. Jane Freeman was again my wife, the young couple were played by Tina Martin (ideal casting) and Jeffrey Shankley, who had his wicked way with the choreographer and ultimately married her, before going on to play leads in several West End Musicals including *Starlight Express.* Stella Moray, was superb as the dancing instructor, Vicky. There was a constant stream of Managements coming to see if it had West End potential, along with 'luvvies' like Maggie Smith and Robert Stephens (ex-Morecambe) to see if it was for them. I realised I was on a loser as far as London was concerned – but you never know. It was rumoured that it was to be put on by Theatre Projects.

Thirty years later I saw a wonderful Australian film, *Strictly Ballroom,* in which the details of the plot were amazingly similar, even though the genders were reversed. I couldn't help wondering if ......... but no, of course not.

The next production was an adaptation by the Associate Director, Michael Simpson, of Labiche's farce, *An Italian Straw Hat.* 'Dad' was again me, in pursuit of my daughter's groom on their wedding day. I was after him and he was after a straw hat. A great chance for comic invention and of course, all ends happily. Little did I realize however, that my performance was to do me a considerable disservice. Some time later, Dews confessed that he had originally wanted Jimmy Edwards to play Arthur Bradshaw in '*QQS*' but that he had turned it down. When the production was to be mounted in the West End by Theatre Projects, the script was sent to him again and he accepted. When asked why he had changed his mind he stated:
'Well, it played so much better than it read.'
'But you never saw it,' Peter pointed out.
'I did. It was when I came up to do some late night cabaret in Brum, I dropped in to see it.'
'That was *The Italian Straw Hat* you saw' said Peter.
'Well, it was a damned good part' said Jimmy, stroking his handlebar moustache.
So my part in a play was taken away from me on the strength of the performance that I gave in another play – is there no justice?
In fact, the production (which I was to be in) at the Palace Theatre, was withdrawn a week before rehearsals were to start

12

due to domestic and financial problems within the management.

I worked with Mr Edwards, however, sometime later on a television serial called *Jorrocks,* with Jimmy in the title role. His enthusiasm to play the part was indicated by the fact that he shaved off his famous moustache to do so. I played some chinless wonder and on the 'exteriors shoot' prior to working in the studio and before any of us had met or discussed the text, the director asked me how I thought I should play the role.
'With a dropped R and a lisp,' I suggested.
'Perfect' he agreed.
I regretted my hasty decision, for I was lumbered with it for six episodes. In the series was a favourite actor and a close neighbour of mine, Michael Bates, and we spent the entire time talking to each other in our General Montgomery 'voices'. Although I have used the Monty vocal tones in my comedy repertoire, Michael, who looked somewhat like Monty, did even better with him. He heard that a film was being made with a somewhat unfavourable slant on the man, so he phoned up the production company, using Monty's voice and said he wished to speak to the Director of the film. They were fearful that he wished to take out legal action and did delaying tactics. When they found that the call could not have come from the man they feared, they traced it to Michael and he was ultimately cast as our famous military leader, with George C. Scott playing the lead in *Patton.*

Back to the plot. I was not seen in the production following *Straw Hat,* but was heard. Little did I realise that *Saved* by Edward Bond, was to be of ultimate benefit to me. I was told that the voice of Winston Churchill was heard over the radio in the course of the action.
'We can't lay our hands on a recording of him doing the speech. Have you got any contacts at the 'Beeb' John?' asked the stage manager.
'I'll record it - they won't know,' I said with overbearing modesty.
'You?'

I did and they didn't. I considered that could come in useful sometime.

*Henry IV, Pt 1* gave me the chance to show off my linguistic capabilities. Owen Glendower, the fiery Welsh wizard from Bangor, is required by the Bard to speak in his native tongue.
"I think there is no man speaks better Welsh," says Hotspur.
Our beloved Will, however, wrote no text in Welsh, so Hugh Griffith, in a Stratford production, wrote some lines and poor fools like me have had to learn them ever since. I was coaxed, parrot-fashion, by a native of the land of the leek, for weeks. Peter Dews, who had not directed the production, said after the first night:
'You only missed out a couple of words, luvvy – I don't think they would have noticed.' Sod.

'Michael wants to see you immediately, John,' I was informed as I arrived for a matinée.
'Hugh Sullivan has been taken ill, will you go on as Falstaff?'
'What about Glendower?'
'You'll have to do that as well – there's no time to quibble, Sybil.'
Padded up for Falstaff, 'carrying the book', quick change into Glendower 'without the book' (just), back into Falstaff to finish off. The 'book-carrying' children in the matinee audience hardly noticed a thing until I had to drag off the body of Hotspur. Having to put the book in my mouth did give rise to a degree of childish merriment.
'You're rather good at being thrown in at the deep end,' said Michael Simpson.
'Anytime,' I replied. I wish I'd kept my mouth shut.

The Christmas fare was *Toad of Toad Hall* in which I rehearsed happily as Mole  - "Hang Spring cleaning!" On the Saturday before we opened there were portents of things to come. On such a day as this we would rehearse in front of the '69 Club. This was a group of young enthusiasts (of the drama), who would watch

14

and ask questions. Michael button-holed me as the noisy throng settled down.

'We have a problem.'

'Go on, tell me.'

'Desmond (Macnamara – Toad), Hugh (Sullivan – Badger) and Geoffrey (Case – Ratty) are all hors de combat and cannot make the rehearsal. The theatre is full of kids, can you entertain them?'

'I'll do the show for them.'

I knew taking over Falstaff would lead to trouble.

The following Monday afternoon was the 'technical'* and we were to open with a preview performance on the Tuesday, with first night on the Wednesday. As I rolled in, having spent the whole of Sunday relaxing in the bosom of my family, I was immediately dragged into 'the office' by Michael Simpson and the general manager, John Greenwood.

'The good news is that Geoff and Hugh are pretty well restored to health but Des is not and could be off for days, if not weeks. Will you play Toad?'

'What and Mole at the same time!'

'John, this is serious.'

'You want me to learn Toad overnight and open tomorrow?'

'Yes. Ellis Jones will be playing Mole.'

Falstaff *had* led to trouble – deep trouble.

Suffice it to say, Ellis and I opened that next night without books, although Toad did go into a short 'stand-up' routine in the final scene in Toad Hall on that first night. This remained a feature (when I played the part) for the rest of the run – not for the purists perhaps, but the adults in the audience seemed to approve. After a fortnight, Des returned and I resumed as Mole, hoping I was in the right position at any given moment. After four days he collapsed and I went into my 'about turn' routine for another fortnight and then he came back again – I didn't know my 'ole from my 'oad. To have played two such diverse characters in the same production was a fantastic experience. There were two particular memories for me. The first being at the Boxing Day matinee, when doing one of my spectacular (if somewhat under-rehearsed) leaps, I sprained my ankle. Only a toad can know the discomfort I was in and I had to have painkilling injections – but the show must go on and we'd run out of understudies. As the audience was expecting to see Mr Macnamara at the evening performance, the company manager went before the curtain and addressed the packed auditorium.

'Due to the indisposition of Desmond Macnamara, the part of Toad will be played tonight by John Baddeley ….. on one leg.'

The other particular memory was a Mole moment, when the family happened to be 'out front'. Mole finds himself in 'The Wild Wood', which is dark and frightening to the velvety creature. He is confronted by a massive spider, which almost causes him to have a nervous breakdown. However, it was the spider that had the breakdown that day, for the wire suspending him from the 'flies' snapped. The huge lifeless hulk layed spread over most of centre-stage. He had to be 'struck'[**] as it would have looked ludicrous to see another deceased spider later in Toad Hall. The day was saved, as dear Moley went into dialogue never before heard at this point in the drama. He experienced a life-changing conversion and expressed his warmth, indeed, affection for the creature of many legs, picked it up, cuddled it and took it to safety in the 'wings' off left. As they disappeared to another part of the Wild Wood, a child in the audience shouted:

'That's my Daddy!' The audience screamed with laughter and Louise just screamed. I fear my 'cred' had gone.

Consecutive plays brought guest artists to join the Company. The first was Alec McCowan playing the moody one in *Hamlet*. Dews said he was going to give me a play 'out' for which I conveyed my appreciation for the generosity of allowing me to have the evenings off whilst still being paid.

'Yes, luvvy, I just want you to play the Gravedigger.'

So that's a play 'out'!

Performing from the 'trap'[***] with just the upper torso and head in view and having water poured in the boots by comedians under the stage, was assistance that I did not require simply for me to say:

"Your water is a sore decayer of your whoreson dead body."
Perhaps it was the Bard's word "argal" that persuaded me to play
him with Bristolian tones – seemed to work.

Although it was supposedly my 'play out' it still meant that I had
to be in at 'the half', **** so in the long wait before my entrance in
Act V (the audience must have been desperate for me by then), I
was able to watch Alec's performance. For those studying this
great part, it could not have been more clearly defined than by his
detailed interpretation of the role. I was in agreement with the
critic who felt that whilst lacking the passion one might have
expected of someone so besotted with Ophelia, the intellectual
content left one in no doubt that Hamlet was a graduate of
Wittenburg University. Some years later I had the pleasure of
reading a delightful book that Alec wrote about his childhood. It
prompted me to write and tell him that I had no idea that I was
working with a budding author, when he played Hamlet to my
Gravedigger.

I was given permission to record a couple of serial readings of
books for the 'Beeb', fitting them in with theatre rehearsals. One
was for *Story Time* recorded in Birmingham, called *John Halifax,
Gentleman* by D. M. Mulock (Mrs Craik), whose Victorian values
I found somewhat hard to swallow but I could accept anything for
a ten-episode engagement. I then fitted in another ten episoder,
this time in London for *Book at Bedtime* of *Three Men on the
Bummel*, the sequel to *Three Men in a Boat* by Jerome K. Jerome.
I had to record a couple of episodes at Broadcasting House in
Portland Place one Saturday morning and was concerned that I
might not get back to 'Brum' in time to play my Gravedigger at
the matinée. Dews said:
'Don't worry, luvvy, if you're not back, I'll go on – I know it
better than you.' Sod again. I did, however, get back in time and
his look of disappointment as I walked through the stage door
touched my heart. He had an incredible reputation for taking on
bets that he could recite the whole of any one of Will's plays,
making no more than half a dozen mistakes – it was astonishing.

Whereas Alec was quiet and unassuming, our next guest made you feel as if you were caught up in the eye of a storm – an electrical one at that. John Wood was up to play another cerebral character, Frederick the Great, the intellectual and military genius, in *The Sorrows of Frederick* by Romulus Linney. John was the only actor I knew that you could sense when he was in the building without seeing or hearing him – you just felt him. The staging was amazing on that tiny stage. By having a rise from the back of the stage and a descent to the front, there was a deceptive feeling of distance and size. Playing the part of the General, I represented matters military and my time of 'square bashing' came to my aid. Dews would shout abuse at the young actors playing the soldiery, for many did not know their left from their right. An army drill instructor was brought in to put us through our paces. It was one of the rare occasions I have seen grown actors weep. Come the first night, it was electric and we would not have been out of place on Horse Guards Parade for Trooping the Colour.

I found John somewhat threatening off stage but loved being with him 'on'. Dews asked me to evolve a powerful military first entrance as the General. This I duly did in rehearsal, to the chagrin of Fred the Great who had to stand by and watch this somewhat elaborate procedure.
'Have you finished?' Mr Wood asked of me.
'Nearly' I responded.
He went ballistic.
'What the hell does he think he's doing?' he asked of the director.
'What I asked him,' fired back Mr Dews.
'Is this a play about a f------ General's entrance?'
There then ensued a quarter of an hour's heated debate between leading man and leading director. In the end I did what I had presented and it remained so to the end of the run.

There was an interesting aspect in the play, which demonstrated theatrical discipline. There was a forty-minute scene set in Sans Souci, where Frederick and his friend and sparring partner,

18

Voltaire, had an intellectual debate. Sitting round the table were the Doctor, the Chancellor, the Bishop and the General. We had to listen every night, without dialogue, assimilating their argument. It was essential for full and fresh concentration to be present at every performance for the scene to hold. The idea that if you do not speak you are not an important part of the scene is rubbish – you are the scene. A great lesson for amateurs and some 'pros'.

One scene that gave me great pleasure was the beheading of a soldier (remember, I had hanged William Corder). The young man's execution was performed down/stage, in full view of the audience. He placed his head on the block and the axe descended and with one blow removed his head from his body, to the horror of those who had come for an enjoyable night out. Let me assure you, the same actor played the part for the entire run. How was it done? Do contact me.

I learnt about one of my numerous personal shortcomings in this production. After our original hostilities, Mr Wood and I became on good terms. On one occasion, he called me into his dressing-room and postulated:
'Are you ambitious?'
I was somewhat taken aback but after brief consideration said:
'Yes.'
'Well, for f--- sake show it!'
I don't think I ever really did.

There then followed several great pieces: *Three Sisters* (perhaps the best of them all), playing Chebutykin, *Pygmalion* (Doolittle) and *Staircase* (Harry). *Pygmalion* taught me about the fickleness of the Press. As Doolittle, I thought I had given rather a 'good one' on the first night. The next day the notices were pinned on the board, and I was a touch miffed to see that I did not get a mention in *The Birmingham Mail*. Phoning my mother on some pretext, she happened to say:
'What a marvellous notice for you in the *Mail.*'

19

'They didn't mention me,' I retorted.

'They did, you got a paragraph to yourself.'

Having read it to me over the 'phone, I shot into the Publicity Dept. and relayed my annoyance. I was aware that quotes would be bannered at the front of the theatre and I wanted that one to be considered. It was and they duly placed it to catch the passing theatregoer's eye. When the paper was asked how this situation had occurred, they simply said that they were short of space for the second run and the sub-Editor thought cutting that whole paragraph was economical – as it was with the truth. There was praise from another critic who said:

"Until he came to the Birmingham Rep., I had only seen John Baddeley on the television and then with no particular pleasure, but he makes us realise every time he comes onto the stage, that he is a much better actor than we had given him credit for."

Praise indeed – he had obviously spoken not only of his own regard for my ability but for the entire Nation.

Dews told me that I was the third best Doolittle he'd seen. So of course I had to enquire as to who had pushed me into the bronze medal position.

'Well, first were Wilfred Lawson (whom, you may remember, I could imitate without knowing who he was) in the film version with Wendy Hiller and second was someone you may not have heard of, Charles Victor.'

I had in fact watched Charles every night for the week I was dressing 'Beau' Hannen and had nicked my nasal tones from him.

'No, Peter, I don't know either of them.'

During autumn, in a rehearsal break for lunch in the Market Hotel, Michael Simpson stated they were not sure what to finish the season with the following June. I said it was simple, that if there was money to play with, *Cyrano de Bergerac* with me in the title role or if strapped for cash, *Staircase.* An hour later Dews called me into the office.

'We've been thinking about the end of the season, luvvy, and we thought you and Hugh for *Staircase* (note the 'we'). Hugh

20

understudied Scofield in Town, so him for Charlie and you for Harry.'

This was not the scenario I had in mind but that is what it became. I thought the fact that Hugh, who was bald and would have to wear a wig for Charlie's golden locks and that I would have to have a bald wig because Harry was an alopecia sufferer, might be an expense that they would not wish to go to but no, it was hang the outlay. Perhaps Mr Dews remembered my '*Cyrano*' BBC audition, when he first met me fifteen years before, and that the memory was too hard to bear. So *Staircase* it was.

Peter approached Hugh and I and told us that he had asked the TV Trainee Director, who was there on work experience, to direct the play. He implied that the two of us could really direct it ourselves. I was somewhat apprehensive, feeling that Hugh and I needed a strong guiding hand to keep us in order. I felt sorry for the young man, who had directed me in a couple of late night shows, which were extra shows (we had so much free time) that we slotted in mainly for the benefit of students. He had overseen my playing Ubu in Alfred Jarry's *Ubu Roi*, but I felt that in a two-hander we needed to feel confident. He went on to have a successful career in television and he never used me!

Dews came back to us with the suggestion of the actor that had played Pickering in our *Pygmalion*, who had recently joined the professional ranks from being a lecturer at Edinburgh University. Hugh and I agreed that he was ideal and so Oliver Ford Davies had his first professional production as a director.

In its day, the play was thought daring, near the knuckle or unacceptable. Homosexuality was still considered by many to be unsuitable for public viewing, indeed, when I had seen the play a few years before, several sensitive members of the audience had walked out. Of course, I now realise that when they stormed out of *Godot* it must have been because they suspected that the two tramps were 'gay' – come to think.....

21

I was a touch peeved that they did not do so in our production. At the same time that we were doing Staircase, there was a touring production of *Boys in the Band* (very much in the same genre) down the road at the Alexandra Theatre. Every night, for them, the front few rows were filled by young men wearing purple carnations – why weren't they there for us? However, at the end of one of our performances, Oliver, who had been watching, saw two members of the audience, a man and a woman, in earnest conversation. He caught up with them, hoping to catch their critical remarks only to hear:

'Ergth vots poznevrt gest imop vos unprima.' They obviously loved it.

My main concern had not been its contents but its length. I was worried that a play lasting only two hours and a quarter (inc.15 min. interval) would be considered by the audience to be far too short for their money. Thirty years later it was considered the ideal length for a play – how do they manage with Will's works?

So the season ended and for those booked for the next one, there was a full fortnight's holiday.

* Anthony Jackson was always called Tony or 'Jacko' by those who knew him. Any reference to 'Tony' in this book refers to him, not to the 'Tony Jackson' who is a different Equity member and not known to the author.

** As previously mentioned, this is a staggered rehearsal where all the technicalities of the production are seen to be in place.

*** An aperture, centre stage, through which a performer can appear from or disappear into, particularly used by demon kings, wicked fairies and the occasional gravedigger.

**** 35 minutes before 'curtain up'.

# THAT CRAZY OLD TOWN

A week's holiday in Lyme Regis, walking The Cobb, climbing the High Street, shrimping the rockpools, was far too brief and I knew Penny was feeling the strain of being a 'single parent'. Although my conscience was getting to me, I had agreed to return to Birmingham. This was not only because I enjoyed the work but because the Company was going to Chicago as part of the Ravinia Festival. So after the break, it was back to rehearse Noël Coward's *Tonight at 8.30* which would then play in Brum, before taking it with *Pygmalion* and Pinter's *The Caretaker*, across the Pond.

The three one-act plays that comprised our *Tonight at 8.30* were *Ways and Means, Still Life* (Brief Encounter in the film with Celia Johnson and Trevor Howard) and *Red Peppers*. It should have been a piece of cake for me as I was only in the latter play but Jane Freeman and I, as the broken-down, bickering, man and wife variety act, had to work overtime on our dance routines. I don't think we ever achieved 'sync' but I did enjoy performing "Has anybody seen our ship, the HMS Disgusting" etc. and anyway, we were supposed to be 'tat'. No sooner had that opened, than Hugh Sullivan, Geoffrey Case and I went into rehearsals with Peter Dews for *The Caretaker,* which was to be performed solely in Chicago. At the same time there was polishing up to do on *Pygmalion.*

It was at this time I thought I might lose my reason. I found learning the part of Davies in *The Caretaker* immensely difficult. The precision of the text was vital, particularly the non-sequiturs and those Pinter 'pauses'. With all the other work we were doing, I think that Hugh (Aston) and Geoffrey (Mick) were also having to pull out all the stops. Apart from the lines, they were demanding parts to play physically – ours being a somewhat violent production. It is a terrible feeling knowing you are not at all confident that you can actually do it, and that somewhere on a foreign shore they are happily booking in expectation. Years later, Alun Armstrong and his wife Sue, had dinner with us the day before he started rehearsals for *Sweeney Todd* at the National Theatre, in which he was to play the lead. I asked how he felt and he said:

'Terrified. We haven't rehearsed a line and the show is already sold out for the entire run.' (I would add that he went on to win an 'Olivier' award for his performance).

Feeling in a similar state, I went to my cousin, Michael, a consultant at the General Hospital in Birmingham and he prescribed me tranquillisers. As we boarded the plane, Peter said:

'It's a long flight, luvvy, so we'll have a word-rehearsal on the way over.' I just wanted to bale out.

After one false start at Birmingham Airport due to an IRA bomb scare, requiring the Police and Fire services to be in attendance, we finally set off for O'Hare Airport via Shannon. I was in a state of tension, not because we might have been blown out of the skies by a bomb, but by the likelihood of Mr Dews doing the same when he realised just how 'dodgy' I was on the lines. I would have to find a solution. I complained of a headache and Mary Miller, our Eliza Doolittle and self-appointed Matron and general medical advisor to the Company, prescribed some tablets she had about her hand luggage. I took this opportunity to close my eyes. Whether it was the potent medication that I had taken or my seeking a 'get out clause' but I slept for the next seven and a half hours, being awoken as we hit the runway at O'Hare Airport.

The theatre and the hotel were on the outskirts of Chicago. The Murray Theatre in Ravinia was acclaimed proudly to be of historical interest, as being perhaps the oldest theatre in America, a hundred years old – I wondered what that made the Theatre's Royal Bath and Bristol. The Orrington Hotel was in nearby Evanston opposite the Northwestern University. There were four

24

days before the opening night of *Pygmalion* but there was to be no escape from rehearsals for those of us in *The Caretaker* that started the next morning. Fortunately, I found that my comfortable suite in the hotel made learning Davies' lines much easier. No pressure of performances for a few days and Doolittle was a yankee-doodle for me – I even forewent the tranquillisers but kept them in case of emergency.

For most of us this was our first experience of the American way of life, like having breakfast in 'The Huddle' and being served eggs (sunny side up) with hash browns etc. by our regular waiter of Oriental origin, who bore the name on his lapel of 'On Q'. I presumed he had been employed specifically to serve actors and asked him if he had considered what should go on his tombstone when the time came. I suggested 'Here Lies Dead On Q', which he did not appear to comprehend or appreciate. There was a car laid on to take you wherever you wished, be it rehearsals, performances or down town – do remember 'no loitering'. The opportunity to visit the stunning Art Institute packed with the Impressionists, to be entertained at the top of the John Hancock Center, where aircraft would fly past below the level of the window, or to visit the theatre for a matinee on our occasional free afternoons to see Sandy Dennis in *Bus Stop* and Eve Arden in *Butterflies are Free*. They were all wonderful opportunities for a greenhorn like me. There was also the chance to see American Baseball at Wrigley Field and cheer on the Chicago Cubs, which would give me something to talk about when I next met my sister-in-law, Sylvia, and she spoke non-stop of her San Diego Padres.

We opened with *Pygmalion*, which was moderately well received in the barn like theatre. Doolittle's broadness was well suited to the surroundings and was appreciated not only for his philosophy but also for bringing on clouds of pollution with him (thanks to a liberal sprinkling of Fullers Earth powder). At the party for audience and cast after the first night I was asked:
'Why did you decide to cut the musical numbers?'

On the second night I gave my pièce-de-résistance. Doolittle appears in full dustman's attire in the 1$^{st}$ Act and then "spruced up and looking in his prime" in wedding outfit in Act V. For the characterisation I had donned a droopy moustache for the role and since my debacle at Bristol, I had always used my reliable Nathans glue. In Birmingham the 'tache was stuck on before the first entrance and remained firmly in place until the end of the play. I had not taken into account, however, the different climatic conditions to be found next to the shores of Lake Michigan. As I reached the wings in this un-airconditioned theatre for the Act V entrance, I realised that perspiration was spouting from every actor's pore and that all was not secure on my upper lip. Pushing it firmly into place, I said to the Stage Manager:

'Get thee to my dressing room and bring thou my spirit gum, I may need it for the brief moment when Doolittle comes off.'

With that I swept on and holding out my hand addressed my host:

'Professor 'iggins.'

Simultaneously, my moustache, which was in one piece, not two (I had learned my lesson), departed my right upper lip and hung limply like the Union Jack on the Lord's pavilion after another Test defeat. The audience decided that this was 'humor' of the highest degree. I refused to do anything so it just hung there. Mr Sullivan, in the role of the speech-teaching pedant, feared I was unaware of the situation and attempted to improvise in a Shavian manner.

'Mr Doolittle, would you care to have a shave?'(much laughter)

'No, thank you guv'nor.' (even more laughter) 'I have come here today, very heavily disguised. This guv'nor, is the new image.'

With that I ripped off the offending hairpiece from its dangling position to reveal a clean, tonsured lip and stuffed it into my pocket (thunderous ovation).

At the party following, a literate theatregoer simply commented:

'Wasn't it incredible that that line about the new image happened to be there at that very moment?'

Incredible indeed.

While the rest of the company took off for holidays in New

Mexico and Canada, the 'real talent' stayed behind to give what was without doubt the hit of our season, *The Caretaker*. It surprised me how knowledgeable and appreciative of the play were the theatregoers of Illinios. They may not have been sure about Shaw but they were positive about Pinter. It was a tour de force for the three of us and most rewarding. As you know, I was off the tranquillisers but they did come in useful. As we approached 'the half' on our first night, Alison, our excellent stage director, came to me and wept.

'I don't think I can do it, John.'

'What, dear heart?' I asked, fearing a personal indiscretion.

'Run the show – my confidence has gone.'

To be honest, my confidence was feeling a little shaky at that point. The last thing the three of us needed, as we faced the foe, was a lack of adequate back-up. Our troops would have this feeling, thirty odd years later in Iraq. This was an emergency I was prepared for.

'I've got just the thing, as long as you PROMISE not to tell anyone else. Take this one pill and I assure you that you will be fine.'

I gave her one of my cousin's tranquillisers, knowing that they were only of value if taken over a period of time.

'Oh, thank you, John. You've saved the day.'

The show went without a hitch and she/we were all a little high at the party afterwards. What a psychologist.


Being such a success with both critics and audience meant that the three of us felt like Gods and what's more, it was Dews' only production out there. The set, which always got a 'round', was an exceedingly grotty room in a derelict building. Being a somewhat violent production, my body was taking a terrible hammering through being thrown about by Geoffrey Case (Mick) and indeed, the audience used to verbally wince. I knew I couldn't take this punishment for the whole run and that the abuse would have to be re.choreographed. There was, however, a brief respite, when Aston delivered a seven-minute speech, telling of the electric shock treatment he had been put through. I lay on my bunk up-stage, withdrawn from the scene and listened - I had learned how to 'listen'. One night, I saw out of the corner of my eye, a rat come onto the stage and rummage through the detritus and fragments of stale food that was lying around. I knew that Davies would be familiar, perhaps at home, with rats, so as it made its way towards me I simply ignored it. The audience were now aware of the creature and there was a buzz of :

'It's a rat, it's a rat.'

Hugh needed all the powers of concentration he could muster just to do the speech, but to have this added distraction made it doubly difficult. As the creature drew closer to me, I still ignored it but thought if he wants to go up my trouser leg, he can forget it. Should this event come to pass, I intended to let out a blasphemous Welsh oath and Hugh would have to fight his own battles. However, it did not do so and vanished down-stage-left amongst a pile of old *Evening Standards* and *News of the World.* As the curtain came down at the end of his big speech and the second Act, Hugh turned to me and enquired as to what the f--- I thought I was doing. He had to be assured by the tranquillised Alison about what had actually taken place. I never quite forgave him.  A search was made in the Interval but the creature was never seen again. It was the opinion of some that it must have been a chipmunk, but whatever it was the audience must have been impressed with the lengths that we would go to create reality, indeed, we considered keeping it in. Of course, they may have thought it was simply a way of distracting them from Mr Sullivan's performance.

On the Sunday between the first and second week of *The Caretaker,* we went to one of the many hospitable occasions to which we were invited. This was a lunch, in which the holy trinity had to go easy on the alcoholic beverage as we had a matinee and an evening show to do. Doing two performances, both on the Saturday and the Sunday, was somewhat demanding – in fact it was knackering. No performance on Monday helped and it was certainly welcome.

During the lunch I told my millionaire host, in his vast and exceedingly lavish house, the trouble I was having with the multiple bruises that now covered my body.

'John, I want to say just one thing to you.'

I thought if he says 'Plastics', I'll scream.

'Come with me.'

He then took me in a lift down into the lower depths, well below cellar level. We entered what appeared to be another residence, a sort of semi-detached dwelling only downwards. It comprised a sitting room, kitchen, storerooms, bedrooms, bathrooms, games room and seemingly a small hospital.

'This John, is our Fall-Out shelter. In this day and age you need to be prepared.'

'Now, getting back to your bruises. This is the sauna (that was the 'one thing' he wanted to say). Come round tomorrow and I'll get a couple of Swedish girls in to birch you. It's the only thing that will help and you'll love it.'

I'm sure I would have, but my co-mates and I had already arranged to take the next day and a half off to see the Mississippi. Damn.


The triumphing trio had been lent a Chevrolet for a couple of days. We were not sure what our aim was, so like good young men we decided to go west. It is was then that one appreciated the vast distance that one covers in our brother (or is it sister) country, to go only a short way on the map. We achieved our goal of seeing that mighty 'ole man riber' and then passed through the rather dreary town of Caso Moline and continued on. The weather had been fine but as evening arrived it started to bucket down. We had to find somewhere to stay and through the racing windscreen wipers we could dimly see a sign indicating a motel. We pulled into the darkened, empty parking area and could detect only one single light coming from a small building stating 'Reception'. As we got out, I simply called in a high-pitched tone:

'NOORR- MAANN…'

My companions leapt back into the car and said:

'Let's get the hell out of here.'

Pity, I'd always wanted to meet Anthony Perkins.

We decided to return to the security of dowdy Moline, found a modest hotel and went out for an haute cuisine burger. We made our way back to Evanston and the Orrington post-hast the next day, with a vow never to reveal our wimpish story.

Of the numerous invitations we received from our wonderfully generous American hosts, a few stand out. After one theatre party, I was invited to the home of the General Administrator of the Chicago Symphony Orchestra.
'Come and play tennis and bring some of the girls with you.'
I pointed out that we had not come kitted for tennis.
'Don't worry, we'll provide everything.'
Indeed, they did. Their vast house came with tennis courts and they were able to provide tennis wear for both genders and even pumps for my size six feet. Following lunch, I walked with our host to the bottom of their lengthy, manicured garden where there was a large expanse of water, and commented how fortunate they were to have such a wonderful aspect on their doorstep, which I could only imagine was one the Great Lakes.
'Well actually, it's *my* lake' he stated modestly. Silly me.

We were entertained several times by the British Consul General, Alan Rothnie and his wife at their Embassy residence. I liked them both very much, so I looked forward to attending a luncheon with them, given by the Ladies Drama League of Chicago at the Shereton. The whole Company was under muster for this occasion and as we drove down the boulevard to the hotel, I became aware that the road was lined with police facing alternately to the road and the crowd. I had no idea we were so popular and so protected. The lobby seemed a veritable hive of activity and I had only been there a moment, when a gentleman bearing a close resemblance to James Cagney (only taller) said:
'Who are you and what are youse doin here?' I didn't appreciate his attitude and was about to say:
'More to the point, who are you and what are youse doin here?' but thought better of it and pointed out that I was a distinguished guest. After discussion with other mobsters, I was allowed

through – somewhat reluctantly I thought. I enquired, after I reached the room where we were to lunch, as to why I had been grilled.

'Well, in half an hour the President arrives for another function.' As it so happened, I was on a staircase when in swept Richard Nixon who came within an arms length of me – he just wanted to be near, I guess.

I sat next to 'our man' in Chicago at the top table for our repast as I had been asked to say a 'few well chosen'. Alan and I had hit it off on our previous encounters and he stated that he thought I would be well fitted for the Diplomatic Service, and amusingly awarded me his own personal knighthood.

'Well, Sir John, I trust you will deliver a few bon mots.'

It was at this point that I had a salutary lesson in handling foreign affairs. In my speech of thanks, I first of all apologised for my unshaven appearance (grown for 'Davies') and turning to Mr Rothnie, noting his well-trimmed beard, pointed out that if I wished to become a diplomat I had to start somewhere. Alright so far. Because the room was packed with members of the 'monstrous regiment', I suggested that the President needn't be shy of the ladies and to –

'Come out, come out wherever you are.'

If the ceiling had opened and the Arctic's entire ice quota had fallen through, pre-empting global warming, the atmosphere could not have been chillier. I continued, without glancing at 'our man' and his lady and managed to charm the frigid members of the Drama League in my usual sickly, sweet manner, which they seemed to appreciate. There was, however, an official complaint made, which surprised me, as I thought that 'Tricky Dicky' was not that popular in Chicago.

'He's not,' I was assured 'but he is our President. You wouldn't speak in that fashion about your Queen.'

So they thought 'Dicky' was a Queen.

I think I might have been stripped of my knighthood that day.

*Tonight at 8.30* was panned by the critics except for (I hesitate to say this) *Red Peppers*. The most eventful event relating to that production, however, had to wait until the last day. Hugh Sullivan and I had adjoining dressing rooms and as we came to the 'five' at the matinée, I was aware of groaning coming from next door. I did not go on until the third act but Hugh was a 'beginner', so I knocked on his door and enquired after his wellbeing. He bid me enter.

'I can't go on' he stated, throwing up into the hand basin.

'What's the matter with you?' I asked.

'I think I must have eaten something at the luncheon I was invited to and there was something wrong with it,' he suggested, throwing up yet again.

I grabbed the adjacent phone and dialled the stage manager's room to speak to Alison. On the opening night of '*8.30*', she had again repeated her nervous concerns and asked for another of my magic pills with the promise not to tell. It was just as successful as the first time but I was concerned that the effect might have worn off by now.

'Hugh is very ill and can't possibly go on. You'd better get across here.'

Within seconds, perhaps less, she and our Gen. Manager, John Greenwood, were stooping over Hugh's prostrate body.

'What are we going to do, it goes up in 'five'?' said the boss. 'Do you know it, John?'

'What?'

'The part of Toby.'

'Of course I don't,' I stated emphatically, seeing what might be coming.

'Have you seen it?'

'Once at the 'Dress.'

'Then you'll have to go on.'

I bloody knew it.

As Hugh's costume of silk pyjamas and Noël Coward dressing gown were being thrown on me, I glanced at the text.

'You're discovered in bed with Mary' said Alison

'When was that?'

'What?'

'Nothing.'

'I see the script says that Toby is reading, so get me a book large enough to mask the French's Acting Edition. Furthermore, he will be reading throughout the entire piece,' I stated with authority.

I was then jostled into the bed with Mary, with one final alarming instruction from Alison:

'The revolver is in the top drawer of the table on your side of the bed. You'll need it when the intruder comes in.'

It is no wonder that I have suffered ever since from the actor's nightmare whilst asleep, of being in a play and not knowing who you are, who anybody else is or what you're doing there – this was IT.

'Good luck, darling,' Mary sweetly breathed into my ear as we lay side by side as the curtain rose.

In desperation, I had adopted the 'Noël' voice so that our tolerant audience might be deluded into thinking they were seeing a Coward play. I only once resorted to my Ken Dodd technique when Stella (Mary) said, as per the text:

'Oh Toby, darling, do stop reading,' to which I replied:

'After tonight, I doubt if I will ever be allowed to 'read' again.'

It was the unanticipated, however, that brought about my comeuppance. The intruder, in the course of the action, cuts off the electricity, hence darkness, hence I couldn't see a damned thing. I now fell even closer into Stella's arms and whispered tenderly into her ear:

'What the f--- do I say?'

Mary then whispered a rough outline of the plot into my 'shell-like' and I then passed on the information to those who had paid to hear it. In fact, we got away with it and having taken our 'call', I had enough time to go into my 'Stanislavsky' for 'George Pepper'.

Hugh was also unable to perform in the evening show or attend the last night party. He simple lay alone, feverish and miserable, in the comfort of the Orrington. My second reading of the part was only slightly more polished than the first. At the farewell function, a well-oiled, theatre-loving reveller said to me, as he knocked back another glass of Californian white:

'I saw the play three times and I thought you were better than the other actor in *Ways and Means* – in fact, I thought you were better in that than in *Red Peppers.*'

With praise like that ringing in my ears, I was overjoyed to board British Airways and get the hell out of there.

## 36

## BOTTOMS UP

If the Company had somewhat disappointed the good people of Chicago, we hoped we could restore amends with our production of *A Midsummer Night's Dream* on home soil. This was the chance to show off my Bottom. At school, I had given my scornful Lysander to J.A.H.Hammond's Hermia, with C.J.Benjamin as Oberon. Now, twenty years later, he was giving his Bottom, which seemed a natural progression for the King of the Fairies, for the Bristol Old Vic, at the same time that I was presenting mine to the townsfolk of Birmingham.

I was taken aback when I received a letter from a Mr Hammond, enquiring if I was the same Baddeley that he had been at school with and if so, could he 'come round' and see me after the performance. I was so excited at the prospect of seeing my cherubic Hermia again that I bought a small bouquet. When the moment arrived, into the dressing room came what appeared to be a portly, red-faced, family butcher, with fingers that resembled the sausages he obviously sold. No point in greeting him with:

"How now, my love! why is your cheek so pale?
How chance the roses there do fade so fast?"

My heart was quite broken.

How striking my performance was I could not possibly say, but I do know that the electricity workers were definitely striking. At any given moment the theatre, and indeed, the City, could find itself plunged into total darkness. They usually chose the moment that I made my first appearance, so my opening line would be: "Are we all (blackout) ….met?"

We would continue with a BBC Radio 3 performance, whilst still loyally attempting to do the moves. After several minutes, the stage director would bring down the curtain and we would stumble into a candlelit, front-of-house bar to imbibe with the customers. After another three-quarters of an hour blindly drinking, blind drunk actors and equally blind drunk members of the audience, were told that that was it – full refund. To overcome this situation the theatre hired two huge gas burners, placed one on either side of the stage, which threw an eerie and mysterious yellow light on the action. This took place at one performance and although impossible for there to be any change of light within the action, the audience found it magical and it did allow Pyramus (Bottom) to proclaim:

"Sweet moon, I thank thee for thy sunny beams" directly at one of the gas lamps. Again, you may not approve, the Fire Authorities most certainly did not, the theatre being threatened with closure if it ever happened again. I didn't think it was that bad a gag.

'We've had a request from British Road Services, for an actor to give a bad lecture to a group of trainees and we thought you would be ideal,' said Mr Greenwood.

The idea was for a 'bad lecture' to be given, illustrating all the 'don'ts', but that the trainees must be unaware that it was deliberate. Afterwards, a discussion would take place to see what they had noticed.

'How long would this 'bad' lecture be?' I enquired of their senior lecturer.

'Half an hour?' he suggested.

I pointed out that any lecture I gave, of whatever length, might be bad but to do it deliberately for that period of time was impossible and could lead to a mass walkout. We were having enough trouble with the electricity workers, let alone the road haulage drivers.

'What do you suggest?' asked the head of training.

'I'll do ten to fifteen minutes and then make a weak excuse and leave. I will return a few minutes later to pour oil on troubled waters and see how they react.' So that was agreed.

On the morning, I arrived unkempt, unwashed and undone, to deliver my lecture on life in the theatre. I was introduced to the students by their mentor who then departed leaving us to our fate. I told the thirty or so HGV drivers that I had little time to spare but would just say a few words. I did everything to alienate; poor vocal delivery, far too much of my back to the listeners, illegible use of the blackboard and general disinterest in my captive students. After ten minutes I said my time was far too precious to be here and without apology, departed.

Whilst I tidied myself up and changed into some clean clothes, my employer returned to ask how they had found it. They were all exceeding angry and indicated that it had been a total waste of time.

'Really?' he declared. 'In that case you'd better tell him yourselves.' To their horror, I reappeared.

I was to discover that they were all in fact graduates, destined to be high-fliers in BR Services. We then spent an hour and half discussing what they had seen and I asked them for their observations. They told me at the end that it had done more to show them how not – and how to – deliver a lecture than they had ever had before.

That evening, as Bottom made his first appearance (for once the light plug not being pulled), twenty patrons in the gallery stood and gave a cheered entrance round. It was of course, my lorry drivers, who confessed afterwards that although most were not enthusiasts of 'The Bard' or indeed of the theatre, they had been enthused to give it a try and had loved it. You see; something can come out of poor diction.

If the employees of BRS were loyal followers, they were not the only ones. I received a continual flow of musical scores with appreciative personal comments from a woman living in Solihull. She had heard me sing and wanted to share her passion with me. She invited me to visit her, so that she could show me what she had. I felt I had been down this avenue before and wrote, kindly thanking her and again used the 'pressure of work' line as my excuse. For some reason, this led to an even greater flow of correspondence regarding matters both musical and theatrical, and also conveying the problems she was having in her marital life. I decided simply not to respond. The one-sided correspondence continued. As she had never sent me a photograph of herself, I visualised a woman of somewhat mature years, in need of solace from someone – perhaps, anyone. On one occasion, arriving for a matinée, Kathleen the stage door keeper, handed me a large envelope. Once again, numerous musical scores.

'Kathleen, was this delivered by hand?'

'Yes, luv.'

'To you?'

'Yes.'

'What did the deliverer look like?'

'Oh, she was a rather good looking woman.'

'How old?'

'I'd say around ….. 35.'

"Dear John,

Just to let you know, I've changed my job and my desk looks out over the stage door, so now I'm able to see you come and go all the time."

I never dared look left, right and certainly not upwards for the rest of my days at the Station Street theatre. Ian McEwan's *Enduring Love* sums up my predicament expertly. (The first chapter, incidentally, being one of the most gripping I've read).

I was sorry to see the end of *The Dream* but in a way, relieved. In the scene where the rustics perform for the Court, there was the usual Morris Dance with much jingling of bells and clashing of staves. Dear John Gill, as Moonshine, seemed incapable of learning the precise timing required in the stick-banging department, leaving my knuckles bleeding, bruised and permanently swollen – I felt I was back in *The Caretaker*. However, it was worthwhile for one moment. As Pyramus, I had been given a skirt to wear by the designer and at the final fitting, it was found to be too large round the waist (those were the days), but I was assured by the Wardrobe Mistress that it could be taken in. I begged them not to for I had found that by disciplined use of my stomach muscles, I could keep it in place for the whole of the 'play scene' and at the conclusion of the dance, as we raised our arms and cudgels in celebration, timed to the second, I could release my stomach muscles and the skirt would drop to the ground. Anything for a laugh.

The last production of the Birmingham Repertory Company in the Station Street Theatre was announced. I was to play the Common Man in their ever popular *1066 and all That*. It was to be given a three-month run, for the audiences to see the Company perform for the last time on the stage that had been graced by Olivier, Coward, Richardson, Scofield, Pasco, Finney, Jacobi, Gambon, Ashcroft, Evans, Ffrangcon-Davies, Leighton, Christie, to name just a few.

The schoolboy humour reflection of history delighted both readers and audiences alike but I found it somewhat tedious, just not my thing. Peter, however, said that I could have five minutes at the start of the third act each night for me to do my own stand-up spot.
'Like ye did in '*Toad*', luvvy.'
So at least I had something to occupy my mind each day. David Glover, playing the compere, acted as my stooge. I think he loathed it. He said he always knew when I felt on top because I referred to him as 'Dave' but when I wasn't so confident, as 'David'. He took particular exception to one comment I made when I said:

'Dave and I have been doing this show so long, we're known as the Butch Cassidy and Sundance Kid of the Birmingham Rep. I'm Sundance and he's Butch.'
Why?

He was not the only one to object. One night, whilst doing my five-minute 'spot', a voice called from the gallery:
'You're rubbish.'
I sensed a lack of ease in the audience but decided to ignore the remark. A comment of this nature was not expected in a theatre that had such a 'classical' reputation – it was not the Palace of Varieties. There came a second cry of a similar nature, which prompted even more discomfort from the stalls and then one further cry.
'You are rubbish!'
By now there was positive resentment coming from the rest of the House, which I felt I could not ignore. Lines like 'move closer to the wall, Sir, that's plastered too,' I did not feel erudite enough for a Playhouse of its esteem. Fortunately, G. B. Shaw came to my rescue. I remembered what the great man had said to a barracker making the same comment to him on one of his first nights – *Pygmalion* perhaps. I raised my eyes to the 'Gods' and cried:
'I quite agree with you, Sir, but who are we amongst so many?'
The house erupted with approval and no more was heard from our man on 'the top shelf'.

Although my critic from on high did not appreciate my work, allow me to defend my performance by quoting the *Guardian,* which stated: "Mr B....... is a tremendous hit – cheeky as Chester, sly as Morecambe, he has his own brand of comedy – a flippant melancholy". So put that in your Brew XI, sir, and swallow it.

The last performance was followed by former 'worthies' rendering their party pieces, in a one-off presentation entitled The *Mighty Line*, a reference to words written by John Drinkwater on

39

the opening of the Theatre in 1913.
"We have the challenge of the mighty line.
God grant us grace to give the countersign."

James Bridie, author and co-founder of the Glasgow Citizens Theatre, wrote the following in 1938, the Silver Jubilee Year of the Birmingham Rep., which was recalled at that final curtain:
"If we are to be bombed, a thorough razing from Piccadilly Circus to Drury Lane and down to the Strand would do less harm to the Theatre, than one bomb on Station Street, Birmingham. Good luck to you."

# THE CHOICE WAS MINE

A musical in town would be ideal. An audition came up for just such, in an adaptation of Henry James' novel, *The Ambassadors*, starring the French film actress, Danielle Darrieux and the American actor, Howard Keel, perhaps best known for his role in the film *Seven Brides for Seven Brothers*. Towards the end of the show there was a scene that required a compère, with a great deal of free play to the audience. The American director took a liking to my irreverent approach to the audition and thought I could be just what was wanted. After three auditions, all on the production side agreed with him, as long as Gillian Lynne, the choreographer, was happy with my twinkle toes. I had a session with her and was offered the part. All that remained was the negotiations. At this point I received a call from – you might have guessed – Peter Dews. He was directing Robert Bolt's *Vivat! Vivat Regina*! at the Piccadilly Theatre, which had been brought up from the Chichester Festival.

'Could you meet me for lunch at that 'Italian' next to the stage door alley of The Piccadilly, tomorrow? Something I want to put to yer.'

After the spaghetti vongole he said:

'How about being in the opening production of the new Birmingham Rep? It's a musical of *Pride and Prejudice*, called *First Impressions* which, as you know, was its original title.'

'Was it?'

'I think it's a good title for the opener of the new theatre.'

'Who have you got for it, or am I your first choice?'

'No, luvvy, there's Francis Matthews as Mr Darcy, Patricia Routledge, your Mrs Bennett, Cheryl Kennedy as Elizabeth, Angela Browne, (that's Mrs Matthews to put you straight from the start,) as Caroline Bingley, Madeleine Christie as Lady Catherine de Burge and a couple of young crackers in Gemma

Craven and Mary Tamm, as well as the other usual suspects.'
'Where would I fit into this?' I enquired.
'I thought you would be perfect as the odious Mr Collins.'
'Thanks for that, Peter.'
'You've got a great number with Cheryl. There are parts for you
in the next two plays and beyond, if you want it. You'll be on our
top whack and the Rep. playgoers would love you to come back.'
'The problem is, I've been offered a part in *The Ambassadors*.'
'Where is it going in?' he enquired.
'Her Majesty's.'
'How long do you give it?'
'Having read it, three months,' I boldly stated like Mystic Meg.
'Well, it's up to you luvvy.'
To the chagrin of those who had put their faith in my stand-up
ability, and in spite of the fact that I really wanted to rub
shoulders with Mr Keel and in particular, Mlle Darrieux,
Birmingham won the day. Had I ruined a promising career?

*The Ambassadors* ran for three months and with 'Her Majesty's'
usual history of success, was ranked as a disaster.

'I've got a couple of tickets for you and Penny to see *Vivat*. Meet
me at the stage door after and I'll introduce you to Eileen.'
Having seen what was another impressive play by Robert Bolt
(the father of Penny's youngest  dancing student), we met Peter.
As we went into Eileen Atkins' dressing-room, he broadly
proclaimed:
'Eileen, this is my leadin' lad from Birmingham.'
Miss Atkins appeared to show no interest in me, for her glance
went directly over my shoulder.
'Penny,' she gleefully exclaimed and they fell into one another's
arms. What the hell was going on? The star of the Midlands felt
his nose being severely put out of joint.
Penny had omitted to remind me that her first job as an actress
had been a Summer Season at Butlin's Holiday camp in Skegness
and that she shared 'digs' with a young woman, whose only claim
to fame up to that time had been as a national junior tap-dancing

champion. Also in residence was a handsome young man called Julian, who later married the talented 'tapper' (for a time) so she became Mrs Glover and then later, Dame Eileen. As a dancer herself, Penny is still waiting to be 'Damed' for her services to dance, albeit not tap.

*1st Imps* was a pleasant enough show but one realised why it had never taken off after its run on Broadway. It was cast, costumed and choreographed well enough and while not setting the town alight (which apart from the Luftwaffe in the war was always a difficult thing to do in Birmingham) it was a dainty enough dish to set before a Princess Margaret, who graced the Gala opening. I was somewhat taken aback but not surprised when the Mayor, at the curtain call, when making a speech welcoming not only HRH but also the audience to this new home of the drama said:
'I hope you like this lovely theatre that we've built. I also 'ope that the Company put on plays that the people of Birmingham really want, not just Shakespeare and that lot.'
Obviously a man of some discernment.

At a banquet to celebrate the opening, our leading man's wife was sitting next to a city counsellor, who was something 'big' in the production of meat provisions encased within pastry, as per. Sweeney Todd and Mrs Lovett.
'I gather your husband's a well-known actor. What's he done?'
'Most recently, he's been playing Paul Temple in a television series' replied Angela, in a matter of fact tone.
'Really. I haven't got much time for television myself.'
'No, I understand' she replied. 'It's very much the same for us with your pork pies.'

The singing of the company was more than acceptable but I most enjoyed hearing Patricia Routledge's strong contralto voice. I had worked with her in *Follow That Girl* and admired her dedicated professionalism. I also enjoyed seeing her feet being in a balletic 'ten to two' stance as she let rip a number. Cheryl, as Elizabeth, sang well but I wasn't sure if her Balham tones were quite right. I attempted to woo her as the appalling cleric, but was rejected in a number simply entitled 'No'. So that was that.

I have to say I wasn't sure about the following play, *Roll Me Over*, either. It seemed to be a pale imitation of *The Caretaker*. Set in a tyre distribution yard, three vagrants live out their miserable lives. It was written by Bill Canaway, whose claim to fame had been writing the film script of his own book, *Sammy Going South*, which was the Royal Film of 1963, and also for co-writing the screenplay for *The Ipcress File*. This play did not match either of them. The quarrelsome threesome were played by Jane Freeman as the blousy Ellaline, Paul Henry as the simple-minded Gordon, et moi as a senile old codger, Cottie. Later, Paul was to gain celebrity status as Benny in the television 'soap' *Crossroads*. I asked him how he arrived at his character of Benny and he said:
'Simple, for Benny read Gordon' – as if I hadn't noticed.

Paul told me of a conversation that he had overheard on a Corporation bus, which I fear summed up my theatrical standing.
Woman A: 'Are ye going to the Rep to see that *Roll Me Over?*'
   "   B: 'What's it about?'
   "   A: 'It's a sort of Steptoe and Son, I think'
   "   B: 'I don't think I'll bother. Are you?'
   "   A: 'Might as well. That John Baddeley's in it – he's always good for a laff.'
And me a classical actor.

The stage area of the new theatre was supposed to be the second largest in the UK. Made for 'big' productions like musicals and tyre yards, it would have swamped *Staircase*. The only real lesson I learned from the 'rubber tyre' show was how to roll tyres in a straight line over a considerable distance. Try doing it and you'll find they go in circles. I might need to use that skill again sometime.

The Christmas offering seemed to be more interesting fare. It was an Edwardian musical slant on *The Merry Wives of Windsor*, by James Gilbert and Julian More, entitled *Good Time Johnny*. The strong cast included Ronnie Barker as Sir John (Falstaff) and Joan Sims as Queenie (Mistress Quickly). I was to play Forbes (Ford) and Paul Chapman, Paget (Page). The director/choreographer, Alan Lund, was imported from Canada, and had directed *Anne of Green Gables* in London, which was selected as best musical in 1969.

The production was to run for eight weeks and it had been agreed that I would take over the role of Sir John for the last two weeks, as Ronnie had other commitments. On the first day of rehearsal, I saw Ronnie sitting on his own in the foyer café, having a coffee. I introduced myself and welcomed him. We hit it off at once, when he enquired if I knew how the bookings were going and I informed him that I understood that the last two weeks were a sell-out and that the previous weeks were not doing too badly either. This appealed to him and we became sparring partners for the rest of our time on the show, which was to be regrettably brief.

I noticed after a couple of days into rehearsal that Ronnie's voice seemed husky and tired. It is true that Mr Lund was a hard taskmaster and I wondered if Ronnie was feeling the pressure of having to sing so much. After four days, he seemed hardly able to speak. He confided in me about his concerns with his 'Hobsons'. 'There's something wrong, apart from tiredness,' he said. 'You ought to see Norman Punt,' I said. 'The trouble is, he's in London and we are up here in Brum. Might I suggest you see my cousin, who is a Consultant here in Birmingham, and take it from there.'

I arranged for Ronnie to see Michael, who on examining him sent him to see a colleague of his, who was an ear, nose and throat specialist. Ronnie then confided in me that the medic had found a growth on the larynx. This would have to be removed and hopefully it would be found to be non-malignant. He was ordered not to use the voice for rehearsals and to stop smoking

45

immediately. He asked if he would be able to open in the show, which was a sell out, to which the Doc said:

'We'll wait and see.'

Although I was to take over Ronnie's role for the last fortnight of the run, I had made it clear that I was not his understudy. However, the situation was ludicrous with me rehearsing his part and trying to do my own part at the same time. I therefore approached the Management and asked if they wanted me to be ready to take over if necessary.

'Oh, please, John, if you would.'

Now I had done my share of taking over in recent months so I asked what arrangement they were willing to make regarding financial reward.

'Well, we could either put you on the same salary as Ronnie for the rest of the run....'

'Or?' I enquired.

'Or ...... we could pay you so much extra for each performance that you have to take over. If Ronnie were not to miss any performances, your pay would remain as is.'

I knew that Ronnie's wage was not that much higher than mine, so having discussed what the exact 'extra' per performance would be, decided to take the latter option.

'Paul Henry will have to take over your part – what do you think he should get?'

'Well, that's a matter for his agent,' I stated 'BUT, I suggest ....' I then put forward a figure not a great deal below mine.'

I hastened to see Paul, told him of the scenario and suggested he went along with my negotiations, which he did.

For the next three weeks Ronnie watched my every rehearsal move, whilst at the same time keeping his mouth tightly shut.

The day of the first night came. I did a full dress-rehearsal in the afternoon as Johnny Falstaff and then with Ronnie 'miked', 'we opened in Broad Street' to a full house. It went well but Ronnie's voice was not up to scratch. Not that I had time to worry about that, I was too busy trying to recall what Forbes was supposed to be saying and doing. The outstanding moment that night for me

46

came when Falstaff and Forbes were to have a duel. Totally unrehearsed, we selected our pistols, stood back to back and walked the required number of paces, before turning to fire at each other. To give the impression of supreme confidence, I twirled the gun on my trigger finger, as if it were *High Noon*. It would appear that the cast and the entire audience saw the bullet fall out of my gun. But not me. What should then have taken place in the action was that as we turned to face each other, Forbes would fire his gun before Falstaff could do so and the noise of the weapon discharging would cause Forbes to faint in a heap. However, as I pulled the trigger there was no response. I expected the 'off-stage stand-by gun' to be fired, as is traditional in these circumstances – but nothing. I lowered my weapon, as did my opponent and we raised our revolvers for a second go. Nothing happened, either 'on' or 'off'. I felt we could be doing this all night, so I uttered the plaintiff cry:

'Oh, sod it, BANG,' and collapsed.

To which Ronnie responded:

'And that's not the only bang he'll have tonight.'

Ronnie managed two more performances and was then told that he must have the 'op' immediately in the Queen Elizabeth Hospital. As he sang his final number, 'The Laugh's on Me', that Saturday night, I saw tears in his eyes, for the future was uncertain for Ronnie. It was imperative that the Press did not know what the problem was with Ronnie and when it was announced that he was having to leave the show, they headlined: "Barker dissatisfied with show – walks out." Nice, isn't it.

Joan Sims, who seemed to be in a constant state of uncertainty about everything, was made even more insecure by Ronnie's departure. However, she warmed to my counselling skills and even my performance, for the show went well. I called in to see Ronnie in his private room at the Queen Elizabeth Hospital, the day after the 'op'. He was not allowed to utter a word. During rehearsals we had vied with each other over an excessive piece of 'business' required in the opening of a bottle of champagne. This had felt like déjà-vu time for me, as memories came flooding back of my initial debacle when I was a student at the Alexandra Theatre and I had feared I might have to report to Derek Salberg again! Ronnie handed me a note, as I stood by his bedside, which stated:

"Do the champagne business" and he stretched under the bed and brought forth a bottle of Veuve Clicquot and a couple of glasses. I duly did as I was bid, using every aspect of the ward, bed (both actual and pan), temperature-chart, medicine cabinet etc. I, of course, delivered our usual coarse dialogue. The door burst open and in walked an irate Matron.

'Mr Barker must have complete quiet and not be disturbed. Would you please leave at once.'

Ronnie, under orders not to vocalise a sound, was unable to rally to my defence and I was sent packing with a flea in my ear (which is a damned good play).

All's well that ends well (another good one), for it was found that the growth that had been removed was non-malignant and his future distinguished career was saved. I had the 'run' of the play to myself – although for the last two weeks they put me back on my normal wage! However, I had become the first actor at the 'Rep' to earn a weekly three figure salary and Paul, who had recently married, would come in and report to me on some piece of kitchen equipment he had purchased, which would not have been the case but for the extra finance he had made by playing Forbes.

With the final curtain of *Johnny,* I decided it was time to move on from the theatre that I felt I almost owned. This had been prompted by my youngest daughter, Louise, enquiring of her mother one Sunday morning, as she climbed into bed between us: 'Mummy, who's that <u>man</u>?' At least it had not been: 'Who's <u>that</u> man?'

There were fond farewells, but I did not really appreciate the headline of a half page article about me in *The Birmingham Post,* which stated: "Goodbye to a First Class Second String." Thanks!

*Champagne Charlie*

## FRINGE BENEFITS

Hardly having time to assure my children that I was their father, a call came from a public house. A group of occasionally unemployed directors, actors and writers living in the Richmond area thought they would like to do something rather than nothing. These were led by Sam Walters, who had contacted me when I was in Birmingham asking if I would play Toby Belch in *Twelfth Night* at the Swan Theatre, Worcester, where he was Director (one of several occasions that I was unable to do that play professionally). With Michael Richmond, actor/writer, whom I did not know and Jeremy Paul, who I did not know, having attended prenatal classes with him, they trailed round pubs in the Richmond area seeking a room where they could start a lunch time Fringe Theatre. Having failed to achieve their endeavours at all the likely venues, they finally came to a run down 'boozer' opposite Richmond station, The Orange Tree. If it had more than three men and a dog as customers at any given time it was considered to be a busy session. The landlord was desperate for anything that could bring life and light into the gloom and despondency of establishment, and said there was a room upstairs which was only used occasionally by the 'Queer Fellows' – or something like that – and that the three dramateers could do what they liked with it. Then Orange Tree Theatre therefore opened in January 1972 with *Go Tell it on Table Mountain* by Evan Jones. The pub was so full with those wishing to see the play at that first performance that half of them could not get into the crowded upper room. They were asked if they would care to stay on and for the cast to do a repeat performance immediately after the first. They said they would, so the players did.

It was for their third play that I received a call from Mr Walters.
'I gather you've just finished in Birmingham. If you're not doing anything, would you like to be in our next production? It's a

three-hander, written by my younger brother, Matthew. Its title is *Googlies*, which I thought might appeal to you.'

So it came to pass that in that small upper room, Paul Chapman (whom I had just been with in Birmingham) and Jeremy Paul's gorgeous wife, Patricia Garwood, (playing my gorgeous wife) and I performed a fifty-minute play about a man who is visited by a stranger, who claims to know him from their schooldays. The innocent and unassertive husband, who has no recall of him, cannot find it in himself to challenge him and ask who the hell he is. The wife returns from wherever, at the end of the play, to add more complexity to the scenario. The situation carries constant menace and like the 'googly' in cricket, you are not sure which way it will turn. It was well received and apart from Miss Garwood walking into a door at the first performance and entering with blood streaming from a cut over her left eyebrow that Henry Cooper would have been proud of, adding somewhat to the surreal atmosphere of the piece, all went smoothly.

Those taking part in the production went unpaid, except for expenses. For the two weeks of rehearsals and the three-week run, I received the generous reward of £5.

By this time I was getting into the strange world of 'voice-overs'. In the late 60's it had been suggested that I should contact a Wendy Noel at the Bryan Drew Agency. I had worked with Bryan when he was an actor, during the brief time I had been at Sheffield.

'What the hell are voice-overs?' I asked.

It was explained that it was putting one's voice to television documentaries, replacing actor's voices in films and also doing the 'sell' lines in Radio and TV commercials.

'You mean a sort of vocal salesman? I didn't become an actor to be a salesman,' I pointed out altruistically.

To be seen in a 'commercial' at that time, was considered to be scraping the bottom of the barrel and detrimental to one's career. Would being a 'voice-over' be any different?

'Well, it might not be de rigueur but if you're any good, you can make more money in a week out of doing them, than playing a lead in the West End,' said my almost namesake, Ron Baddiley.

I hastened to the offices of the Bryan Drew Agency in Shaftesbury Avenue faster than I had run against the Olympic athlete and forcing an entry, ascended the stairs two at a time and demanded to see Ms Wendy Noel. I presented her with a cassette tape of my 'voices', which she passed on to her predecessor, Mary Harris, for her candid opinion, to which she gave the thumbs down. Wendy, however, took a chance and slowly introduced me into that rarified world. She asked me what was the minimum I needed per week to fulfil my financial requirements. On being told the modest sum, she assured me she could guarantee at least that – a rare statement for an actor to hear.

'But take a word of advice,' she sagely stated, 'don't let it distract you from your other work.'

Perhaps I should have listened to her with more consideration.

Late one evening the phone rang. Could this be an advertising agency requiring my services at nine the following morn?

'Is that Mr Baddesley?'

'Nearly.'

'This is Heathrow Airport. We have a Mr Patrick Blackwell here who says you are a friend of his.'

'Do continue.'

'He wonders if you could collect him from the airport?'

'Well, yes,' I stated, somewhat confused as to why he couldn't get a taxi or phone me himself.

'Please come to the Medical Centre, where he's being kept isolated. I think I should warn you that you may not recognise him.'

Was this some form of retribution on his part to gain revenge for the time he had to visit me in Hammersmith Hospital following my car accident? On arrival, I was taken into a side room where I came upon the Incredible Hulk. His face was swollen to twice its normal size, his torso was expanded so that every button and zip was wrenched open and his fingers resembled Cumberland pork sausages. He muttered some incoherent sound through swollen lips and clenched teeth.

'It appears, Sir, that he must have been bitten whilst in Africa and that he swelled up on the journey. We believe it to be an allergic reaction. Hopefully it's not a virus.'

I too, was hopeful it was not a virus and furthermore wondered what kind of reaction the woman in the seat next to him must have had, watching him turn from Jekyll into Hyde.

As fast as the Citroën would take us, I made for London and the Hospital for Tropical Diseases. Nurses fled down corridors, terrified at the apparition they saw before them but after three days of assiduous application of drugs and diuretics they brought him back to a reasonably normal size. Pity – I had found the transformation somewhat of an improvement, as well as being exceedingly funny.

--------0--------

Peter Dews could be relied on to offer me work. This time it was to play the part of Bert (I've been a Bert many times) in a play for Granada entitled *Goddess of Love*, in a series called *The Man in Room 17*, featuring Denholm Elliot and Richard Vernon. I was getting used to trips to Manchester, so I drove up the day prior to the first rehearsal, confident that one of my previous landladies or hotel proprietors would accommodate me. But there was no room at the Inn. Everywhere I tried, including The Midland Hotel, was full. I would like to have had the opportunity of displaying the sophistication of the celebrated Austrian actor, Anton Walbrook, who when on tour with *Call Me Madam*, arrived at the Midland to be greeted by the Manager with the words:

'Mr Walbrook, your suite is ready for you.'

To which he replied:

'What do you mean – ready? I will inspect several.'

Not even an airing cupboard was available for me.

In desperation, I went to the studios to seek help. I entered the Wardrobe department and proclaimed:
'Which one of you girls will I be sleeping with tonight?'
On hearing of my plight Ethel, a kindly seamstress of mature years, offered me a bed.
'The only trouble is, love, we are doing the final recording this evening of *Family at War*. There's a 'wrap'* party afterwards, so if you could come back at 10.30, you could drive us to my place in Salford.'
I had no alternative, so for the next four hours I filled in at The Bombay Nights with a fish pakora, chicken vindaloo, mutter paneer, washed down with gulab jaman – I've always loved Chinese. I returned around the witching hour to find a well-oiled cast, headed by Patrick Troughton and Colin Douglas, and a similarly imbibed Ethel from Salford.
'John love, would you mind also taking Edna home, she lives in Ashton-under-Lyne?'
If you think my landlady was drunk, you should have seen her friend, Edna. Having vomited a couple of times in Quay Street, we levered her unwilling body into the back seat.
'If you could give a helping hand love, we'll have to undress her and put her to bed.' The sights I've seen in the name of art.

'Now John, when we get home, you'll see my lovely Willie.' A chill ran through my body, fearing this could be a Mancunian euphemism for what I dared not imagine.
'We've been married forty years – he's lovely.' My relief was tangible.
As we entered No.43 she called out:
'Willie, come and meet John, he's staying the night.'
William approached me, extended his hand and belched.
I was unaccustomed to this northern manner of greeting and although I have always had the ability to 'burp' to order, was not certain if that was the required response, or indeed, passing wind of any kind, so I meekly shook his hand.

'Brtfg mrtgr dluf' he gurgled, beckoning me into the back parlour.

Throwing open the doors of a large cupboard, he indicated what appeared to be several hundred bottles of alcoholic beverage. Taking one, he poured me a glass.

'Buwthlun.'

I thought, I've been down this road of incomprehensible dialogue with Mr Blackwell at the airport and feared that my host might have formed an allergic reaction to me. I realised that was not the case, nor was this the language of a native of outer Mongolia, but that he was suffering from the removal of his voice box due to cancer and that he was bravely using the 'Jack Hawkins' method of communication. This assumption was later verified by his loving partner of forty years. I admired his courage enormously.

Buwthlun translated is Dandylion.

He was determined that I should sample several examples of his winemaking expertise.

'Werbefur; (Elderflower)

'Urbuk' (Burdock)

'Weunup' (Parsnip).

It was at this point that I became aware of the room taking on a life of its own. I pleaded that I wished to retire for the night (or what was left of it) but found it difficult to make an exit as the parlour door kept moving to a different position as I approached it. Finally, I groped my way up the seemingly endless flight of stairs, to fall into bed and watch the ceiling as it throbbed at me, with the walls spinning like a carousel. Sleep took me briefly out of this nightmare, only to be awoken by a shot being fired in the street outside. Terrified, I hid under the blankets, waiting to hear the wail of cars bearing the lads in blue. I just prayed that I would live out the night (I didn't want to let Mr Dews down) and gratefully subsided again into a welcome unconscious state, only to be awoken by yet another revolver shot disturbing the peace of gentle Salford. I had heard about gang warfare but did not wish to be a participant. I felt convinced that I could hear the sound of bodies being dragged down the street but in no way was I going to get out of bed to part the lace curtains and see.

At breakfast the following morning, I touched upon the matter of the assassinations that had taken place the previous night, and expected to be told to forget it and not get involved but Willie simply said:

' U tugh kaws umpn ut u bobbes.'

Translated: 'It were the corks coming out of the bottles.'

Whilst my gratitude knew no bounds, there were limits. I was exceedingly grateful when I managed to obtain a room at the New Theatre Inn for the rest of my stay. This celebrated pub, offering B&B, was well-known to touring actors and much appreciated because of its close proximity to the stage door of the Opera House. Sadly, this historic hostelry and home to many an Equity member during their week's stay, was pulled down a few years later. Opposite to it, before this sad happening took place, were the new impressive Law Courts. Staying at the Inn at that time was a senior actor of charm, elegance and dignity, Gerald Cross. He was approached by a fellow guest (of the non-theatrical variety) who addressed him in broad Glaswegian tones:

'It's a teerrribul day fur you'se profession, today.'

Gerald sipped his pre-prandial champagne.

'Why is that?' he enquired.

'One of you'se profession was fust on, when they'se opened the new Law Courts, today.'

'Really, who was that?' our esteemed actor enquired, with a mild degree of interest.

'David Kossoff.'

Gerald was wide eyed with disbelief and was now intrigued beyond measure. David Kossoff was of foreign, Jewish extraction and had made a name by presenting a one-man performance of dramatised readings from the Bible – the King James version. The thought of this holy man being hauled up in front of the beak seemed hard to comprehend.

'What was the problem?' our actor enquired.

'Well, it seems he sucked his penis.'

'I beg your pardon?' spluttered Gerald, choking on his bubbly.

56

The informant repeated the offence.

'Good lord, how terrible, poor David.' Gerald's imagination began to race and to the surprise of the Celtic supporter, he asked: 'Where did this take place – a public lavatory?'

The bemused Jock said:

'How the hell would I know? It seems this wee guy had been his penis and musical director for years and your Kossoff just sucked him on the spot, with nay notice or compensation – so the penis is suing him.'

Gerald ordered another bottle of Bollinger.

<sup>*</sup> End of production celebratory binge

# 39

## FUNNY GOINGS ON

The Albert Hall is impressive but you can be in it for too long.
Ronnie Barker, as a way of showing his gratitude for my Florence
Nightingale act in Birmingham, invited Penny and me to be his
guests there for the SFTA (later BAFTA) awards occasion, where
he and Ronnie Corbett were in the running for the Best Light
Entertainment category with *The Two Ronnies*. They duly won
this accolade, which was a relief having had to sit for hours whilst
awards were made for every conceivable aspect of the business.
'The award for best eyelash make-up artist goes to .......'
Thank God the food was reasonable.

The most memorable aspect, apart from Ronnie's moment of
triumph, was when Dame Sybil Thorndike came to the podium to
announce the winner of 'Best Film of the Year'. As she entered,
carrying the golden envelope, the entire hall rose to applaud her.
Aged 90 and with the vocal power of a Regimental Sergeant
Major, she announced the winner, relishing each word of the title.
*'Sunday, Bloody Sunday.'*
The director, John Schlesinger, went up from the main body of
the hall to the stage to receive the accolade from Princess
Alexandra. To do this he had to walk past Sybil and on doing so
he realised he had passed theatrical royalty without an
acknowledgement, so he stopped in his tracks and returned to
Sybil and made good his error. Having duly received his prize at
the Royal table, he returned to collect his celebrated announcer to
escort her to her table, as previous recipients had done. Sybil,
however, gestured for him to carry on by himself, whilst she, a
non-award winner, went to speak to the Royal personage. Having
done so, she made her own way to her place, to an even greater
reception than her entrance. I bet the winners wished their
reception had been as vociferous.

Three days later I worked with her, recording the 'son' aspect of a *Son et Lumière* for Windsor Castle or was it Hampton Court – I did several. I told her how much we (the audience) had enjoyed her returning to have a private word with Princess Alexandra. She simply stated:

'Well, I knew her father so well.'

I remembered how on one occasion she was seen with her husband, Lewis Casson, standing in the pensioners queue at the Birmingham Repertory Theatre for a matinée of *Saint Joan*, with Anna Calder Marshall in the title role. The management rushed out to the line of 'oldies' to give her and Lewis the 'house seats'. They found her happily chatting to all her fellow senior citizens, waiting for their turn to pay. I wonder how many of her 'friends' in the queue were aware that the play had been written for her by George Bernard Shaw and that it had made her a star – she was certainly a most unpretentious one.

Although Woodstock is in Oxfordshire, it was transported by the BBC to the Forest of Dean, being the most suitable location for the TV serial adaptation of Sir Walter Scott's novel *Woodstock* and David Maloney, whom I had been at Drama School with, was the Director. It was the story of Charles I v Cromwell in 1649, the year of Charles' execution and I was cast as Roger Wildrake, a flamboyant and devoted supporter of Charles and perhaps, the most colourful character in the book. In the Editor's Introduction in a 1969 edition he states:

"The life and soul of the story is Roger Wildrake, who never fails to put the reader in good humour. Few other writers could have depicted with such mastery a character, as the roistering, loyal, endearing Cavalier of broken fortune".

I hope I achieved that for the viewer – it most certainly sums me up – particularly the 'broken fortune'.

We stayed in a hotel in Gloucester, which was at least as old as the story we were depicting. Hitting one's head on beams and losing control of legs going down lop-sided corridors, was hilarious. David became so enamoured of the area that he and his wife Edwina bought a cottage in the Forest as their holiday retreat. They called it, naturally, 'Woodstock', which they still had when they both died thirty-four years later. It was David who encouraged me to write this memoir. I'm sorry he cannot read it.

Whilst I had been taking Birmingham by storm, the Greenwich Theatre had opened. Peter Dews yet again offered me employment, this time in *The Inferno*, in the very theatre that I had done my pub act to raise funds for. Perhaps the author thought it was the Green Witch Theatre, for that is what Michele Dotrice was supposed to be. Dealing with religious persecution, she was burnt at the stake, as she would not compromise her beliefs for either Edgar Wreford or Hugh Sullivan (my gay partner in *Staircase*). It was a powerful play but paled somewhat in comparison with Arthur Miller's *The Crucible*, which I was to be involved with years later. I seem to have been a regular witness to burnings at the stake, hangings and decapitations, so naturally, I was made priest in attendance at her execution.

Sometime later, they risked employing me there again, this time not in drama but a *Summer Music Hall*, starring one of my favourite funny men, Max Wall. Made up of old timers from the Green Man Pub, we did a seven-week season. The underlings did the first half and Max took over the second half. With either Mr Geoffrey Robinson or Mr Fred Stone in the Chair (hot-foot from the Players Theatre) and a cast including (in alphabetical order) strutting their variety of pieces: Mr J. Baddeley, Miss Jacqueline Clarke, Mr Derek Griffiths, Miss Marion Grimaldi, Miss Ruth Madoc, under the direction of Mr Ewan Hooper and Mr Alan Vaughen Williams. Apart from other items, it gave me the opportunity to do my *I Wonder What Happened to Him* striptease act again, which seemed to go down well with the patrons (and matrons) of Greenwich and even Max. For me, the main delight was being able to watch that superb comedian/clown every night and to observe him 'work an audience'.

Max had been having a difficult time. He had recently had an affair with a young lady who was in the London musical of *The Pyjama* Game, in which Max starred. She had been a one time Miss United Kingdom and the Press virtually destroyed his career and his marriage, even though he married this mistress of glamour (for a time). The public turned against him and work dried up. During this bleak period, I had worked with him in a radio play at the BBC and was somewhat embarrassed because the story hinged round a young comedian (me) whose act was based on a down-and-out old comic (Max). It was too near the truth and the fact that I had to impersonate Max made it even more gut wrenching. Of course we did it, and Max never made an untoward comment. Having lost everything, he was now in lodgings on Blackheath Hill, with the most caring of landladies, Mrs Moreton-Pritchard. The reopening of the Greenwich Theatre was just the opportunity he needed to regain his original stature.

He invited me to have supper with him in the theatre restaurant after the show one night. I was flattered by his generosity, knowing of his financial plight and touched because I was not aware of others in the cast having had a similar offer. I recall him saying, as we had our paté and Melba toast:

'The trouble is John, I don't 'go'* north of Portsmouth.' A somewhat limited area of approval.

Having completed the meal, I went to collect my coat, car keys etc., from the dressing room. To my horror I found that it was totally locked back stage.

'Harold's closed up and gone,' said the restaurant manager.

How the hell would I get back home?

'Knock on the back door of the pub across the road and tell them that George has sent you and explain the situation.'

The street outside was black, the sky was black and certainly the pub was black. There was not a chink of light visible and I was certain, it now being 1am, that the landlord and his wife would be safely tucked up in bed asleep – or something. Terrified, I rang the side doorbell, which was hardly visible in the Stygian gloom. All was silent. Suddenly, the door was flung open by a man who bore a close resemblance to Mike Tyson, except he was bigger and uglier. The noise of alcoholic revellers from within was deafening. A policeman's helmet lay nonchalantly on the hall floor. 'Big Mike' appraised me for a moment and then brusquely enquired:

'Ye, what do you want?' With shaking limbs and sweating palms, I mentioned George's name and the predicament I was in.

'Wait there a minute,' he ordered, shutting the door in my face. The pitch-black night took unto itself once more its deathly hush. After a four-minute wait (I was counting every second), the door was thrown open and bedlam ensued from within.

'Where's the car?'

Stumbling and mumbling, I led the way to the adjacent car park. In his hand, like a jailor, he was a holding a vast bunch of keys, comprising of at least a hundred of various shapes and sizes.

'Where is it?' he enquired.

I pointed out my Austin Countryman in racing green. He glanced at his collection and instantly selected an insignificant item hidden in the centre of its bedfellows. He placed it in the door lock and the door immediately opened.

'Wot a bit a luck,' he commented and removing it from its companions, he simply stated:

'Let's have it back tomorrow.'

What it is to have connections in low places.

'They're auditioning for a Christmas musical at Greenwich with an American director. His wife, the well-known Revue artiste Thelma Ruby, will be playing the lead. As you're down there you might as well have a go,' suggested my agent. So I did.

I sang a number for the man, which he seemed to approve of and then he asked in North American tones (which would not have been out of place in The Actor's Studio, New York):

'Mr Baddeley, do you mind improvising?' I said that I didn't, that it was learning the lines that was the problem. As he seemed confused by this comment, I asked what he had in mind.

'Could you imagine that you are a retired army officer, reflecting on past times and of the people that you knew.'

I thought for a moment he was taking the 'michael' and that he must have seen the show I was performing in each night in that very theatre, for it was exactly the format of *I Wonder what Happened to Him*. I realised, however, that this was not the case.

'Just one extra thing I'd like you do,' he requested, 'for a brief moment I want you to become a young man again, and then you slip back into your old age.' That was different. I said that it would be a pleasure and I turned my back, cleared my throat, and within an instant faced him again and went straight into:

"The India that you've read about and may have been misled about ............. etc." Of course, no striptease, and just a brief moment for a touch of the Dorian Grays. He appeared to be staggered. He called to the stage manager:

'What time is it?'

'12.45.'

'How many are waiting to be auditioned?'

'Three.'

'Would you tell them to come back at 2 o'clock?'

He turned to me with a smile on his face and a twinkle in his eye.

'Mr Baddeley, I am taking *you* to lunch!'

He obviously felt he had seen a genius. He had – Noël Coward.

At a smart restaurant nearby, I partook of his generosity in the company of Ms Ruby and he offered me the part.

The following day I turned down his kind offer, somewhat doubting his credentials but most of all fearing that I might not live up to his expectations if I was supposed to improvise regularly in the manner of 'The Master'.

I wonder what happened to him?

* To 'not go' is a theatrical term for failing to gain audience appreciation, not a refusal to travel.

## THE RETURN of the NATIVE

*"They came from Birmingham which is not a place of promise, you know, Mr Weston. One has not great hopes of Birmingham. I always say there is something direful in the sound."*

*Emma* by Jane Austin

Having left Birmingham, what the hell was I doing back there? 'It's a revue type show about the city's history and we need an MC, general audience 'chatter-upper' and we thought of you, being one of their 'favourite sons'. The title is *Up Spaghetti Junction.'*

In theory, a good idea. It was devised by Malcolm Totten and written by himself, John Clarke, David Edgar and David Turner. A group of builders, who are "tearing it down and putting another one in its place" took us through the strange eventful history of the second city. Leading the lads, who were more committed to tea and bacon 'sarnies' than putting bricks on mortar, was Our Kid, played by your author. The sketches were written by the talented playwrights but the 'links' with the lads, of which there were many (links rather than lads), were left to the 'workers' to improvise. So, while Michael Simpson and Christopher Honer were directing the easy stuff, the men of the Midlands: Gareth Armstrong, Lionel Haft, Paul Henry, Olu Jacobs, Geoffrey Leesley, Frank Moorey, Colin Starkey et moi, would go up to the top bar and improvise from morn to night until we had worked out our act. It was a great opportunity to insult the City Council, football clubs, hotels, the local press – indeed, anyone who had got up our noses. I'm not sure if it was due to us or not but the Gas workers went on strike and the audience were advised to wear coats.

"Lovely comin' in on the bus today. The daffodils were out."
"Does that affect us?"
Just one of the shafts of wit that was forced on the customers.

The stage area of the new theatre was vast. Hugh Durrant managed to virtually fill it with scaffolding and half demolished and half built buildings, which left an acting area the size of a postage stamp, smaller than the old Repertory Theatre stage, which was quite an achievement. It did allow me just enough room to welcome the audience and to pour venom upon latecomers. I instructed the front of house staff to admit all latecomers and for them to be shown to their seats – always good for 'embarrassing' moments, which I had learned from Max.
'Have you come far, sir?' I would enquire, as they were settling into their seats, hopefully, unnoticed.
'I beg your pardon?' might be the response.
'Where have come from?'
'Balsall Heath.'
'Oh, so you managed to get a Visa then.'
'Does you husband know you're out, Madam?'

Sentiments like:
"You can always tell a Brummie by the shamrock in his turban" littered the lyrics of the songs and Olu Jacobs, a black actor with a superb voice, was challenged during one matinée with the reality of life in that fine City. With all the workers on yet another tea break, we were lulled into quietude by him singing a mournful song of how ethnic minorities were unwelcome. The general theme ran on the lines:
"We can sweep the streets, we can clean the hospitals, we can drive your buses –
(Refrain) But you don't want us living next door."
This sentiment was repeated at the end of each poignant verse. One matron of the city, coming in for a matinée on her senior concession and sitting in the front row, was so carried away by the depth of feeling conveyed by the performer, that as he sang

65

the refrain yet again, she supported him with heartfelt conviction by saying most audibly:

'True, very true.'

His fellow workers all then appeared intent on burying their faces in their sandwiches for some reason. It became a constant statement both on and off stage, for the rest of the run.

In its way it was quite successful. Whilst taking a short holiday afterwards with the family in Studland, I was horrified to read that the main writer of the show, Malcolm Totten, also on holiday, had fallen off a rock, a distance of only three feet, struck his head and died. In the midst of life ………

After our brief seaside interlude I played the kindly doctor, Mr Lloyd in a BBC TV serial of *Jane Eyre*. My lasting memory of that production was of the children taking part. I thought they were all appalling and asked the director where they came from, to be told they were students at the various drama schools, catering for those with the acting bug but who were still of school age. I was to find over the years that this standard, although not total, was pretty general and it seemed these 'would be's' were there more to feed their mother's wish to live out their own dream, rather than for the benefit of their offspring. "Don't put your daughter on the stage, Mrs Worthington." I determined my children would never go down that path. The girl playing the young Jane, however, had got ability and intelligence and seemed to be the only one with any talent. I enquired as to what Drama School she went to.

'She doesn't. She goes to an ordinary private school and was recommended to us.'

I asked the young girl if she wanted to be an actress when she grew up.

'No, I don't. I hope to become a Doctor.'

I'm sure she did.

Where some of my jobs came from, I have no idea.

'It's the City of Bath's 1000th anniversary of the Coronation of the first monarch of all England, which took place in Bath. He was King Edgar and we'd like you to play him.'

This royal millennium was reason enough for there to be a celebratory occasion in the beautiful city of Aquae Sulis. The one-week production was mounted at the University and then recorded for transmission by Harlech TV. The title was *Good Edgar or A Knight of Saxon Violence*. The author and composer was a young man, who like us all was slaving to make a living but unlike myself, was a dab hand at DIY. I was not only impressed with his composing talents and with his dexterity at the keyboard, but the fact that he completed *The Times* crossword over breakfast each morning. Not long afterwards I saw him in a TV series giving DIY tips, then adding a touch of cabaret to the proceedings. Finally, the DIY was dropped and he continued as the writer and entertainer, Richard Stilgoe. Amongst his many successes, he wrote the book and lyrics for *Starlight Express*.

The cast of *Edgar* comprised: Jill Fletcher (daughter of celebrated comedian, Cyril Fletcher) playing the Royal nanny, Ethelmerman; Patricia Michael (who I had persuaded to alter her surname from Fitt) as my daughter and Charles Collingwood (to become well known as Brian Aldridge in *The Archers)* as Leograed, an impresario. Richard himself played Carlos, a lame troubadour. The King's son, Ethelred, did not appear, as obviously he was never ready. Our Director was David Bellamy, not the TV pundit on matters ecological, with the pronounced dropped 'R', but a man I had met in Harrogate some years before, when he worked backstage at night and in a shoe shop during the day. He was not hugely popular with the cast for calling them in for 'notes' at 9am, the morning after the first night and then turning up an hour late himself. He had one particular skill that I have never been able to emulate. When I asked him in the bar what he would like to drink, he nonchalantly responded:

'Two pints of Guinness, please.'

Looking round to see who his partner was and seeing nobody, I naturally checked the request:

'Two, did you say?'

'Yes, please.' It was then apparent that he required one for each hand.

Obviously, a man who had been on an Assertiveness Course.

Presumably thinking that we had a thirst for theatrical knowledge, Cyril, the father of Jill Fletcher, who had come to see the show, regaled Messrs Stilgoe, Collingwood and Baddeley in the bar afterwards with a master class on how to play comedy. Unfortunately, he failed to raise a smile among the three of us, for he was indeed a very odd ode. I longed for Max Wall to walk through the door.

Switching on the TV the following morning, I heard the news of the murder of John Lennon – you can't forget these things.

'You really should be a member of the MCC,' said Charles. I had discussed my passion for cricket with him and although I had not played against his old school, Sherborne, I rather imagine he may have played for it.

'I'll get Peter Howell to second you.' I knew Peter from BBC radio – another man of class. I put it out of my mind because I knew there was a waiting list of forty years. However, due to the MCC urgently needing extra funds, three years later they decided to expand the membership by a couple of thousand and I got in under the wire. Dickie (Richard S) missed the boat to his chagrin, and it took several years and a few cabaret performances in the Long Room before he got in.

'Oh, it's you again, Sam. Another feast for the upper room?'

'No, this is in an actual theatre' bristled Mr Walters.

There had been a successful run in Town of a collection of short plays under the title *Mixed Doubles*. Sam was to direct a follow-up, with a try out at the Capitol Theatre, Horsham. Had I gone to Christ's Hospital, I would have known it well. This was another collection of short pieces, which had been put together by Andree Melly and her husband, Oscar Quitak, entitled *Mixed Blessings*.

The theme being, anyone affected by having children. The authors were: Alan Ayckbourn, John Bowen, Lyndon Brook, David Campton, Denis Cannan, David Cregan, Alun Owen, James Saunders and Fay Weldon.

'Your task will be four one-man pieces written by Andree's brother, George, and is about those also affected by but not having 'mixed blessings' of their own. It will also allow time for the others to do their costume changes.'

Basically, I was there to do 'front cloth' work – nothing new. The author, George Melly, was the celebrated jazz singer, critic and man of wisdom and what he had written seemed to be right up my street. First there was 'Uncle Ted', a children's party entertainer who loathed children; then a 'camp' shop attendant in a 'kiddies' boutique; a Scottish nanny; and a headmistress. My joy knew no bounds. My main concern was finding costumes for the latter two parts. The dear ladies of the company, Andree, Marion Mathie and Ann Penfold kindly brought items from their wardrobe for me to try but none seemed either to fit or to be quite to my taste – I could be very fussy. I resolved to find my own solution. I had noticed an Oxfam charity shop in the town and so one wet and windy Wednesday afternoon, I entered and enquired if they had a tweed two-piece jacket and skirt, silk blouse, lisle stockings, brogue shoes, a three-quarter length long sleeve dress (floral if possible) with pinched waist, high heel shoes and fish-net stockings. Fortunately, it was a quiet day in the shop. They asked if I could help them with the sizes. Those of you who were loyal enough to read of my Southsea exploits will see where this was leading.

'I'm not quite sure,' I truthfully informed them.

'Well, who are they for?' they asked.

All right, you guessed.

'They're for me.'

It has to be said that the Oxfam ladies hardly blinked an eyelid, but before they could say:

'Oh, we get a lot of your people in here,' I explained my need for these attires. They were wonderful and provided everything, all for the cost of three complimentary tickets for the first night and a 'fiver' to go to their worthy charity.

I enjoyed every moment of performing Mr Melly's work, particularly when I was in my dresses. Years later, I thought Dustin Hoffman must have raided my wardrobe for his performance in *Tootsie.*

--------0--------

When I left Drama School, I had written to Hazel Vincent Wallace, which was not the name of a solicitors practice but that of the director of the Leatherhead Theatre Club (later to be called the Thorndike Theatre), and I had received a clear response.
"Dear Mr Baddeley, I am sorry I cannot be helpful, but I am afraid it is unlikely that anything suitable will crop up for you here."
Well that seemed pretty clear to me. I was surprised therefore, when twenty years later, I was to hear from her again.
'Jonathan Lynn would like you to play Don John, the bastard.'
'Jonathan's not that awful,' I assured her.
'No, Don John's the Bastard in *Much Ado About Nothing.*'
'Oh, really?'
It was a challenge, for I was used to playing mainly comedy roles and Don John was not a bundle of laughs. I put this to the young director and he said:
'Exactly. I want you to play this dreadful man with humour – to make him even more sinister.'
I had worked with Jonathan in a TV series called *Doctor in Charge* which he had written with George Layton, whom I had acted with briefly in a 'soap' about a football club called *United –* what a network it all is. Jonathan went on to fame and presumably fortune, as co-author of *Yes, Minister* etc.

Benedick was played by Terrence Hardiman with authority, and Beatrice by Hilary Dwyer, somewhat less so. Barry Stanton was excellent as Dogberry and I was a moderate Don John. My legitimate brother was Hugh Sullivan (he couldn't keep away from me) and one's eye was drawn to a waiting-gentlewoman, Barbara Kellermann. There was much delight when Dame Sybil Thorndike came to see the show. She sat in the front row and during the masked ball scene I was able to observe her leaning forward with rapt attention. After the performance, as had become her tradition, she remained in her seat and the cast came to her to show respect and to hear her comments. As she had played the role of Beatrice many times, my heart sank when our leading lady asked her what she felt about her performance. Sybil was charm itself and said:

'I heard everything, everything.'

I was told later, that when in doubt this was her stock response. Sitting in the front row, it was to be hoped she could hear it, for even at her age she had excellent hearing, but I was not sure how she would have fared a couple of rows further back. There was the story of her seeing *The Changing Room* by David Storey, an all embracing tale of Rugby footballers spending most of the time getting into or out of their shirts, shorts and boots, or indeed, being totally naked. When the lads went to hear Sybil's comments, sitting in the front row as usual, she was asked how she had found the play, to which she warmly stated:

'I saw everything, everything, and the gentlemen's little arrangements didn't bother me at all.'

That Dame certainly kept her eyes and ears open.

# 41

## EDUCATION, EDUCATION ....

'What about Frensham?'

Mark was an unusual boy, but then every parent thinks there is something that makes their offspring stand out from all others. From an early age he seemed to prefer the company of adults rather than children, girls rather than boys and generally being by himself rather than with others. He most certainly did not enjoy playing sport but did relish writing and in particular amassing facts and figures and records. There is no doubt he was demanding and required his parents, siblings, friends and loving neighbour, Helga, to be as interested in his research as he was himself. Over the years, one was never aware of him reading and yet he was able to refer to literature with some authority. Due to behaviour problems, it was considered that he should go to a Child Guidance Clinic. There he formed a strong rapport with his psychotherapist, a most charming woman with whom Mark formed a close bond. It was felt that it might be best for him if he were to be educated in a more unusual, indeed, special school, rather than the hurly burly of State Education. Several of these 'special' schools were suggested but we did not feel that the ones we saw were suitable choices for Mark.

It had not occurred to us that a boarding school was a good idea. The fact that both Penny and I had been to one did not make us feel that our children should go down that path, nor indeed, was there a Dotheboys Hall syndrome entering into the equation. In the end, however, we felt that Frensham Heights School, near Farnham, had the progressive, freethinking, non-regimented approach that would give Mark the stimulus he would benefit from. This was a school that stood alongside Summerhill founded by A. S. Neill and Bedales by John Badley.[*] What about the cost?

It was one of the most expensive schools that could be found. Ask not how, for ours is not to reason why, but the local Education Authority agreed to fund the fees, as they felt it would be beneficial and more appropriate for his needs. Over the next few years we were to see a great deal of Rowledge and the Ponds at Frensham.

Birmingham called yet again. How was I fixed for doing three plays and taking them to Hong Kong for the Festival, which would be sandwiched in between their being presented at the Repertory Theatre? With so much happening on the home front, I felt that the project would take up too large a slice of the year, so I turned down the chance of doing an overseas tour to far eastern shores and of being in Middleton's *The Changeling*; workshop performances of Edward Bond's *The Pope's Wedding*; and *Henry V*. I said I could only have done *Henry* and was sorry not to be going with them. To my amazement they came back a couple of days later and said:
'Alright then, just come and play Pistol.' Perhaps they saw me as a mascot – it was irresistible.

The flight out was made up entirely of artistes taking part in the Hong Kong Festival i.e. the Birmingham Rep. and the London Symphony Orchestra, under the baton of André Previn. It is a lengthy flight to HK and if you think actors can drink you should have seen the LSO. As we disembarked at Kai Tak Airport, having seemingly flown the last few miles down a street looking in through bedroom windows observing Chinese couples co-ordinating, the Leader of the Orchestra fell down the length of the steps, broke his arm and had to be returned to the UK the following day as damaged goods. When we arrived at our hotel on Kowloon side, one exceedingly well-oiled actor had his comeuppance. When passing through the lobby he demanded 'a woman' and was totally phased when one arrived at his bedroom door a quarter of an hour later. Not being up to his act of bravado,

73

he had to pay her to go away.

As I lay in bed, I wondered what all the buttons over my head were for. It reminded me of a film that was frequently played when I went to parties as an eight year old, of a mad inventor who had a similar arrangement in his bedroom. Although The Miramar Hotel on Nathan Road, Kowloon, did not have buttons that made the bedcover shoot to the window to become curtains during the day, or another to send the bed vertically into the wall to become a roaring fire with mantlepiece, at least there was one to open and close the curtains without rising from the prone position.

I loved the bustle of every street at any time of day or night, so full of humankind it felt like the exodus from Wembley after a Cup Final and also the fact that for the only time in my life, I stood out in a crowd. I really could see and hail my colleagues at a hundred paces. On my first evening I wandered into side streets, where chow mein was being sold from woks, chickens were being slaughtered from coops and sex potions dispensed from jars. The latter fascinated me because the viagra seller sat between what appeared to be two pudding basins and throwing a coin in each with particular dexterity, they would spin round the bowl like a motor bike on the 'wall of death'. At the same time he would extol the virtues of his product like a Covent Garden tradesman selling cabbages. As the coin was slowly dropping to the bottom of the basin to lie dormant, he would give the basin a quick flick with his nimble fingers and the coin would shoot back to the top. I felt this was a symbol of how one should address life. Keep several options in the air and make sure they are never allowed to fall away.

The cheapest boat journey in the world was the Star Ferry from Kowloon to Hong Kong Island for two old pence. I did not enjoy the constant hawking and spitting that took place but it gave me pleasure to go behind an unsuspecting friend and clear my throat in the most audible fashion, and see them cringe without daring to look over their shoulder. *Henry V* was performed in the City Hall, which also housed the Concert Hall where the LSO were performing. We would 'nip' out of our rehearsals to hear them rehearse but they never reciprocated – philistines. My problem was that the long haul from 'Blighty' had disturbed wax in my eardrums and I could not hear my fellow artistes utter my 'cues'. Two visits to the HK General Hospital and presumably using sledgehammers, they cleared out the problem. There was a bigger one to follow, however. Part of the duties of artistes touring abroad is that they are also considered to be amateur diplomats and expected to attend constant receptions and parties. Being charming to Chinese millionaires, saying the right thing in front of the Governor General and fighting off the attentions of wives of Foreign Office personnel who have been away from the UK for far too long, can be demanding. Prior to going, I had foreseen one major problem, which could affect my flag-flying responsibilities and also my personal social pleasure – leeks.

Not leaks, leeks, this was not an incontinence problem, simply dietary. Have you ever eaten a raw leek? Following their altercation (Act V Sc 1), Fluellen forces Pistol, "the rascally, scald, beggarly, lousy, pragging knave" to consume the leek that he, Fluellen, wears in his hat and adds sauce to it by striking him over the head with his cudgel. Aunchient Pistol finally addresses the audience with his parting speech. I was told that even the Birmingham playgoers, who were used to coping with anything, found the smell of my leek issuing from my mouth overpowering, reaching as it did up to five rows back in the stalls. Eating a raw onion would seem as a mildly flavoured Menthos mint compared to the mind-blowing pungency of a raw leek. I found partaking of this lethal mixture on a daily basis gave me a terrible migraine – something I was prone to and being struck over the pate with a cudgel every performance did not help. At the opening-night party in Hong Kong, presumably overwhelmed, not by my looks, charm or personality but from the aroma issuing from my mouth, one of our very attractive hostesses recoiled from me at our first meeting, as did Paul Totellier, the celebrated cellist – and he was French. This form of odoriferous breath had worked for me in the

RAF but not here. I determined that a solution must be found. Stage Management, 'Props' and even Wardrobe could find no resolve. As I wandered the streets of old Hong Kong, stopping at a stall selling Chinese vegetables, I found the answer. Chicory. I rushed back to find June Callier, our head of the Wardrobe Dept., presented her with the chicory, separated the leaves of a leek from the white danger end and said:

'Stitch those leaves onto the chicory and nobody will notice. I'm sure it will work.' Nobody did, so it did. Chicory, being the most bland of all salad vegetables, meant that my breath was as sweet as Listermint and the cast could stop humming the Halitosis chorus.

Our arrival had overlapped with that of the Royal Shakespeare Company, who were playing the fortnight before us in the same theatre. They warned us that we would be approached to do an extra matinee for schools (gratis).

'If you agree to do it, don't let the English School 'buy' the whole 'House', which we did and they were the dullest bunch you could imagine. We'd suggest that children must come themselves to the theatre to buy their tickets, which will allow them off school that afternoon.'

We took our fellow thespian's advice, the result being that we played to a full house of children, made up of 95% Chinese. They were wonderful, having far more knowledge and understanding of their Shakespeare than any English schools audience one plays to. They were also quite normal kids, in that they giggled if there was any kissing or lines of double-entendre nature. They were even amused with my abuse of the Bard when the French prisoner addressed me:

"Je pense que vous ...." as I grasped him by the throat and interpolated:

'Ponce .. moi?'

Damned clever, those Chinese.

I was delighted to meet Martin Boddey and yet at the same time felt slightly guilty. Martin was a singer and actor but more importantly a cricket follower of immense enthusiasm. He took on the part I had rejected in *The Changeling* and also played the Bishop of Ely in Henry and something in the Bond piece. I did not know that he had recently had a heart attack and that he lived under the constant threat of a masterstroke and should not be overstretched. However, he wanted to go to Hong Kong, to see the Hong Kong Cricket Club before he died, which was downtown in that crowded Isle, next to the salubrious Hong Kong Club. That cricket pitch must have been the most valuable 22 yards in the world.

Martin was an habitué of the Tavern at Lord's, and around 6pm on a match day it would be full of actors, literati and other alcoholics. It was Martin's idea to form a Club, in humorous opposition to the MCC, its sole purpose being to raise money for charity and to support children that wanted to play cricket but had limited resources. It was also an opportunity to exchange unlikely stories and drink to excess. Martin was therefore founder and member No 1 of The Lord's Taverners. Unfortunately, he had another minor attack while we were out there but he was determined not to miss a performance or of attending a lunch at the HK Club, which had been arranged in his honour. There he would have regaled them with the story of how he had asked the Duke of Edinburgh to be the President of The Taverners, which he regretfully had to decline but that Martin's second suggestion, of him being their permanent 12th Man was accepted.

On his return home from Hong Kong he was taken ill again and I visited him early one morning in his private room in hospital and he immediately offered me a whisky.
'Open that cupboard, you should find something you like.'
It was full of his favourite tipple brought in by his wellwishers. His doctor had said that one a day would be good for him but I am of the opinion that he was intending a glass, not a bottle. Two weeks after my visit, Martin was 'padding up' for the Elysian Fields CC.

Several years later, I was invited to become a member of The Lord's Taveners and my first 'occasion' was a celebration dinner at the Hilton, Park Lane, in honour of Sir Garfield Sobers. It was 'Bod', however, who was foremost in my mind.

--------0--------

Hazel Vincent Wallace phoned.

'We're putting on Alan Ayckbourn's play *Time and Time Again,* I'd like you to play Graham. If you don't know it, get yourself a script and tell me what you think.'

As we were on holiday, I read the play as we sat on the beach, flinching as the seagulls swooped over us as we partook of our picnic lunch. Penny became more and more irritated with the man sitting fifteen yards away from us, offering bread to the seashore vultures, which would fly past an inch from one's nose. There were large, clearly written notices on the promenade stating:

**DO NOT FEED THE SEAGULLS**

Having just lost her smoked salmon to a herring gull, she approached the beach-bum and requested that he desist, pointing out the Town Council's notice adjacent to us.

'Why not?' he retorted 'I'll feed them if I want to. They're only human, aren't they?'

I assured my indignant partner that there was no answer to that. It was at that point, as she passed me a ham sandwich, that I decided to take the role.

The cast of Vivienne Martin, Elaine Donnelly, Drew Henley and myself were headed by Trevor Bannister, who was well-known for being in *Are You Being Served* on television. He had just come hotfoot from playing the same part at the Theatre Royal, Windsor, thus having a head start on the rest of us. It was a play right up my street – or so I thought. The rehearsals went smoothly and I felt confident with myself and with my fellow actors. Then came the first night. Our star then gave a somewhat individual performance, in that his moves seemed to bear little relationship to what had been rehearsed. Dear old Eddie Reindeer might not have kept to the script but at least I knew where he was! I

78

suspected the rest of us must have looked somewhat incompetent not knowing where to look. My pantomime experience, however, was a great help and I thoroughly enjoyed the challenge. Years later, Trevor and I would meet on the golf course or in the club bar where he was always charming and witty company – but I never took my eye off him just in case I missed him!

\* In 1965 I had received fan mail, redirected to me by the BBC, congratulating me on my fine voice for a man of my age. Although always seeking approbation, I felt this was going a bit far being only in my early thirties. It was when I realised that the letters were addressed to John Badley, who had recently been interviewed on radio on the occasion of his 100th birthday, that I felt compassion and forwarded the mail to its rightful recipient at Bedales.

# 42

## SOAP IN MY EYES

'Soaps' are not for me. However, there was a void and the opportunity to earn a modest crust came my way by being offered a few weeks on *Crossroads*. Like being involved in an accident, most of the details of that engagement have been blocked from my mind. 'Roy Warwick' was some kind of hard-dealing theatrical agent trying to promote one of the young regulars. The chance of living again with my mother and stepfather in Weoley Castle, made the stay bearable. The pressure of producing four, if not five episodes a week is quite demanding and the standard could not be high. As Noël Coward said, on being asked what he thought of television in its early days, it felt very much like - 'Amateur theatricals in an iron lung.'

With Noelle Gordon as Meg Richardson (the Elsie Tanner slot of the series) and Ronald Allan as David Hunter, the suave manager of the motel, there were some experienced old hands aboard. There were other audience favourites, like Roger Tonge as Sandy and Ann George, not to be confused with Susan George or even Boy George, playing Amy Turtle. She was of local stock, having been a member of an amateur society and had been given her chance to make the 'big time'. My character of Roy Warwick was somewhat acerbic, boring and did not tolerate inefficiency. He did not respond well to Amy's slowness on the reception desk. I was, however, surprised when the producer of the programme took me to one side and asked me to 'ease off' when rehearsing the scenes with Ann. I enquired as to what he meant. He informed me that she felt that I, personally, was not satisfied with her and might be trying to get her the sack from the programme. I pointed out that I was simply saying the lines that were in the script.
'I know. It's just she's nervous about you. Of course, on the recording you can play it with the stops out.'

I said I'd never had such a request before but that I would do my best. The moment of truth came in the last scene of my last episode. Whilst hopefully seeming as professional and pleasant as I could be, I could not wait to say farewell. Although the episodes were recorded, they might as well have been broadcast 'live', for they never stopped for retakes. What you did was what was broadcast. If you 'dried' you had to ad lib your way out of it. If you took the option, as a dear old Norman Mitchell did, of putting in unacceptable expletives, thinking that would stop the recording, you would be mistaken. They simply kept on recording and the sound of the foul oaths were blanked out on transmission, so that it was only viewers with hearing impairment who could lip-read, that 'phoned in to complain. As we reached my last scene, to end that strange eventful interlude at the Crossroads Motel, I was aware that the studio manager was standing with arm raised ready to give me my cue to enter the reception area, approach the desk and to go into dialogue with Amy Turtle (Ms George). I tried to indicate to him that there was a problem but he chose to ignore me, as he was terrified of missing his director's instruction in his 'cans' for me to enter. The problem was that Miss Turtle was nowhere to be seen. I entered upon my cue therefore to an empty desk. I had noted that there was a hand-bell on it so I just hoped it was 'practical'. Ringing it, with success, several times, I heard the scampering of feet crossing the studio floor and finally a florid Amy rushed up to me on the wrong side of the desk. She could hardly speak with breathlessness and confusion.

'Oh, sorry luv.' I suspected that this was not characterisation but a personal apology to me.

'Just get behind the desk and get on with it,' I demanded.

She was uncertain if that was my 'character' improvisation or my personal annoyance. It was both.

'Let me have my bill.'

At this point the young couple that I was to have the bulk of the scene with entered. Having overcome the faulty start, I felt confident and full of authority. I turned to the young man to deliver my first line to him and realised that I had now 'lost it' and had no idea what was to follow. In desperation I said:

'This cannot be allowed to go on,' hoping that all those in the control room would realise the situation and for once, call a halt. No. The camera kept rolling and my fellow actors offered no helping hand.

'How do you mean?' said the terrified youth.

I knew that I was supposed to be annoyed with the couple for some reason but that was all. I looked them in the eye and stated:

'You will just have to pull yourselves together.'

Fortunately, the young man took the bold step of making a suggestion.

'Do you mean about us being seen on the boat with Diane?'

'EXACTLY,' I responded and the scene, my last thank God, fell into place.

I was assured that it all looked fine, so I bid the company and the management a dignified farewell and stepped out into the exhilarating cold night air of Broad Street, Birmingham and escaped to freedom.

One piece of escapism that I had during those weeks had been to cross the road and see the 'Rep's' production of *Equus* by Peter Schaffer, which helped me to keep my sanity. In a fascinating and disturbing play, I admired the two young actors for their love scene in the stable, in which they were totally naked, which gave a moving intensity to the play. They shared the scene with the 'horses' all played with great beauty and sensitivity by the other actors, - indeed, Geoffrey Leesley looked almost Stubbs like. It has to be said that through the publicity received surrounding the naked lovers, the production played to full houses. There was a moment of audience participation at one performance that was not appreciated by the performers. It was not totally surprising, coming as it did from a man of the Midlands who, at the most poignant of moments, called from the back:

'Look out, Red Rum's watchin' yer.'

Perhaps because I had been tempted to contact them for help

during my stay at the 'Motel', I decided to offer my services to 'The Samaritans'. I was not sure if I was suitable but felt my personality might be right – might be. The interviews, grilling, training and induction made it, quite rightly, a commitment to be taken most seriously. I was accepted. I was to find out that often those who think they would be perfect for the task are not and those who call their capabilities into question are frequently ideal. It is not a matter of anyone being better than another, just that some have the particular qualities needed. Non-judgmental listeners, who do not bring their own agenda to bear on the situation, are essential. Those who 'know what it's like', however caring, would not be. Being a Samaritan requires anonymity and a pledge of total confidentiality. I was to remain with them for several years, which was a privilege, and my respect for those with whom I worked alongside, who were so skilled in simply listening, knew no bounds. What impressed me was that they came from all sections of society without pretensions or side, be it the clergyman whose personal beliefs and faith would not enter into his attitude, to a wonderful West Indian bus driver who brought a deep understanding of humankind. Without doubt it was one of the highlights of my life.

--------0--------

A call from that Pub again.

'We want to do readings of a play by the Spanish playwright, Alfonso Vallefo called *Fly By*' said Sam Walters. 'The main reason for it being a reading rather than a staged performance is that the characters are expected to fly, and with the best will in the world we could not rig up Kirby's Flying Ballet in a room that size. The play has been banned in Spain under the Franco regime, as it carries challenging political undertones. After the reading, the audience will be invited to ask the cast questions.'

The theme was that the hero, read by Brian Cox, believes that he can fly. His passion drives him to convince others that they can also do so. To demonstrate this quest for freedom, he takes charabanc loads of passengers to a cliff's edge and they jump off and attempt to fly. The result being several deaths and holidays being cancelled for the local hospital staff. Of course, this could be interpreted as an uprising, a seeking for political change. Our intrepid flying man, although constantly in plaster, will not give up what he believes is possible and will jump off anything over three feet high. His wife, tired of caring for a cripple, beseeches him to forgo his dream. He points out that he managed to 'take off' that very morning, even though it was only to rise seven inches. She heartlessly dismisses this fantasy.

"Good God, Maria, doesn't an elevation of seven inches mean anything to you?" he enquires.

Concern is shown from those in high places, that should he be able to achieve this seeming impossibility, of the effect it might have on commerce. What would happen to the Airline business? Shoemakers would become redundant. It needed to be stamped out. Eventually, the day arrives when he promises to show the world that he can achieve human flight. With a vast crowd gathered outside the hospital, he stands on a balcony, like the Pope uttering 'Urbi et Orbi' and launches himself into space. This time he rises higher and higher. He has achieved the ultimate freedom. At that moment, a shot rings out from the crowd and he plunges like Icarus to earth – destroyed. The symbolism presumably being, that once there is a step beyond the accepted limits and the seemingly impossible is achieved, we have to destroy it.

Consider and discuss.

*A Flea in Her Ear (La Puce à l'Oreille)* by Georges Feydeau, offered by the Birmingham Rep, really caught my fancy but would I ever get away from the capital of the Midlands? The chance to play the double of Chandebise/Poche, however, was not going to be missed. I regretted not having seen John Mortimer's translation of the play at the National in 1966 with Albert Finney playing the double but at least I came to it fresh. Perhaps this was

84

the master of farce's best play.

From the moment that Chandebise first appears, it is non-stop action for him both on and off stage. With two dressers to help, I was constantly changing in and out of costumes. I knew that by the end of the second act, I could not manage another 'change' before the interval, for they had to be accomplished at such speed. One of these changes I could not see how it would be possible to achieve. Exiting down left as Poche the hall porter, to appear completely changed into the bourgeois Chandebise, up centre, less than ten seconds later, seemed impossible. However, if Feydeau had constructed it then it must be possible. I also appreciated that Velcro did not exist in 1907 when first performed at the Comédie-Française. Detailed study of the text, however, (for there was no stage instructions), showed it was possible, which seemed to the audience like a conjurer's sleight of hand – I loved that. Not all my ideas to assist the quick changes were perfect. Remembering the shoe routine with my Noël Coward striptease, I found a large pair of galoshes for Poche, which could be slipped over the patent leather shoes I wore as Chandebise. It only let me down once, unfortunately on the first night. Scampering round the 'set', as Poche, my right galosh left my foot, revealing the elegant black boot of Monsieur Chandebise. My secret was out. How was I to cover this debacle? Sitting on a bed (there is always a bed in a good farce), I stared with amazement at my extraordinary right foot and declared:
'It's no good, I will definitely have to wash my feet.' The ensuing round of applause gave me the time to pull my boot back on. There was unfortunately a dearth of dialogue at this point and the action needed to be moved on, so I simply threw the ball back to Madame Chandebise with:
'You were saying?'
The director took some convincing that this was not a deliberate variety act.

I greatly respect motivation and truth in a performance but when I was asked by a fine young actor in the cast, Paul Jesson, what my mother was like, I was somewhat taken aback.

'What do you mean *was*? She's still alive,' I informed him.

'No, your characters' mother, for your motivation.'

I told him for a play of this kind my overriding motivation was getting laughs. I think he considered me a philistine. I was, however, able to show my credentials when I suggested a piece of 'business' that I thought would benefit us both. In true farce style with no pretence to political correctness, his character, Camille, had the physical defect of lacking a roof to his mouth, making his diction virtually incomprehensible, a problem that could only be overcome by having a silver plate in his mouth. In one moment of general hysteria he attempts to explain a situation to Poche, minus the silver plate. He had been given one brief line by the author, so I suggested to Paul that he extended the line until I, or rather Poche, stopped him. He asked what else he should say, so I said:

'You know the story, use that to improvise. You could even mention your mother.'

It worked wonderfully well. He went on and on in a totally incoherent manner, whilst Poche studied him with amazement, finishing it off with a thump on his back. Apart from the fact that it always got a 'round', there was appreciation for this moment in the 'notices', extolling Mr Jesson's comic invention. Thanks.

It is impossible for me to have one favourite play but *Flea* comes very high.

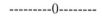

There was a salutary happening around this time. ATV asked to see me about a series they were doing, showing the working day of various jobs, - 'a day in the life of' format. They wanted to do one on an actor and wondered if I would play him. I said I would and they asked if I had any ideas. I threw out a few and they said why didn't I write it. They asked for a 'treatment' and I gave them a three-page detail of who, what and where. I received no reply, nor was I approached to play the part. Some time later, that episode was broadcast with Richard Pasco playing my role. I had no complaint that Dickie should be cast instead of me, but what amazed me was to see that the suggestions I had made, including where to do it and the people to be involved, were all taken up. I contacted ATV about this and was told that they had no recollection of ever receiving anything from me.

Moral: use an agent and trust nobody.

# 43

## HI HO TORONTO

*"A cold coming we had of it, just the worst time of the year for a journey"*
'Journey of the Magi' by T.S.Eliot

'Triumph Productions are doing a season of plays at the Phoenix. There's Lee Remick and Alfred Marks in *'Bus Stop'*, Rock Hudson and Juliet Prowse in *'I do, I do'*, Douglas Fairbanks Jnr., in *'The Pleasure of His Company'* and then Glynis Johns and Louis Jourdan in an adaptation of a 'Feydeau', which has had several titles and this time it's *'13 Rue de L'Amour'*. You're into farce, so how about doing another? It goes to Billingham, Toronto, Norwich and then into the Phoenix for a couple of months. Your country needs you.'

Billingham in mid-winter with blizzards blowing, was not a pretty sight. An air of depression and despondency pervaded the atmosphere, which I believe to have been a hangover from the Depression of the Thirties, from which it had never recovered. Unemployment in the North East was rife and although actors know the feeling well, at least there is the chance that something might turn up. The air was filled with fumes from nearby iron foundries, causing most of the actors to suffer with chest infections and the celebrated 'Billingham throat'. Even the sparrows were coughing as they fell out of the trees.

Peter Dews had assembled an hilarious cast, for apart from our two stars, there was James Grout, Margaret Courtenay, David Stoll and the two young trouble-makers, Michael Cochrane & Baddeley. We got the thumbs up at the 'Forum' but rehearsals still continued. With deep snow and a cast of invalids, we were all anxious to escape from Cleveland. I did venture out on the middle Sunday, to have lunch with relatives in Gateshead. The snow and ice made the car journey feel like Scott's journey to the South Pole and I feared for the same outcome. My cousin, a biology PhD with the Open University, and her husband, a local GP, lived in some style. Patrick invited me to see his wine cellar and I feared that corks might explode again. He had inherited a great deal of wine from his father and insisted on decanting a bottle of Château Lafitte 1914. I begged him not to as I was totally lacking in sommelier appreciation. I decided that whatever passed my lips I would laud it to the skies. As I sipped the wine the most velvety, perfect taste touched my palate. My expression of pleasure required no award-winning performance for it was sensational.

I eagerly anticipated my first trip to Canada, the birthplace of my grandfather. The theatre that we were to perform in was owned by a self-made millionaire, Ed Mirvish. He had started his business life selling goods from a barrow to become one of Toronto's wealthiest citizens. Apart from the theatre, he also owned a string of restaurants that I looked forward to making acquaintance with. Later he was to take over the Old Vic in London.

By the time the fortnight's run in Billingham was over, however, I was feeling very unwell. There was a gap of a week before we flew to Toronto but as the days went by I grew worse and was bed-bound. With two days left before my departure, the doctor said that it was out of the question for me to fly. I was desperate to go but this was 'flu' like I'd never experienced. So the show opened without me the following Monday at the Royal Alexandra Theatre, whilst I lay in bed waiting for a flight on the Thursday. I boarded the plane still feeling dreadful, but I knew that they did not expect me to go on until the Friday performance. I was met at Pearson Int. and driven straight to the Lord Simcoe Hotel on King Street. There being a five hour time gap it meant, that although it was just 6.0pm in Toronto, for me it was 11.0pm. I threw up in the bathroom and fell into bed. An hour later there was a knock at the door and Mr Dews entered.

'Thank God you're 'ere, luvvy. I want you to go on tonight.'

'It was agreed it would be tomorrow, Peter.'

'I know, luvvy but I've been playing your part since it opened and I have to get back to London tomorrow. Glynis and Louis are complaining that I have not been able to watch the show since we got here and give them 'notes'. You've got time for a kip, the show doesn't go up until 8.30, you're not a 'beginner', so if you get there at the 'five', you'll be fine.'

'Where's the theatre?' I asked through a veil of tears.

'It's two hundred yards to the right outside the hotel, you can't miss it.' As he closed the door, I made for the bathroom, vomited again and took an early bath.

My associates greeted me warmly as I staggered through the stage door. The sound of a full house, usually so encouraging, was alarming to me. Although I had performed on the set in sunny Billingham, I knew the layout would not be exactly the same, being a different space. Furthermore, I had not been able to see the auditorium to get 'the feel' of the House. Let it be said, however, that for my two scenes, I received exit rounds on both. The lesson being, make sure you have a temperature of a hundred and two degrees, vomit a few times and see that your body clock says it is five hours ahead of reality. As far as I was concerned the curtain fell at around 4.0am.

'Let's get round to the 'Shakespeare' for a drink, John, and have something to eat.'

Gagging but not joking at the thought, I asked the waiter for a modest sandwich. A twelve-inch tall, multi-decked, multi-coloured, multi-flavoured object was placed in front of me.

89

'Your sandwich, Buddy. Enjoy.'

In the cast was the charming actor, David Stoll. His grandfather had created the Stoll chain of theatres – I knew their theatre in The Kingsway well. David had the reputation of being the last of the 'farceurs' and his personal seriousness made his performances hilarious. He seemed to find any decision a challenge. There was no On Q to serve our breakfast in the Lord Simcoe as it was a help-yourself facility. David would enquire as to what I was having and then ask me what he should have. An innocent like that is always at the mercy of the other boys. On one occasion, he courteously escorted Glynis back to the hotel, as the rest of us wished to stay imbibing at the 'Shakespeare'. Seeing them walking out together arm in arm, set our evil minds racing. We all knew that Maggie Courtenay (who continued to worry about her performance on a daily basis and demanded continual support from anyone willing to give it) was able to do a brilliant impersonation of Glynis, with her high-pitched, throaty tones. We arranged for a cassette-recording to be made of Maggie making a phone call to David in Glynis' voice, thanking him for his kindness of the night before, and stating that she was feeling lonely and would like him to come to her room immediately, because she felt a great need for him. There were no pauses in this one-sided dialogue, which was very much in keeping with Glynis. A call was made to David's room at ten the next morning by Jimmy Grout, asking if he would like to go out for an early lunch with some of us. He agreed and so it was arranged that we collect him from his room at noon. On the dot of the appointed time, nearly everyone in the company, including Maggie C, stood outside his door. With stopwatch in hand, a loyal ASM phoned David's room, and as his receiver was picked up, started playing the cassette recording into the mouthpiece. As we heard the phone ring within his room, we knocked on the door. David opened the door, with telephone in hand, in a state of confusion, surprised to see such a gathering. We all entered, with David seemingly in torment over the call that he was receiving. He looked at us

90

distractedly with hand over the mouthpiece, stating:
'It's Glynis, it's Glynis!'
He tried desperately to interpolate without success.
'She's pissed, she's pissed,' he informed us.
As 'her' demands became more sexually explicit, one feared for his sanity and indeed, his heart. Because Maggie was present in the room, he knew it was not her deceiving him – it must be our leading lady. His room was fifteen floors up, looking out over the Toronto skyline with the C N Building, (at that time the world's tallest, somewhat phallic, structure), dominating. Perhaps fearing an observer from this huge erection just across the road, he begged someone to:
'Shut the window, shut the window.'
This was too much for those gathered, who burst into paroxysms of mirth. The man was so shaken that he would not believe the truth until the recording was played to him face to face.

An unusual aspect was that the Toronto 'workers in the sex industry' would advertise their telephone numbers for appointments on television. Of course, Cochrane could not resist requesting one to phone David's room for a booking. His victim had to deal with this and told us:
'You won't believe this but a 'tart' phoned me and I had to say it was all a terrible mistake.'
'Good heavens!' we cried. He was a true innocent abroad.

It has to be said, however, that unbeknown to him, the rest of us had our 'comeuppance'. We knew that he had recently married and wondered what kind of woman would take on this insecure gentle Gent. At the first night party, when we opened at the Phoenix, we saw David standing with a stunning looking woman – his young bride. The sound of jaws hitting the floor was audible.

--------0--------

An interesting post-show outing in Toronto, for those in the

91

company who loved dancing in the dark, was seeing the great Ginger Rogers in cabaret. Although advanced in years, she could still put it across, but one did miss Fred Astaire. We were invited round 'after' and it was interesting to meet her face to face, although in many ways I wish I had not done so, as she was now more 'tucks' than tuxedo.

We ate and drank a great deal at the 'Shakespeare', which always had a lively and welcoming atmosphere. One lunchtime, however, I was aware of it being unnaturally quiet - almost funereal. Frankie, the barman, seemed to be unwelcoming and dismissive of me. His attention was totally given to three other customers, obviously businessmen, wearing pinstriped suits and dark glasses. It was only when they left the building that the mood of our home-from-home lightened. It had been my first experience of the Mafia, who had called in to collect the 'rent'.

My stay on Canadian soil seemed to be all about food. Ed Mirvish invited the Company to take lunch with him in his restaurant next to the theatre. He knew exactly how to cost everything and this included the menu in his eating-houses. It was very much on the 'Bernie Inn' style, with each meal laid out exactly to a plan. Choice was limited, price was good. However, I caused a minor incident by asking for a different colour of wine to go with my main course from the one allowed in the instructions. I thought my request was modest but the waiter was taken aback and had to consult Ed, before he dare acquiesce.

Penny was now working for Social Services and one of her colleagues suggested that I contacted a friend of hers in Toronto. I did so and she invited me for tea. On the day in question, Cochrane and I with two others from the company hired a chauffeur-driven car to take us to Niagara Falls. We saw this awesome sight from on high and then donned the yellow sou'westers to see it from down under. Feeling peckish afterwards, we had a lunch of somewhat larger portions than I would have wished. Everywhere is further away than you imagine

92

in Canada, and as we drove back to the 'Simcoe' I realised my
5.30 tea date was going to be a difficult call. At six o'clock I
phoned to apologise.
'When do you think you will get here?' my hostess enquired
'We're waiting.'
'I'm on my way,' I lied.
Throwing myself into a cab, I gave the address to a slightly
surprised cabby. He drove at hair-raising speed due north,
presumably to Alaska, for we entered the snow-belt en route.
Arriving at my destination, I looked forward to my cup of tea and
an iced bun. The door was opened by an extremely glamourous,
delightfully décollétaged, woman.
'So glad you've made it, we're all through here.'
'All' – I thought that 'we' referred the happy couple of my
hostess and her partner. In fact, it meant the happy dozen waiting
in the sitting room.
'We'll serve dinner as soon as we've had an apéritif.'
Having had a large lunch, I now partook of an even larger dinner.
I pointed out to my host the problem of having to perform at the
theatre very shortly.
'I know - we all loved the show. I'll drive you there. What is the
latest you can make it?' he casually enquired.
Having phoned the theatre, they agreed to 'beginners' – like that
first night all over again. Having bid my hostess a lingering
farewell, her husband then drove me at even greater speed than on
my outward journey, to downtown Toronto and I staggered into
the theatre to be greeted by Glynis:
'Oh, darling, I've been looking for you. Louis and I are taking all
the company out for dinner at the 'Shakespeare' after the show
and Louis has asked if you will escort me.'
'It will be a pleasure, Glynis.'
I fell into my dressing room and, as was becoming a tradition by
now, 'threw up'.
My shipmates from the lower decks, who knew of my
gastronomic achievements of the day, grinned with satisfaction as
I forced down yet another dinner, whilst wrapt in small talk with
Miss Johns.

The night was not over, for several members of the cast decided to extend this long over-due celebration and remained on the premises, partaking of whatever was left in the establishment of an alcoholic nature. At around 4.0am the mafia-sponsored host of the establishment came to us, with a vast platter of eggs, bacon, mushrooms, beans and hash brownies.

'I guess you're all in need of breakfast!'

I was not able to look at food after that for at least the next couple of hours.

Years later, I heard that they had pulled down the 'Simcoe' but hopefully not the 'Royal Alex' and most importantly not the 'Shakespeare' and that it remains to nourish the people of Toronto.

On returning home, I knew I was back in dear old Blighty, with a letter awaiting me on the coconut matting, bearing the good tidings:

"You have been elected to membership of the MCC."

Recognised at last.

* Originally called Monsieur Chasse or Monsieur Chasse Goes Hunting, it was first performed in Paris at the Palais-Royal in 1892. Our version had been adapted by Americans Mawby Green and Ed Feilbert, who were perhaps best known for their economically costumed hit Pyjama Tops.

94

# 44

## HOMELAND

On our return we were immediately despatched to Norwich. That beautiful city, comprising fifty-two churches and three hundred and sixty five public houses, was very much to my taste. Its fine Cathedral I knew from having attended, with my mother, a service of dedication there in 1950, for a memorial to all those of the Norfolk Regiment who had lost their lives in the Second World War. My father had been seconded to that Regiment from the Royal Artillery and so his name appears in their Book of Remembrance. Whenever I was in the city I would call into the Cathedral, to light a candle and request the verger to open the glass cabinet holding the Book and turn to the page bearing my father's name.*

We were to play a week at the Theatre Royal before making our way to the Phoenix. Not having made a prior arrangement, I asked of the others what 'digs' they had fixed and Mr Grout's held most appeal. It was a Country Club about 15 miles outside the city and seemed perfect, so I phoned and booked in. After the show we made our way to an Italian restaurant that seemed happy to stay open (behind closed doors), and let us sample their moderate wines, for as long as we liked. Jimmy Grout left for our place in the country at around 1am and I said I would be following shortly. At 3am I felt it was time to make my way for my night's slumber. At this point I realised I had no idea where my home for the week was. The only clue I had been given was that it was off a road leading out of the city to the east, immediately after a large dairy. More in hope than certainty, I had been directed to a road, which a local thought might be the one in question and somewhat in an alcoholic haze, I made my way along this virtual snow-bound thoroughfare, becoming acutely aware of how "very flat, Norfolk" was. To my relief I saw a dairy and took the next turning. I drove down a deep and crisp and even lane and although partially snow-blind, saw a large house appearing with an impressive drive, with frozen pond in the forecourt. There were no cars to be seen, nor indeed did there appear to be an entrance to the building. Instinct directed me round the back where there were some cars parked. I returned to the front, to discover an inconspicuous door but seemingly not a main entrance. There was no bell to ring or knocker to knock to summon the sleeping proprietors. It could have been the opening of *The Rocky Horror Show*. I turned the knob and to my surprise it opened, leading, not to a reception area but a lounge with dying embers in the grate. A door opposite led at last to the Desk and as with the *Crossroads Motel*, nobody behind it. There was, however, a key and a message saying;

"Welcome Mr Badley. We did enjoy the show and look forward to meeting you. Your room is No 4, first floor." On the threshold to my bedchamber lay a note written, it would seem, in a somewhat grouting manner:

"Dirty Stop Out." I knew I was amongst friends.

The run at the Phoenix went well, having received moderate notices, with Maggie Courtenay taking the honours. Having craved reassurance from the rest of her teammates, during the whole of the pre-London tour, that her performance was satisfactory, she pulled out all the stops on the 1$^{st}$ night in Town and gave a rendering hardly recognisable to what had gone before. An old trick, which I had witnessed before. My somewhat Clouseau-ish performance as the Inspector of Police was also well received and I was amused when working with Maggie some years later, when she reminded me of how concerned *I* had been about *my* performance – the mind plays funny tricks.

As I was 'off' stage more than 'on', I was able to look out of my dressing-room window and study life in St Giles' Passage. On matinee days, I took the risk of parking my car in this cul-de-sac, leading only to an alleyway. Hopefully, to protect me from the vicissitudes of the Parking Warden, I left a note on the windscreen stating "Delivering at the Phoenix" which seemed to work. Having arrived early for one matinee, I glanced out of the window and noted a black Mercedes, which had been parked by the alleyway. In attempting to drive past my Citroën, it scarred the side from stern to stem and then come to a halt. I raced out to confront the driver. He had three passengers who all seemed to be carrying bleeding wounds to their persons and most certainly chips on their shoulders. When I questioned the driver, he told me to something 'off.' I pursued the matter, at which one of the passengers, with blood seeping from an eye had to be restrained, for he intended, it would appear, to end my life. I remained calm and reasonable and the occupants all got out of their car. At this point, members of the Company were arriving for the matinée, the 'half' being nigh upon us. They asked if there was a problem to which I replied in the negative. The next three minutes, however, became bedlam as the passengers of the Mercedes, for no apparent reason, turned on everyone except me. My innocent friends found themselves in a brawl, which left them battered, bruised and bewildered. Michael Cochrane was mainly concerned that his overcoat had been torn.

'That was my father's,' he tearfully stated.

The storm abated as quickly has it had arisen and our opponents got back into their somewhat dented vehicle and departed the scene, having given me prior warning not to call the Police or they would obliterate me.

I called the Police. They informed me that there was a Club at the end of the alleyway, frequented by the likes of the Kray Brothers and others of a similar calling.

'Take my advice, Sir, forget it.'

I did but I haven't.


As I arrived one evening, I saw a 'gentleman of the road' lying sprawled on the pavement of the same thoroughfare, being either drunk, drugged or dead. His head was in the gutter and I saw a car reversing at a pace down the narrow road that I knew so well, with its nearside wheels in that very gutter. In another five seconds it would have crushed the poor man's cranium. My scream to stop must have penetrated the windows not only of the car but most of the offices in the Charing Cross Road. A few feet from squashing time, the car halted and the woman driver got out. She could hardly speak, realising what might have taken place.

'I had no idea. I didn't see a thing. Thank you for stopping me. It would have been terrible.'

'I know' I responded 'It could have ruined your tyres.'

From that moment, I felt insecure when arriving at the theatre and trusted I would not have to return there for a future production, fearing it could be the Phoenix too frequent.

For gallantry shown with no consideration for self, I had been awarded the MCC as previously mentioned and I could then walk through the Members Pavilion and the Long Room with my head held high – as long as I wore a jacket and tie. For the enquiring mind, *the* tie, recognised all round the world, of red and yellow diagonal stripes, represents an egg and tomato sandwich. The two things at that time never allowed in those hallowed surroundings, were women and a mobile phone. In the 1990's they struggled with their conscience and Government legislation and gave way to the former but *never* the latter.

I had by now just started to get into 'voice-overs' in a reasonably big way and I had heard, a couple of years earlier, of trials of a device called a 'bleeper', being carried out in the Reading area and had put my name down for one. When at last I received the object, I informed my agent, Wendy Noel, that she could contact me anywhere at anytime.

'Nobody else on our books has got one of those,' she informed me.

'Well, you'd better just use me then!'

I knew how long I had been on the waiting list, so I reckoned I had two good years ahead of me. Within a week I saw Miriam Margolyes with one. When I asked how long she had been on the

list, she responded tenderly:
'Well, I heard about them on Tuesday, contacted BT and they sent me one by return.'
Life can be so unfair.

* As mentioned earlier, his name is also on the Roll of Honour at the Commonwealth War Cemetary, Medjez-El-Bab, in Tunisia.

# 45

# MEMORANDUM

As with being a regular broadcaster, being a regular voice-over artist, means there are too many productions to recall. As my life changed, bringing its increased financial rewards, so the dramatic stories declined. I had found to my concern that I could make more money in an hour from a voice-over than I could in a week in the theatre and found it impossible to turn my back on the golden egg for the sake of exhilarating theatrical penury. I do remember, however, when doing one of my first voice-overs being asked to 'dub' a performer's voice in a Strongbow commercial. It depicted an archer stripped to the waist, displaying an impressive and muscular torso, firing his flèche d'Or into a cider barrel saying:
"Strongbow for men".
'Just lip-sync that line, John.'
'Why?' I enquired.
'We can't have his lisping, mincing voice coming from that body. It would destroy product credibility.'
I found it hilarious, which I suppose is the point. So I 'butched

up' the archer – which is more than I did 'for the everyday story of country folk'.

For a few years I had played, on a very irregular basis, Ambridge's 'copper' in *The Archers*. When asked to play the role, they said they did not want the Tony Hancock rural tones performance but a man out of Hendon Police College – whatever that meant. The result being, I fear, that I made their Police Constable more dreary than Drury. After some years they contacted me to tell me that I would not be required in future, as the Constabulary were getting a Panda. My initial concern was the availability of bamboo shoots and then I pointed out that I did possess a driving licence. This argument was accepted and for a time I stayed on at the wheel. However, the programme Producer at the time, William Smethurst, was obviously desperate to get rid of me and I received a letter eventually telling me that Drury had been promoted and transferred to Borchester. He went on to say that he thought this was all for the good as:
"Drury never seemed to work somehow and we were wasting your abilities as an actor. I look forward to welcoming you back at some point in a role which has more promise."
I still await that call but am encouraged to know that at least I had been promoted.

Mark's time at Frensham Heights had not all been plain sailing. We were aware that he was not completely happy there but wondered where else he would have been. Mark had been accepted into the school by a progressive headmaster, Maurice Bridgeland, however, when he arrived at the school for his first term, a new Headmaster had been installed. Perhaps the school had been getting too progressive and influential parents were looking for some better academic successes from their bright children, so Alan Pattinson was brought in to batten down the hatches. This was perhaps unfortunate for Mark. We received a letter from the Head shortly after his arrival, questioning whether

Mark was suitable for the school, due to his rather unusual behaviour. We pointed out that it was because of his unusual approach that he had gone to the school in the first place. I was asked to go for an interview with Mr Pattinson. Prior to presenting myself at the Headmaster's study, Mark had informed me that my inquisitor and I had been to the same school. I did not recall him and imagined he must be younger than myself – how galling. The interview was conducted in a professional manner in his large study looking out over the rolling Surrey hills.

'The main problem is that Mark seems to be somewhat eccentric and is constantly drawing attention to himself and talking to others in class, to the distraction of pupils and staff. He sees himself as a Court Jester and is quite amusing but work has to be taken seriously.'

I expressed surprise at this seemingly disturbing egocentric manner and was unable to imagine where it might have come from.

'May I ask' I said sardonically, 'Is there no room in the education system for the eccentrics of this world?'

He considered this with care and philosophically.

'Why, yes of course there is.'

'I'm very glad to hear it' I responded 'otherwise, if it were not the case, what would happen to the teaching profession?'

He paused only briefly and said:

'I take your point, let us say no more about it.'

He then mentioned that we had played together for the Old Boys, of which again I had no recall but didn't say so. He asked me what I felt were the essential ingredients of a good education. I expounded for twenty minutes, to which he expressed a modest degree of interest. Three months later, attending what Frensham called Founders Day, I heard the Head deliver a profound summing-up, to the assembled gathering of parents and Governers, of "The Meaning of Education". I sat with open mouth as my words came out of his.

I should have had Alastair Campbell's role.

Perhaps the life of a schoolmaster would have suited me. Sam

Walters offered me the leading part of Josef Gross in *The Memorandum* by Václav Havel. Havel spent most of his time in jail because of his uncompromising and outspoken condemnation of the political regime in power at that time in his home country, Czechoslovakia. Ten years later he was to become its President. The play deals with the absurdities of the ruling dogma and its ludicrous effect on office routines and the threat under which they all live. There were two other parts that caught my eye when reading the play, which appealed to me rather more than the part I had been offered. One was Mark Lear, a pedantic teacher of a "synthetic language built on a strictly scientific basis. .... a thoroughly exact language, capable of expressing with far greater precision than any current natural tongue, all the minutest nuances in the formulation of important office documents. The result of this precision being the exceptional complexity and difficulty of Ptydepe."

I found it hilarious. The other part, Mr Column, says nothing so as not to compromise himself, always responding with varying shrugs of the shoulders. The parts were totally opposite in complexity, one, an horrendously difficult part to learn and the other conveying all, or rather nothing, in mime. Sam opted to give me the former.

The first performance in that small upstairs room over the Orange Tree was riveting. Although Mr Lear had a group of students, all bar one wearing blank masks to indicate their lack of comprehension at what their tutor was saying (also allowing a subtle doubling-up of the cast), the audience themselves felt that they too were part of the class. Many were terrified that they would be asked questions, including critics such as Bernard Levin and Michael Billington, who were in attendance. To be eighteen inches from a row of pencil-wielding newspaper judges can be daunting. It was received extremely well and I was interested to see particular approbation for the parts I had earmarked, which was good for both myself and Paddy Ward playing the silent Mr Column. The production also brought attention to John Challis. Having 'wowed' the critics, I felt extremely confident at the second performance as I entered to my mask-wearing students to deliver my lengthy first monologue. After two lines, the text departed the memory bank and I found myself ad-libbing about the language's extreme complexity and the dedication that had to be given to its study. Knowing there was no prompter in that lonely room, I feared we could be there all night listening to my gibberish, also that Mr Havel might not have been too pleased at the desecration of his text. The students could not help me for they were not supposed to know what I was talking about in the first place. I decided the only action available was for me to leave the stage and get hold of the text to refresh my memory. So, I stopped mid-gobbledegook and informed them:

'You will just have to excuse me a moment, I have to check the chalk.' With that I exited, to find a loyal supporter off-stage, holding the text and pointing to the exact place that I was in doubt about. After a quick embrace, I returned to my class to complete the lesson without a hitch. My only moment of distraction after that hiatus was seeing one of my students in such a state of mirth at the situation, that there were tears running down his mask. 'Checking the chalk' went into common parlance as a euphemism for studying the text.

For sometime, Jack, my step father had been unwell and had been forced to take early retirement from the Gas Board a few months before his sixty-fifth birthday, thus denying him his fifty years long service gold watch (miserable sods). He had been declining physically through a failed hip replacement and mentally, due to the gradual encroachment of Alzheimer's disease. He was cared for loyally by my mother, which proved a great strain on her health, as those who have been in that situation will well know. I would visit them to give her some mental respite. His powers of memory-retention were dreadful. A thirty-minute conversation would mean the same topic would be repeated at least half a dozen times. There were, however, moments of sad amusement for the observer, such as the occasion he insisted on staggering from his chair to speak to a visitor at the front door.

'Harry Barnes – Legal & General,' said the Insurance man, extending his hand.

'Jack Price – Birchfield Harriers,' said my mother's athletic old husband, offering his. In fact, in his youth he had been a member of that celebrated club and for a time held its 440 yards record. One of his running companions had been Lord Burghley, the Olympic athlete. So at least Jack knew his name and the distant past. When he was examined by a Consultant Geriatrician to see if he should be taken into Care, Jack's response to the question:

'What is the name of the Prime Minister?' brought the carefully considered answer:

'Gladstone.' To which the medicine man's diagnosis was:

'He has no mental disfunction – he cannot be taken into care.'

Jack not only knew his own name but that of a distant Prime Minister – great. Now, if it had been Mr Blair that had been in power at that time, his reluctance to answer sanely would have been understandable. Eventually, he was hospitalised and when Clive Perry, the new Artistic Director of *my* Birmingham theatre, offered me the part of David Bliss in *Hay Fever* I accepted, mainly so that I could visit him in hospital. Clive had seen me in *A Flea in her Ear* and presumably liked what I had done and felt I would be right for the part. By this time, Jack seemed to be far away in his thoughts and I was told by his nurse, that he refused to accept his medication, which they felt was essential.

'I've found the answer, however,' she said. 'I put his pill into a jelly-baby and he enjoys that without being aware of its content.'

I witnessed this compassionate offering being put into operation.

'Mr Price would you like a jelly-baby?'

'Oh, that's very kind of you. Are you sure *you* don't want it?'

'No, it's for you, Mr Price.'

With that he put it in his mouth, as she set off on her patrol down the ward. After masticating for a short time, a quizzical look came over his face and he spat out a little white pill.

'Do you know, that's the third one that I've had like that today.'

Jack was never one for a hidden agenda.

Clive Perry directed *Hay Fever* himself, having recently done a successful production of the play in Pitlochry and he brought not only most of the ideas from it with him, but also their leading lady, Edith MacArthur, to play Judith Bliss. I was obviously suffering with some form of delusion, for I was seriously concerned that I would seem too young for the part. The probability was that Ms MacArthur was younger than I but she felt older. The fact that I had children in the play seemed far-fetched. I put this concern to Mr Perry who asked about my own children. I argued that that was not the point, it was just that I might appear too young. He convinced me that it was not the case and I was comforted by a line of Judith's:

"David has retained his youth astonishingly, perhaps because he has had fewer responsibilities and cares than I."

We seemed to spend the entire rehearsal period working on the tea-party scene at the end of Act I, which it has to be said, was the high-spot of a rather smart production. During the run, I paid my daily visits to see Jack because my mother had to forebear going, as her GP had stated that she was too ill to look after him, otherwise he would have had to return to be cared for in her incapable hands – how hellish it all was. Jack would sit staring into space, whilst I would deliver a thirty-minute monologue, hoping to stimulate a reaction from him. I described to him how I had made my way to the Repertory Theatre that day, taking him on an imaginary journey round the centre of the City he knew so well.

'I went past the Town Hall, down New Street, up Corporation Street passing Lewis', down to Snow Hill Station, along Colmore Row, round Chamberlain Square, past The Hall of Memory, up Broad Street ......'

He continued to stare blankly, seemingly showing no interest and then he looked at me in an incredulous and pitying manner and spoke for the first time on my visit saying:

'To .. get .. to .. the .. 'Rep' ??'

He obviously felt deep concern for such an incompetent.

Jack may not have been the only one to doubt my competence, for after the last performance of *Hay Fever* Clive Perry came round to the dressing rooms of each artiste to thank them for their input in the production. Barely putting his head round my door, he bid me farewell with:

'Do come again, John,' and withdrawing his head uttered:

'I thought you were absolutely marvellous.' I could not believe my ears, for I felt certain that he had loathed my performance. As the door closed on him, I just caught his final two words:

'In *Flea.'*

Thus the play ended its run and so did Jack.

Whenever I could, I would return to 'Brum' to visit my recently widowed mother to give her support and succour. She had no car, so one of my tasks was to drive her to wherever she wished to make her purchases, like the grocers, where she would take her list of requirements for the assistant to assemble, pack it up and take it to the car. For those without a car the shop would deliver it to their home (free of charge). This all changed when you were required to walk round a supermarket and collect you own items and transport them home as best you could. Thirty years later, many of these stores 'introduced' a system of on-line ordering, for them to assemble and deliver to you (for a charge) – good, these new old-fangled ideas.

On one occasion, as I stood outside the greengrocer's shop, idling and waiting for my mother whilst she was ordering the 'veg', I was approached by a woman, who I imagined wished to ask directions.

''ang on a bit. Yow were at our Theatre, wunt ye?'

Appreciating my celebrity status, I responded modestly:

'Yes, I was.'

'When are ye cumin back, then?'

I should establish that at this point there had been no suggestion and certainly no offer made for me to return by Mr Perry, who presumably was still recovering from my performance in *Hay Fever*. However, I felt that there was a profound urgency expressed by this good woman of Birmingham and that to give a blunt negative would be unfeeling. She was obviously looking for a ray of hope.

'Well, I'm not ...... not exactly ..... sure ......'

'Yowe are cumin back, int ye?'

'Yes ..... yes ..... I will ..... I'm not quite ..... sure ....'

'Yer definitely cumin back then?'

The woman was obviously desperate.

'Yes, I will <u>definitely</u> be coming back .. I'm not quite sure ..'

'Oh good. Well, I 'ope they giv yer summat better next time – you were VILE last time.'

With that she went on her dignified way.

Very discerning, those Brummies.

## 46

## FUNERALS & THINGS

Having guided my mother through the farewell to her second husband and my stepfather, so began an on-going trend. I was asked to read at the funeral of my best man's mother, Lady Hungerford, which was a great privilege She was a humanist and therefore there would be no priest officiating at the cremation ceremony. The occasion was to be quite simple, with just a recording being played of one of her favourite artistes, Dietrich Fischer-Dieskau, the celebrated lieder singer, followed by my reading an extract of the writings of the 14th century mystic, Julian of Norwich from her *Revelations of Divine Love*. I had been a little concerned at the 'old English' aspect and was not sure of my ability to read Chaucerian-type writings. I was assured that an academic from Cambridge would write a modern rendering and I asked to have this well before the day for me to con, but of course, it only arrived on the day.

I was met at Loughton station by the future wife of my old flat-mate. We had not met before but she said she would have known who I was because of my Italian shoes – so there. She drove me back to the family home, 'The Dragons', which would have suited any Agatha Christie 'Poirot' novel. I was immediately whisked into the Library to study the text that I was to read. I briefly spoke to some of the mourners, one of whom was my old friend, now Head of Radio Drama at the BBC, Ronald Mason – I really did not want his criticism of my reading of olde English. After a lengthy journey, we came to the crematorium in Epping and I enquired as to who would officiate.

'Nobody,' said my grieving friend. I was then approached by a crematorium stagehand and asked what was required. From my limited previous experiences, I gave a brief running order, just as we were being ushered into the Chapel. As we processed down the aisle, I espied the 'Priest's' seat and made a beeline for it and noted the instruction pinned to the desk stating:

"For visiting clergy. To instruct the curtain to be drawn, press bell on right hand side of lectern."

Brian had told me that when Herr F-D reached a certain point in the recording, he would indicate to me from the front row that there was a twenty second orchestral passage prior to the chorus bursting into song. I had to reach the podium and signal to the back-stage crew to 'cut' the recording otherwise the chapel would be overwhelmed with the sound of two hundred voices. Having agreed with my 'behind the catafalque' helper to flash when the music should to be taken out, on the nod from my friend I bounded to the lectern to signal the cutting of the tape. This being successfully accomplished, I then gave the reading and as I reached the final line of this deeply spiritual piece, with timing born from delivering last lines of a play, I pressed the bell to indicate that the curtain should be drawn round the coffin. This went smoothly, with dignity and decorum. As the curtain closed, knowing there was nothing more to come, I raised my eyes to the

Verger standing at the back of the chapel and respectfully bowed my head, hoping he would read my body language and 'do something'. I feared that he might look at me in astonishment and point at himself with a 'what me?' attitude. He, in fact, returned the bowed head gesture, came down the aisle and opened the side door. I resisted the temptation to stand there and shake the mourners hands as they left and swept straight out into the courtyard. He asked me if I would care to look at the floral tributes. I was so punch-drunk by this time that I thanked him and went to the largest bank of flowers I could see and blindly studied them.

'No, no, sir,' he said compassionately and guided me to a slightly smaller (but more tasteful) array of flora.

The flowers were transported back to the family home prior to the guests and were already on display throughout the house on our arrival – I was impressed. Among those present was Irish actor Bill Weisner, who had known the family from the time they had all lived in the emerald isle. I knew him from our days in Morecambe when he slept in the dining room. He expressed appreciation of my pastoral duties at the crematorium but said he had anticipated that I might be 'up-stage' of the curtain as it drew across, and that I would disappear behind it with the coffin. I had more stagecraft than that. I think he was rather disappointed.

All such occasions are moving, deeply felt and painful. However, spirits can be lifted by a joyful farewell. Endings are important for those that are left behind, so that they can grieve for those that are gone, in whatever way they wish. I have usually preferred a church, rather than a crematorium service, in that they can seem more uplifting and not limited by time. This does not mean that one has to have a profound faith but there is the chance for more joy and celebration of a life in a decent 'house'. The devil does not have to have all the best tunes and humans have voices worthwhile being heard, be it spoken or sung. Whilst I remember all the 'farewells' that I have attended, it has been in a church that my heart was most stirred. Like the country hillside church in

Warwickshire, where my Aunt Sybil* was buried and where her husband's ashes were scattered, also where their daughter, Susan's  Memorial Service was held. Climbing up the steep incline in the rain, sitting in the freezing nave warmed by the congregation of 'townies' and farming folk, made it feel like Hardy's Wessex.

There was the fellow actor, who always addressed me as 'young man', whose cremation with just the family in attendance, was followed immediately by a service of remembrance in his local church, with a lone piper from his wartime Highland regiment playing the lament, which seemed perfect. I was to find out afterwards that he had received the Military Cross for his 'D' Day exploits, which he had never mentioned.

There were other occasions, usually with actors present, that seemed more unusual, spontaneous and often humorous. Like being greeted by the well thatched Anthony Jackson at the 'sending off' of an alopeciaed friend, John Hollis, begging me not to say 'hair today and gone tomorrow' or 'hardly worth going home,' only to find myself attending his 'farewell' a year later. Presumably by arrangement with St Patrick, Tony laid on a special offering for us, in the form of a tornado that hit the area the hour he set off. They must have known they were in for something on the 'other side'.

A beautiful service was held at St Paul's, Covent Garden, for the lovely Gwen Watford, where the organist failed to turn up prompting the Vicar to ask:

'Is there a pianist in the house?' A member of the congregation then came to his assistance, playing without a score, so that we were able to sing with as great a gusto as I have heard. A reading was given by John Gielgud, who at the age of 90 gave the impression that he needed the text for "Fear no more the heat of the sun", and then after a couple of lines allowing the book to drop gently to his side, finishing the rest from memory .. how theatrical we all are.

At the same church/theatre venue, I recall hearing Nigel Anthony, at Peter Jeffrey's memorial service, reading an extract on golf from P. G. Wodehouse's *The Clicking of Cuthbert*. Not knowing anything about the game himself he delivered the text with such exquisite timing that he received a 'round' from the congregation – not really done, old boy, but what a perfect celebration.

Just some of many adieus.

* I have a particular treasured memory of my Aunt. Well into her nineties, I walked in on her listening to a Rugby World Cup Semi-Final and asked what the score was.
'France Nil, Jonny Wilkinson 18,' was her immediate response.

# 47

# OLD VIC

'I see Timothy West has been made Artistic Director of the Old Vic, I must drop him a line.'

My brief congratulatory note bore unexpected results. He called me and asked if I would like to do a couple of plays for the Company, which included a trip to Hong Kong for the Annual Arts Festival and then on to Perth W.A. for their Festival. The opportunity to play the Old Vic, where I had been so inspired by my visits there when I was in the RAF, also the chance to visit Hong Kong again and to go 'Down Under', plus working with Tim and Prunella Scales was irresistible. The plays were Pinero's *Trelawny of the Wells* with Tim directing and *The Merchant* of *Venice*, which had already played in The Cut. I was to take over as Launcelot Gobbo for the tour and then back to the Vic for a couple of weeks on our return. All this was to be preceded by a run of *Trelawny* at the Vic. The latter gave me what I thought was a great double of Ablett in Act 1 and O'Dwyer in the last act – a character actor's dream.

Although I had now been in the business twenty-five years, the excitement I felt on the first day of rehearsal, in that long top room of the famous theatre, was as if it were my first day in the 'business'. I was a little disappointed with the read-through but knew that many actors don't 'deliver' at the first reading – some indeed, not until the first night. However, I was touched when Bill Fraser (a wonderful actor, perhaps best known for his TV role of 'Bootsie' – or was it 'Snudge'), playing Sir William Gower, said to me after that first mumble through:

'Well, at least there are two of us doing it!'

With *Trelawny* it is essential to have an actress playing the part of Rose that has star quality – after all, Rose is the 'star of the Wells'. In the play's first production in 1898 the part was played by Irene Vanbrugh, but the charming actress cast in our 'offering' did not possess that aura. We did have, however, a rising star playing Tom Wrench, whose approach to the part was somewhat too 'modern' for me but he played it full throttle and that was Robert Lindsay. There was a real established character actor playing Augustus Calpoys in Ken Wynne. Having a street corner conversation with an out of work actor with whom I was well acquainted, I told him that I was going to be at the 'Vic' and that I was to play Young Gobbo.

'Good God' he said 'who's playing *Old* Gobbo?'

It was to be Ken, of course.

The opening scene of *Trelawny* sees Ablett and Mrs Mossop preparing for a 'Company' celebration for Rose Trelawny. Jo Warne and I spent hours rehearsing the laying of the table, until we could have been employed at the Ritz. The contrast of parts from the London-born Ablett to the Dublin raised O'Dwyer, with flaming red hair and an overbearing voice, really gave me great pleasure – even if the audience needed ear plugs.

I find it is often the 'off' stage incidents that stay in the memory most, rather than the play itself. Coming down the stairs at the 'Vic' after a Saturday matinee, I became aware of an overwhelming smell of fish. The only time before that I could remember such a pungent odour was in ......... no, surely not. I descended the last flight of steps to the stage door and there he was.

'Norman! I haven't seen you since Bristol!'

He stood there clasping his usual bunch of flowers.

'I seed the Matinel and these are for the actress who played Rosel'.

'Norman, I'm going next door to the Royal Victoria for a drink, would you care to join me?'

And he did, which was a shock, as I had never seen him outside his natural habitat of the stage door before.

'How are things with you, Norman?'

'Well, I'm getting married.'

113

I gasped.

'Oh, how amaz... how splendid. Who is the lucky lady, is she from Bristol?'

'No, she's a Russial.'

I had heard of a Jack Russell or even a Ronnie Russell but ….

'A Russian, how did you meet her?'

'Well, I were on a bus tour 'oliday in Russial and she were the Guide.'

'Are you going to settle in Bristol?'

'No, in Russial. She lives in Omsk and theym givin' us a flat and me a job in the Department of Culture.'

I knew fish was good for you.


There was much excitement as The Queen Mother was coming to see *Trelawny*. She requested that she meet the Company after the performance on stage, not as a line-up but in casual groups and that we should remain in costume, otherwise she would not recognise us. On the afternoon prior to her visit that evening, I passed the stage-door keeper Bert (or was it Alf – it's usually one or the other) holding forth on the phone.

'No, you f------ can't. …… you're not b----- doing that…. just do as I s------ well tell you.' He then slammed down the receiver.

'I don't know, John, some mothers.'

I was rather taken aback.

'Exciting, the Queen Mum coming tonight, Alf/Bert.'

'It doesn't mean much to me, John, I'm not a Royalist, except for the pub next door .. geddit?'


How charming she was. She went from group to group saying how much she had enjoyed the play and asked questions regarding the role she had seen you portray. She greatly touched us all because she insisted on the Management giving everyone a glass of the Champagne she had been consuming – she certainly knew her vintages. The other aspect I noted was that she met not only the cast but also members of the stage management and theatre staff. I observed her in conversation with Alf/Bert and the next day, seeing him at his post, I commented to him that I had

seen him having a tête-à-tête with Her Majesty.
'Yes, John, a very nice woman, very nice indeed. In many ways, she reminds me of my own Mum.' A chill ran through my heart.

We reached Hong Kong at 'Kung Hei Fat Choy' time and I was taken to my palatial room in the Hilton, looking out onto the 'Peak'. I was touched by the formality of the Porter bringing tea to the room for the two of us to share as a 'welcome' greeting. Rehearsals for *The Merchant* started the next day, 'working in' us newcomers to the production. Tim was Shylock, as in London, Pru took over from Maureen O'Brien as Portia and Ken and I were the new Gobbos. The following morning, I was informed that due to maintenance work, my room would have to be changed and that this would to be done whilst I was having breakfast. To my surprise, I found that I had been moved up one floor to the exact same position and that all my belongings were in the same order as prior to. Had the number on the door not been different, I would have no idea of the change. I was required for rehearsal at 10am and as I was about to leave for the usual heavy note-giving session on my performance from Tim, the Porter knocked on my door. He brought in yet another tray of tea and we had to go through the same welcome procedure as before, simply because I had changed rooms. The outcome being that I arrived for rehearsal a quarter of an hour late and I am not sure that the director really believed my story, but he had to accept it in case it caused a 'loss of face' situation and a diplomatic furore.

We had not brought any of the 'sets' from the 'Vic', so they were all freshly constructed on site. I feared this would never be completed in time until I realised that they, the Chinese, could put up a twenty-storey block of flats in a day, seemingly starting at the top and working down. The productions went well enough, with the cast looking upon the whole experience as a wonderful paid holiday. Nearly everyone took the opportunity to have several suits and shirts run up by some poor sods working in the 'sweat shops'. I recall at one matinée, having played the first Gobbo scene, changing, getting on the MTR,(the newly installed underground system), going under the Harbour, dashing into 'Sam's' on Nathan Road for a fitting. I returned in good time to do that tedious brief 'Sola, sola, wo ha, ho, sola, sola!' scene in Act V. Well, time is precious.

We spent our days on some sea-going craft or other, being lunched and wined, seeing our nubile young members 'skinny dipping' in the South China Sea, which I feared could be shark infested and being concerned that Peter Marinker (Antonio) might come back having definitely lost a pound of flesh. There were trips to Macau and into China (which was now allowed) and on one such occasion, I noticed that each time the coach stopped, to allow eight hundred cyclists cross our path, Chinese faces peered at us through the windows, as if observing a freak show. I commented to the driver that they were obviously intrigued to see our white faces.
'It's not that' he said 'It's your round eyes.'
'Do they find that fascinating?' I enquired
'No' he said 'They think you look ugly.'
I pointed out to my father, Old Gobbo, one particularly gnarled and wrinkled native of Kwantung Province.
'Look Ken, Margery!' (A reference to Old Gobbo's wife and Launcelot's mother, who is spoken of but never seen in the action of the play). We considered writing in some lines for her.

"You are invited for luncheon at the residence of Sir Run Run & Lady Shaw". Sir Run Run was Chairman of the Hong Kong Festival Committee and also a film mogul of some standing, not that he was that tall. As we embarked on his motor-launch, to be taken to what appeared to be his own private island, I seriously expected the side of the cliff face to open and we would sail into an entombed harbour, for this was a 'James Bond' sensation. We dined in immaculate surroundings, with immaculate white linen tablecloths, immaculate cutlery and immaculate china, bearing his crest and wife's initials. We were already seated as our host entered with the most stunning Chinese woman on his arm.

'Lady Run Run's a belter' commented Ken, only for it to be pointed out that the lady at Sir's side was in fact his mistress. Some actors are so naive.

Sir Run Run was slight of stature in every way, which was no wonder, for he only picked at his food, whilst the actors gorged. I had been intrigued by this powerful man's given name, 'Run Run' not being, I would have thought, the first name to leap to mind when considering a newly born's moniker. I was informed, whether it be reliable or not, that originally he had made his living from the drug trade and that he had started as a delivery boy, going from client to client with such speed of foot that the nickname became fact. No wonder he was so slim, perhaps he could have become the fastest man over 26 miles 385 yards in history had he not had such a high calling.

--------0--------

After we finished the performance each night, we would find some hostelry to quench our thirst. This was either the 'Go Down' Club – so named, I assumed, because you went down to it, or to the exceedingly popular 'English Pub'. This was owned by a British husband and wife, he of gentle manner and she, built like and bearing a resemblance to Henry Cooper, who kept a firm grasp on the attitudes of their clientele. We were told they were so wealthy that they owned the largest private seagoing craft in HK harbour. Returning one night to the Hilton, having just 'gone down', scrambling into an actor-packed lift, I was aware of two 'proper people' being in our midst. We slowly disgorged the giggling thespians, floor by floor. Finally, I found that I was the last of the Mohicans, apart from the two dumbstruck outsiders. As we continued our ascent she, for they were a couple, asked:

'How's Penny?' The bottom could have fallen out of my lift.
I stammered:

'Very well, I think …… but how ……. ?'
'We worked together for 'Shelter' and I remember you doing the commentaries for the Donkey Derbys.'
Now of course, I had nothing to fear about being seen in a compromising situation but instinct told me that this might not be the case with them. When she asked me if I knew where she could buy her friend a silk dressing gown, I knew I was right.

Our departure from HK was more dramatic than either of the plays. As we gathered in the Hilton lobby to be transferred to the airport for our journey to Australia, I felt there was tension in the air and asked if it was my imagination. I was told that the talented actor playing the role of the Prince of Morocco had, under the influence of an illegal substance, gone on the rampage in Room 920 and smashed it up.

"Mislike me not for altering the complexion of my suite" did not go down too well. So Morocco was homeward bound.

--------0--------

Perth was a huge contrast to that floating gold mine called Hong Kong. You could actually walk down town without being forced into the gutter. The air was pure and one could breathe in without going into paroxysms of coughing. The gentle breeze, known as 'the Fremantle Doctor', giving one the feeling of health, energy and of general well being.

The taxi took me from the airport to the apartments where several of the artistes were being housed. When the driver stated the charge, I added a suitable amount as a tip. He enquired why I had given more than requested and I said it was a tip.
'Do people tip you for your job? Does a doctor get a tip after you've been to the surgery?' I conceded a negative to both questions.
'Then why should I be treated any differently?'
I apologised for giving any impression of being patronising and determined that I must remember this attitude when I got back

home with the taxi drivers at Heathrow.

It was wonderful to step out each morning into clear skies and warmth to take my daily run (which I was into at the time), and cool off by running through the water sprinklers that nourished the green sward by the sea. We waited for the arrival of the replacement Morocco from London, who turned out to be Christopher Asante, the most delightful, colourful and 'camp' of actors and rumour had it, of royal blood. He was a Perth showstopper, in that his was the only black face to be seen in that fair city for the whole of our time there. Outside the apartments there was a balcony that passed by all our rooms, which allowed 'Morocco' to troll along, wearing a dressing- gown so flamboyant he would have made Noël Coward look dowdy. A few doors from me was the poet, Roger McGough, doing his thing at the festival, who made a refreshing break to talk to, away from all the thespian tittle-tattle.

I hired a car that was very useful, not only for the daily journeys to Her Majesty's Theatre but for visits to see my cousin, Peter Baddeley, who was a gynecologist in Perth. He was the brother of the Consultant I had taken Ronnie Barker to see in Birmingham. Peter had become part of the 'Brain Drain' in the sixties, having felt that Oz afforded him better opportunities and a more comfortable way of life. Granada TV featured a documentary on him, showing him at work in the 'op' theatre, also at home with his wife, Gill. He exuded his power on the squash court (his brother and he had been Derbyshire Junior Doubles tennis champions) proving that he was the right stuff for Oz. His only condition in becoming a TV celebrity was that the programme was not to be shown until after his departure. *The Delivery Man* (with full front cover picture on the *TV Times)* therefore went out the day after they set off into the wide blue yonder. I was a trifle galled when doing a television play a couple of months later in Manchester, that they were still talking about the programme at Granada and commenting to me:
'And he's a damned good actor,' a little too strongly I felt.

As well as taking me for a round of golf at the Royal Perth GC, having had to scour the whole of Western Australia for left-handed clubs for me (no man out there would admit to being the other way), I had dinner with the family and most of the medical profession west of Sydney. It was there that I witnessed that in 'Oz' the ladies were still required to withdraw after dinner, leaving the men to smoke and exchange dubious comedic material.

'On Sunday, we'll sail out of Fremantle to Carnac Island for a picnic lunch and consume a few crates of 'tinnies'. The fella's are all great blokes, not a shirt-lifter amongst them,' said the Captain. As we got under sail in the 'Nellie Dean' (a 33ft Bermuda rig, drawing 6ft, for you matelots), I was somewhat surprised when Peter commanded me to take the helm. The only boat I had sailed up to this point had been in the bath, but as we were under sail I could not refuse the Skipper, otherwise I might have been made to walk the plank. I quickly learned that steering a sea-going craft is not like driving a car. As the boat keeled over to the left (sorry, port), my natural instinct was to wrench the wheel to the right to bring it into the upright position. Wrong. Having nearly pitched three of our crew into the 'drink', I soon learned to do the opposite to my landlubber experience. Having basked, noshed and drunked on the sun parched Isle, with not a sign of Ben Gun or Alexander Selkirk, we returned to our home port, without my having any recall of the return journey from the moment we pulled anchor to the time we docked. It was home for dinner and I was so tired that I hardly took any notice of the  poisonous Dugite snake that was sleeping in the cutlery drawer. The 'barbie' was fantastic. The company very 'macho', nevertheless they accepted the performing pom with not a hint of derision.

I had been cast for the first time in the role of Equity Deputy. It is his responsibility to calm the actors and present their concerns to the management. A man with a foot in both camps, it could be said, but unlike Long John Silver, I had two to keep me firmly on the ground. I think I realised that I had a degree of diplomatic capability and was never accused of not listening to the views expressed on either side, or of failing to balance both causes with care. I was the representative of the actors and stage management but able to appreciate the points presented by the Management. I never once said 'at this point in time, my executive committee etc' but I was tempted to. It all seemed to work out harmoniously and was a development in my man-management skills. Of course, I had been trained as a Samaritan.

My performances in *Trelawny* went down well but I was at a distinct disadvantage in the bar afterwards, for whilst the rest of the cast were surrounded by fawning 'sheilas', I went unnoticed because of my amazing make-up and stunning performances, which had rendered me unrecognisable. I stood alone and palely loitering with nobody's intent. Then ......

'There's a woman down at the other end of the bar that wants to meet you.'

I almost left my glass partially full in my anxiety to be of service. There stood a wonderfully attractive, tallish woman that made me melt at first sight.

'John, this Marion Montgomery.'

Ms Montgomery, the great jazz singer, was in Perth for the Festival with her accompanist, the composer, Richard Rodney Bennett.

'I was looking for the wild, red-haired Irishman and it's you.'

She was gracious enough not to express disappointment, unlike some I've met.

'Have you been invited to be a guest tomorrow for a day at the Races?' she enquired.

'Yes. I can't wait for the off' I said, hoping I didn't sound or look too much like Groucho Marx.

'Good, you can show me the ropes.'

I did not tell Ms Montgomery that I had never been to a racecourse before. Looking deeply into her eyes, I simply intoned:

'Of course I will!'

As VIP guests at Ascot (that's what they call it) we had every comfort; superb view, running bar and in-house betting arrangements which saved one having to go outside to the on-course bookmakers.

'How do I lay, John?' she enquired. Somehow, her by now ardent admirer managed to control his emotions and 'con' his way into showing her. I was dreadfully shocked and saddened when I heard of her death only a few years later and would always think of her when seeing her husband, Laurie Holloway, at the keyboard in the *Parkinson Show.*

I played one game of cricket in Perth for the Festival side, captained by the director of the Perth Festival, David Blenkinsop, without catching the eye of the selectors. I did see others a few days later that would have, watching Western Australia play Queensland at the WACA. Sitting in the blazing sun, downing 'coldies', stripped to the waist – perfect. During the course of the day, I dipped into my shorts pocket to hand over a few shillings for a charity. Getting a circular stick-on-label, as proof of purchase, I stuck it on my chest. The result being that when I stripped off in the theatre that evening to get into 'Gobbo', I had a bright red body with a circular white spot in the centre of my torso. When questioned by my innocent companions as to what this was, I informed them that I had been to the Doctor who had said that he feared it could be 'carcinoma ringtosis'. I passed on his warning that you cannot be too careful of the sun's rays in Perth and that they should all go on the beach fully dressed, preferably wearing an overcoat. Many took this seriously and although it ruined their tan, they were right to do so, for I found out shortly after, that Perth had the highest incidence of skin cancer in the world. Even practical jokes can pay off.

Of course, it was constant party-time for those taking part in the Festival. Some of 'our lot' had been to see a special matinée of the Canadian 'drag' artiste, Craig Russell, who gave stunningly real impersonations of Judy Garland and Barbra Streisand. At one of these party functions in Perth, in walked – I knew not what. The gender of the guest was difficult to define but appeared to be more distaff than staff. It was Craig. He seemed to take a strong fancy to me – I suppose it's understandable. His constant presence at my elbow became an irritant and as I passed Bill Fraser, heavily into the Malt, he asked me if I was enjoying myself. I commented that I found my companion's close attentions somewhat overbearing and Bill settled the problem by turning on him and stating in his gruff tones:

'Leave him alone, he's mine!'

That put Miss Garland off.

One of my greatest regrets was not seeing Bill's last play before he died, in a production of Priestley's *When We Are Married* at the Whitehall Theatre, in which he played the photographer, Henry Ormonroyd. The cast also included Tim West and Pru Scales. Even though I missed him in that, I will always remember that I was 'his'.

The day following Bill's rescue act, the theatre was abuzz with the rumour that I had been 'picked up' the night before. To gain some revenge, I asked the Company Manager to announce over the 'tannoy' system at the end of the matinée performance:

'Mr Baddeley to the stage door, a Mr Craig Russell for him.' As the announcement was made, I told my two dressing room companions to listen with care. In the hope of observing the meeting of the gaysome twosome, the sound of dressing room doors opening and feet coming out onto landings, was louder than some of them could deliver lines on stage. I then went out and shouted down:

'Tell the bitch to go away, I don't want to see her.'

That taught 'em – how dare they treat the Equity 'Dep' with disrespect.

--------0--------

From the summer warmth and vast open spaces of Perth and Her Majesty's, it was back home to the winter chill of Eastbourne and the cramped Devonshire Park Theatre. Poor Young Gobbo hadn't room to swing his broom let alone a cat. Shortly afterwards we made it to the Old Vic for a final couple of weeks and although there was a mini-tour of Europe to follow, the fact that it was announced that funding from the Arts Council for the Old Vic had been withdrawn, I felt I needed to re-establish myself in the voice-over world fast, to bolster funds and reconnect with the family. So it was farewell to the shades of Lilian Baylis and Emma Conns, and that theatrical mecca in the Waterloo Road.

# 48

## DALLAS

Back at the ranch, Mark had left Frensham without exceptional academic results to his name but with the highest degree of literary ability in the family. The girls were at Waldegrave Girls School, Twickenham, slowly working towards scholastic standards that would take them eventually to University degrees. Penny was continuing to study for more and more qualifications, so much so that I called her, like Trofimov, "the eternal student" and Mark, who was looking for the opportunity to become a DJ, "twenty-two misfortunes." Penny had qualified as a social worker and over the years accumulated diplomas in Drama Therapy, Social Studies and Counselling. Mark and I went to the University of Life – unfortunately, I was failed.

Penny had always wanted the country cottage. As I had not picked up on this, whilst I was caring for sheep in 'Oz', she purchased from her own resources, an estate in the New Forest. This was an all 'mod-con' caravan or, to use its correct term, mobile home. This alternative venue, with one update of the 'van, remained in the family control for over a quarter of a century and became a well used and enjoyed 'second home'.

Not to be outdone, I had linked arms with the roaring Tony Jackson in renting an apartment in central London to facilitate the voice-over kings. Also resident were Ray Brooks and Gary Watson. We moved from one flat to another over the years, usually as a four or fivesome. Various others replaced out-going tenants, like Stephen Greif and the wonderfully outrageous Miriam Margolyes, all trying to be the first to make a million. Having overlooked Leicester Square for a time (where I once found Bill Mitchell, like Goldilocks, sleeping in my bed), we eventually settled for a top floor, one bedroom apartment in

Broadwick Street, conveniently placed for the majority of the recording studios and more importantly, adjacent to the John Snow pub. A considerable amount of carousing took place within those walls, whilst we waited for the call to the next voice-over. Our average turn-over could be about four a day, which made it difficult for one to down microphones and leave for Ardwick Rep. The 'flat' gained quite a reputation in theatrical circles and some of the stories that emanated from it would require a separate book, sold under a plain wrapper.

Elstree featured somewhat for me at that time. I had been auditioned by Jim Henson and Frank Oz of *The Muppets* fame for their extraordinary creation, *The Dark Crystal*. They employed artistes from both sides of the 'Pond' for the voices required for this fascinating and frightening creation. I was cast as The Historian, one of the 'Skeksis', bearing some resemblance to my own features but if difficult to detect, can be identified by the pince-nez. There was a daring approach, which I failed to see could be successful, in that the creators invented a completely original language for the characters. As there were to be no sub-titles, I could not see how the audience would be able to follow the plot. Perhaps they wanted an Oscar for best film in a 'foreign, Foreign language.' It was tested on a New York audience who were of the same opinion as myself, so we had to do it again in characterised English. The actors did not complain – we got two fees. A small fortune must have been spent on the production and how successful it was I couldn't gauge, but it did take on 'cult' status.

I also spent a claustrophobic time dubbing a superb German film, *Das Boot*, into English. This drama set in a U-Boat, was unbelievably real. Superbly acted, written and directed by Wolfgang Peterson. The dubbing was under Louis Elman and won an award at some gong ceremony. He was rightly proud of the contribution of the British voice work but I think it was generally felt that the film was best in German with sub-titles. Some years later, I was in conversation with actor, Ian Ashpitel, who had been a sub-mariner and on hearing of my involvement in the film said I had gone up in his estimation enormously – it was worth doing it for that alone.

At the celebrated John Wood Studios in Broadwick Street (owned jointly by John Wood and Patrick Allen), just fifteen yards from our favourite watering hole, I did a considerable amount of work. A comment uttered by John in his role as the recording engineer, was to have an irritating and lasting effect. At one 9.0am, recording session, sitting in my little booth, peering through the darkness at the screen to which I was lending my vocal tones, John came in to me and for no apparent reason slightly altered the position of my script on the desk. He then whispered to me:
'Everything OK at home?' The implication being that I was not up to speed. Thereafter, if ever my colleagues wished to challenge my interpretation of a role they would always enquire:
'Everything OK at home?'

He didn't say that when Miriam Margolyes and I added grunts and groans to a pornographic movie, which the two of us found hysterical. The additional dialogue, of our own creation, which we offered free of charge, was found to be too explicit and was not accepted.

'They're looking for a cartoon voice for a gas flame in an ongoing series of British Gas commercials – should be just your thing' said Wendy Noel.
(Sometime later):
'They loved your 'test' and want to go with you' she informed me. 'It could be a five year contract – big money.'
(Sometime even later):
'It's extraordinary, they want you to go for another test.'
'I thought they *loved* it,' I grumbled.
'They are going to pay a fee, so just do it' she ordered.
(Sometime even later than that):

'What's the problem,' I enquired of the Director.

'Well, we loved the cartoon voice that we had asked you to create but 'Mr Big' didn't like it.'

'What's *his* problem?'

'He said he didn't want a cartoon voice but a 'real' man's voice. However, we still feel it should be a cartoonish type of voice.'

'Will you tell me who 'Mr Big' is?'

'No.'

'Well, tell me where he comes from.'

'Yorkshire.'

Having seen a queue of likely lads outside and in particular, the bluff Leslie Sands, I did my 'Wilfred Pickles'.

(Quite sometime even later still):

'You've got it, John' phoned Wendy.

'I should bloody well think so.'


Not long after that event, there was a desperate call from the office:

'Can you get down to Molinare Sound in an hour? They're doing a test for a series of radio commercials hopefully using Len Rossiter and Richard Beckinsale from *Rising Damp*. Len's had to go to a funeral, so they want you to do Len's voice for the test.'

'You want me to try and get a job for Len?'

'Yes.'

So I did. I noted that this was to be for a series, requiring different 'end lines' for each one. I suggested to the production company that they should use me for that and they agreed. For each occasion I would say:

'At Wrensons, High Street, Harborne, all this week,' – or similar.

Each time I asked if they would play-over to me what Len and Richard had done for the main body of the commercial, so that I could get the 'feel'. After doing several 'tags' over a period, I enquired if that was the actual commercial that they had been using or was it a 'guide.'

They informed that it was the finished article, to which I felt honour-bound to say:

'I have to tell you that is not Len, it's me.'

Something hit the fan and I was sworn to keep it under my hat, which I did – well, I did get a fee each time.

Texas Instruments were looking for a voice suitable for a computer chip that could go into cars. The idea of the talking car was that it would inform the driver of an impending problem in an audio rather than a visual manner. The man at the wheel would be warned that:

'Your front nearside wheel has fallen off,' so that they would be aware of the situation.

The boffins from Dallas flew over to test a batch of voices to find one suitable – I suppose 'chip' friendly would be the term. They took the recordings back to Dallas to analyse and I came out top of the heap. They needed to do more tests to make sure it suited their high 'tech' recording facility, so I suggested that rather than them wasting their time coming over to the UK, why not fly me out to Dallas – and they agreed.

Stepping out of the air-conditioned Dallas/Fort Worth airport into the State of Texas, I was hit by a blast of heat as if from a furnace and was glad when I was dropped at the air-conditioned Four Seasons Hotel, somewhere out of town. I was collected the following morning and taken to the strange and highly secure world of Texas Instruments. Having once more signed a 'silence' contract, I was surprised that I had to be escorted everywhere, including the gents urinal.

My recording studio floated on a tank of water and I was not supplied with anti-sea sickness pills. The precision needed to produce the speech patterns they needed was exhausting. The slightest incorrect inflection was unacceptable. Nevertheless, it was a fascinating experience, in spite of my 'loo' watcher.

Although, my speech might have been suitable in Dallas for the digital chip, not everyone understood those 'British' tones in the street. I had contacted the leading theatrical agent in town and went in to see her. I thought I could impress her with my Prof. Higgins-like tones, which might be of use sometime. She said in her southern drawl:

'Oh no, whenever we need a 'British' actor we always get David Healy.'

David, whom I knew and greatly admired, was the most charming of men. His performance of Nicely Nicely Johnson in *Guys and Dolls* at the National Theatre won him, quite rightly, an Olivier Award. David, a Dallas boy, with clear Texan tones quite apparent to a British ear, was their idea of the cultured English gent, so I realised this 'Brit' would not be coming into *Dallas*.

On the Saturday, one of the recording engineers (all of them PhD's incidentally) offered to take me round downtown Dallas. Having read numerous books on the Kennedy assassination on Dealey Plaza in 1963, like *Rush to Judgement* by Mark Lane and *Six Seconds In Dallas* by Josiah Thompson, I was anxious to take the opportunity of seeing Elm Street, the Book Depositary and the Grassy Knoll. I was surprised how deserted it was at 11am. Getting out of the car and walking to the stockade fence at the top of the grassy knoll, where many believe there was a second gunman, I was totally on my own. My first impression (as a crack shot!) was that the window in the top floor of the Book Depository where the officially accepted lone gunman fired the fatal shots, was not as far from the target as I had imagined and that a trained marksman should be able to 'take out' his subject. However, the strong feeling held by many in the crowd that a second shot had come from the picket fence, which was nearer the target than the Book Depository, I believe was more than possible. For what it's worth, I believe there was a conspiracy and that the man in the Depositary, Lee Harvey Oswald, was aided by an accomplice(s). Where was E. Howard Hunt, the CIA spymaster and Watergate break-in organiser? Some claimed to have seen him in Dallas that day. Up to his death in 2007 he remained "oddly reticent", only repeating "no comment" when questioned.

I had finished my work by that day and my ticket back allowed me to leave for the UK from wherever I liked. As I had a few days to spare, I wanted to stay on and take in somewhere else in the States. Would it be the home of jazz, New Orleans, or the home of the 'exotic', San Francisco. Taking a late Sunday breakfast at the 'Four Seasons', I found the restaurant was packed with 'brunchers'. I was invited to join the table of a couple of guys, by now well into their muffins. When addressing me, one sounded as if he was doing a James Stewart impersonation. He was a Dallas doctor and his companion was a Dallas chef from another hotel. They said if I was doing nothing, I could join them for dinner that evening, but I had made up my mind to move on that day and told my table companions it was San Francisco here I come. Enquiring if I had fixed a hotel, they told me of one just off Union Square that was far more reasonable in price than most in that area. Giving me the number, they suggested that I phone them up, reversing the charges and book, which I did. When asked by Reception what time I would be checking in, I hazarded a guess at around 9pm, for at that moment I hadn't booked the flight.

I landed at San Francisco Int., at around 6pm and decided to take the airport bus into town rather than a cab. After a short time into our journey, the driver of the single-decker spoke to us over the in-bus tannoy, rather like a tour guide. With his right hand on the steering wheel and his left holding the microphone, he uttered:
'Ladies and Gentlemen, Mr Frank Sinatra.'
He then went into the complete *Chicago* number doing, it has to be said, a very reasonable Frank impersonation. Having received an enthusiastic 'round' from his passengers he then said:
'Thank you. And NOW, Mr Tony Bennett.'
His rendering of *I left my Heart in San Francisco* brought his audience to their feet, which could have been a driving hazard.
I knew then that I was definitely in San Francisco.

The hotel was walking distance from the bus station and I found myself at the Reception desk at 7.30. The Clerk, sounding like my old friend Liberace, waved a limp right wrist at me and in serious tones said:

'You said 9 o'clock, it's only 7.30 – you're too early. Go away and come back later ......... I'm only kiddin!'

It was the gayest hotel in the western hemisphere and I then appreciated where my two 'brunch' friends in Dallas came from. The weather was perfect (no fog on the bay) and I enjoyed my stay in San Fran tremendously, I was only sorry that I had no one to share it with. Walking in the sun to visit the Golden Gate Bridge, to be informed that I was actually looking at the Oakland Bridge; taking a trip to Sausalito and at least passing by the Golden Gate; going on a tour from Fisherman's Wharf over to Alcatraz; climbing the hill to the Mark Hopkins Hotel and dining in the revolving restaurant at the "top of the Mark", with its breathtaking view. Everyone should dine there and declare their love to someone. I was chilled and thrilled going to the St Francis Hotel in Union Square and taking the lift to the top floor restaurant and having for the first time the experiencing going up in a bubble on the outside of a building, so that it felt like being suspended in space. It was that hotel which had been used for the film *The Towering Inferno*.

I roamed Chinatown one night in search for a 'real' Chinese restaurant, to be disappointed to find that they all seemed similar to those in Gerrard Street, with American Express and Visa signs in the windows. Eventually I saw what I was looking for, a restaurant window with no signs displayed, and a group of diners inside made up entirely of Chinese. I ventured in and asked, or rather mimed, if I could eat there. They looked, in their Oriental way, somewhat surprised but immediately offered me a place at their large round table. For the next hour I ate from the 'lazy Susan', encouraged by them to try every dish and to drink their rice wine, all the while communicating in a Marcel Marceau fashion. When the meal was ended they shook my hand and wished me 'welly good fortune.' It was then I realised that it was not a restaurant but someone's abode and that I had walked in on a family meal. It was best 'Chinese' I ever had.

On my last morning, having been served breakfast by a mincing waiter, I mulled over the *San Francisco Times* and read of the death of a film star that had set all male hearts pounding - Ingrid Bergman. Of all the gin joints, in all the towns, in all the world, I had to learn of it there.

## 49

## ORPHANED

At whatever age, it is salutary to know that you are next in line.
My mother's death affected me deeply. Guilt often accompanies bereavement, remembering what you did not do or say, rather than what was good and positive. The Bard's line in Julius Caesar that "the evil that men do lives after them, the good is oft interred with their bones" is hard to acknowledge, but gives us cause for thought. Her final illness from cancer of the oesophagus was an awful throwback to her own mother's death. Having undergone a major operation, with the overwhelming encouragement of her godson (the Birmingham Consultant), performed by one of his own former students, which she survived, but sadly failed to outlive the post-operative period. I said farewell at her funeral, reading a quotation that I had found in her prayer book. It was from the leaf of a day-by-day calendar, of her wedding day to my father. By chance it happened to be its anniversary that day.

*Do you know how love comes into being?*
*It grows like the acorn through the long years, while it feeds on dreams, on sorrow, and song; then suddenly it buds, and in that fleeting moment it has buried itself deep down in your heart.*

Henrik Ibsen

I needed to immerse myself in some project. I had wanted to find a subject for a one-man show that suited my particular sense of humour. I spoke to Sam Walters and he gave me a date six months hence, to put on my offering – I had to find something. Staring down at me from a shelf over my desk, where it had been for some time, was a book that always amused me when I felt low: *The Life and Death of Rochester Sneath*. When at Cambridge, Humphry Berkeley, a man of singular humour, created in 1948 a fictitious minor Public School; Selhurst, near Petworth in West Sussex. He set about writing to the Headmasters of various Public Schools, seeking their opinion and advice on school matters and also to celebrities inviting them to attend the school's tri-centenary[*] celebrations. He arranged for the Petworth GPO to forward this mail to his 'digs' address in Cambridge. His ludicrous requests, (couched in the most convincing terms), was accepted as genuine by virtually every recipient. Their gullible replies, along with his initial letters, make for hilarious reading. Those taken in included the Headmasters of: Marlborough, Rugby, Charterhouse, Haileybury and his own school, Malvern. There were also prestigious names like the architect, Sir Giles Gilbert Scott, the conductor, Sir Adrian Boult and George Bernard Shaw, on his 'hit' list. He was persuaded by a friend, 'RAB' Butler, to place the correspondence under Bank security for twenty-five years and then to publish it, which is what he did. The contents reminded me so much of my own school that it never failed to reduce me to uncontrollable laughter.

I wrote to Humphry Berkeley to seek his permission to use his material for a one-man show and received a positive response from him, also inviting me to dinner. At first, I felt somewhat overawed and outclassed by him and found his slightly effete manner challenging. However, as the evening progressed, I felt more at home and found that there were certain foibles that we shared. Whilst he was far more erudite than myself, I appreciated that behind his serious concerns he found it irresistible not to prick pomposity. This character trait led many colleagues to take exception and for all the good work he did in politics, he was to lose favour with many. A classic example being when he made an adverse comment about the Lord Chancellor, who implied that he might take legal action. Humphry's response to that was to recommend to his Lordship that if he did so, he should seek the advice of a competent lawyer. It was this sense of the preposterous that we had in common and on which we were both hoist with our own petard – "Very good but he doesn't take things seriously."

The format I chose for *A Night with Rochester Sneath* was of a talk given by the Headmaster to possible parents and other interested parties, extolling the virtues of the school, with the help of one of the boys, Fawcett Major, who assisted with the slides that were shown. The pictures of Mrs Sneath, Wotan their son, one of the Matrons, his Secretary, Dorothy Lord (always referred to as 'good Lord') and a Mrs Harvey-Kelly who resided conveniently in Cambridge, all bore a remarkable resemblance to Rochester Sneath himself. There was music, in which the Head sang about the old boys, all of them celebrities of the day and also the school song, with the refrain:
" Up Selhurst, Up Selhurst, Up Selhurst, straight and gay
 Up Selhurst, Up Selhurst, Up Selhurst, all the way."
The main problem was that the audience had to be aware that when a reference was made to the letters they were in fact genuine correspondence, the rest was my invention. This was done by the Presenter (JB) telling them of the actual hoax and then for Mr Sneath (JB) to appear at the back of the auditorium and take over. It was another stunning illusion.

The show was performed initially at the Orange Tree, in that small upper room and on the first night Humphry gave me his guest list just prior to the performance. At first I did not welcome this, for it seemed to include most of the members of the House of

135

Commons, Humphry having been a Member of Parliament for Lancaster. In fact he was responsible not only for the method by which the Conservative Party elected its leader, but was also a leading protagonist, following Lord Wolfenden's Report on Homosexual Offences and Prostitution, in bringing into being the Sexual Offences Act in 1967. This ultimately led to him losing his seat, if that is a suitable way of putting it. In a song referring to old boys of Selhurst and what they got up-to after they left the school, called *Better Things*, there were lines about Jeremy Thorpe and Norman Scott.[**] Mr Thorpe and his wife were sitting in the front row that first night and had I not had Humphry's list, allowing me just enough time to alter the lines, the ensuing embarrassment would have killed the performance – it was very close!

The show was later put on at the Birmingham Repertory Theatre as a double bill, with Rattigan's *The Browning Version* playing the first half. It also went on a mini tour. The Rattigan play was, of course, far superior to my modest efforts and I was particularly interested in the young actor playing Taplow, Sam West, whom I had always felt a strong affinity to. He was making his professional début. The Sneath show was never really satisfactory but I was thrilled to hear that there had been a complaint from the Head of Wrekin College (incidentally the alma mater of my Best Man) that, as there had been performances on two nights, boys had returned to the second in order to record the words of the Selhurst school song and were later heard singing in the corridors of their own somewhat modest school:
"Up Wrekin, Up Wrekin, Up Wrekin straight and gay etc". He complained – damned cheek, considering that they had not sought Selhurst's permission.

There was, however, approbation in a charity performance at the BBC, which will come up later in a different guise. As the show was, to a degree, stand-up comedy with invited comments and questions from the audience allowing improvisation, it led to a remark that I treasure. Bill Mitchell, the deepest voice 'in town', who was a house resident, or so it would seem, of Ronnie Scott's Club in Frith Street, said to me after a performance: 'Man, you were making Jazz.' I liked that.

--------0--------

Mark, who had been writing for several magazines, including *Video the Magazine* as a film critic, at last obtained what he was seeking. He joined Wiltshire Radio, a commercial station that had recently started in Wootton Bassett, as a DJ. The main problem seemed to me was that he did the early shift from 6 to 9 each morning and as he could never rise when he was at home before 10.0am, I wondered how he would manage. He also did evening shifts, the result being that he rarely had any sleep. Mark, who was never good at caring for himself, seemed to be under great physical strain. Within a couple of years he seemed to become burnt out. Apart from that there was something else looming that we were unaware of at that time. However, it was a period that meant a great deal to him and his series *Reflections* was successful enough to be repeated for some time afterwards.

--------0--------

For years I had been going to Cologne dubbing films for an ex-pat Englishman, Ian Cummings and his partner, Bernd Horst. Although I had worked in the 60's in Hamburg, it was working in Cologne that really introduced me to Germany. On one occasion, going to Hanover, I had been met at the airport by the youthful Bernd, who at that time spoke no English. Uncertain how he would recognise me, I told him to look out for a man carrying an umbrella and reading *The Times*. I felt as if I were in a John le Carré novel and indeed, am surprised I was not taken in for questioning. Whilst staying there, I wished to take the opportunity of seeing the formal gardens of Herrenhausen. At the bus station I addressed a likely Transport Inspector thus:
'Vas number bus fur Herrenhausen, bitte,' to which he replied: 'Sieben.'

At this point I panicked, uncertain what number that was, and enquired in my native tongue:

'Nine?' to which he replied:

'Ja, sieben.'

'Nine?' I desperately implored.

'JA, JA est ist sieben, idiot.'

OK, so I don't speak Deutsch.

We were dubbing into English a cartoon series of a delightful character called Urmel, which had already been done in Spanish, Italian and Egyptian. It has to be said that the 'Brits' do tend to find everything exceedingly funny but the work gets done. Rubbing shoulders in the recording booth with characters like Anthony Jackson, Geoffrey Matthews, Nigel Anthony, Norman Mitchell and others meant that I was working and watching the screen through constantly streaming eyes. To observe Mr Jackson, after he had returned from a 'good' lunch, fast asleep on the studio floor and for the sound engineer to ask the studio manager:

'Vas ist das?' to be informed:

'Tony schnarcht,' I found almost unbearable.

Let it be said, however, lest you should think this was a group of incompetent idiots, that after the last day of recording, the overall producer and moneyman raised his glass of Sekt and addressed us thus:

'I vish to say, zat ven you start vurking hier, I zink you no take ze vurk serious. BUT, unlike ze Spanish, unt ze Italian, unt ze Egyptian, you alvays finish ze day unt time – you never vunce vent into OVERTIME!!!

That Herr Oberfuhrer, shows our talent. Skol.

I loved my visits to Germany and always appreciated our friend's caring hospitality. They, of course, as befits occupants of that disciplined nation, expect everything to run to time. Filling in at a local bar with a 'gross Kölsch' before going on to dinner, we found ourselves at a linguistic disadvantage. When the waiter passed and I demanded the 'Rechnung bitte' he brought another round of beers. The next time, I stated firmly 'Rechnung bitte', he brought yet another round of Kölsch. By now we had passed the time for us to be at our hosts, so after we had finished the third round, with head spinning, I screamed:

'Rechnung bitte UNT EINE QUITTUNG BITTE' – somehow or other, he took the hint.

OK, so my Deutsch was improving.

--------0--------

Nice. A word that we were never allowed to use at school, unless it was pronounced 'Neece'.

Texas Instruments were obviously keen on me after my Dallas excursion, for they employed me at their facility in the hills looking down on the Baie des Anges. The view, taking lunch on the terraces, was stunning and driving down the hairpin bends, like Grace Kelly in *To Catch a Thief*, to the hotel on the Promenade des Anglais was breathtaking. Those who know the 'Negresco', one of the great hotels of the World, will appreciate how I felt staying at 'Le Meridien', five hundred yards down the road. I was fortunate to visit Nice a couple of times and found the Côte D'Azure heaven. My first experience of staying in the south of France had been on holiday many years before at St Claire next to Le Levandou and I felt this could be the place for me. I assure you, I did do some work, not only producing odd sounds but doing recordings of stories for children and adults. Texas Instruments also employed me on home soil in Bedford, which did not have quite the same charm – good restaurant, though.

They gave me my first opportunity to appear in a published work. Articles for magazines and programme notes I may have written, but never anything within a hard-back. One of the boffins at Texas was writing a technical and academic work entitled *Electronic Speech Synthesis*. This dealt with techniques, technology and applications. As you can imagine it was right up my street. Open at any page and you can read:

e(n) = s(n) + p/k =1 a(k)s(n-k)

I won't continue, otherwise it will spoil it for you.

'I'd like you to write a chapter, looking at speech synthesis, from the voice contributor's perspective' said Geoff Bristow, the editor of the work. I produced a chapter entitled *The Power of Speech,* for which I received remuneration. I trust this will leave you with a feeling of *some* respect. Do read it sometime.

---

\* It should be 'tercentenary', to be pedantic.

\*\*Jeremy Thorpe, leader of the Liberal party, was tried for the attempted murder of Norman Scott, following a homosexual affair. He was found not guilty and acquitted.

## 50

## CONFUSION & COLLAPSE

'Mr Baddeley, you can read music,' said Miss Appel from BBC Radio Bookings, more as a statement than a question.
'Well, ......'
'Good. The BBC has commissioned an orchestral work by the Australian composer David Lumsdaine entitled *Ballad for Edward John Eyre*, which will be performed live for the Third Programme from Liverpool University. Those taking part will be Elizabeth Manning, soprano, Barry Guy, double bass, with the London Sinfonietta, conductor, Elgar Howarth. The work requires two spoken parts as narrators, who are integral to the piece. I thought that you, with John Rye as your alter ego, would be ideal. I will see that the score is sent to you as soon as possible. You will receive your normal reduced narrator's fee. Thank you.'

Although I had always wished to appear on the concert platform, I did feel slightly overwhelmed. The score arrived by special messenger – or were there two of them, for it measured 18" x 12". I found it not only heavy but totally incomprehensible. On arriving at the home of the BBC Symphony Orchestra in Maida Vale for the first of two rehearsals, I was greeted by a somewhat flushed John Rye, who simply stated:

'I'm just going to follow you, dear.'

I introduced us to the Maestro and stated that we would be keeping our eye very much on the stick and depended on him to bring us in. The orchestra seemed to spend longer than usual warming up, until I realised we were already well into the work. In fact, orchestra, soloists and the additional pre-recorded synthesised music, sounded as if they were warming up for the entire piece, which lasted 50 minutes. Fortunately, I had read that book on Electronic Synthesis, so felt reasonably comfortable. The only real degree of clarity should have come from us, the narrators, which was difficult for we were somewhat drowned out by the band – but then what can you expect of musicians?

Perhaps the story should be explained – for there was one. Edward John (how apt that those Christian names are for a man of great courage) Eyre, was the first traveller to cross southern Oz, going from Wollongong (or somewhere like that) to Fremantle. During this journey, he loses all of his team of bearers but one, not through carelessness but by desertion or death. The torment of the journey is expressed by the music and the narrators speak the words from his diary. At the beginning of this trek, his voice is strong with occasional words uttered from his sub-conscious self, but by the end the sub-conscious is stronger than the conscious, until the destination is reached. For the final moments of the work one hears the conscious-self reading the last words of his diary with clarity and strength (and audibility), with the conclusion coming as the final strains of the composition slowly sustain one note, to finally fade away.

The first performance, in front of a full hall, was memorable in that I was still coming to terms with the complexity of the work with John Rye loyally 'following me'. Relying on the maestro to 'bring us in' over the cacophony of sound coming from the orchestra, the recorded synthesised music, the cello of Mr Guy (seemingly covering every note that his bow could produce) and Ms Manning (having the extraordinary ability of being able to sing two different notes simultaneously), demanded great concentration. At one point, I felt certain that Mr Howarth had failed to bring us in. Sitting centre stage, right in front of him, I directed my laser eyes piercingly at him. He realized that he had overlooked us and desperately gave me the cue. Through sheer intuition, I cut two lines and our spoken section fitted perfectly into the work. Mr Rye said afterwards:

'I just followed you, dear.' Teamwork.

The sustained reception we received after the final note had faded was the kind only heard in a concert hall – an unusual experience for a simple thespian.

We also performed the work later at the Whitworth Hall, Manchester and it was recorded for a CD. There was another broadcast, which was performed at St John's, Smith Square. The two aspects that stand out for me of that occasion was that firstly, having had initially no comprehension of what was being played, I could now understand it perfectly and was able to detect any false note. The other being, how furious my co-speaker, Mr Rye, was when the BBC announcer in Third Programme tones referred to him as John Ray. I told my disconsolate 'echo' that because of the emotional depth of his dulcet tones he was frequently confused for the American popular singer, Johnny (Cry) Ray.

I was foolishly suggested for a programme called *Just a Minute*. The format was that the team had to speak on any given subject for one minute without any repetition, hesitation or deviation. It was recorded, unrehearsed and off the cuff, in front of an audience. I imagined that they would record an hours worth or so and then edit it down for the thirty-minute broadcast. I was wrong, what you heard is what they did. Members of the team were the hysterical Kenneth Williams, the brilliant Peter Jones, the ponderous Derek Nimmo and the overwhelmed moi. In the chair was the capable and pedantic Nicholas Parsons. They all took it in a very competitive manner, apart from Kenneth who, if he felt that proceedings were going flat, would scream abuse at the Chairman or the rest of the team. I felt out of my depth. As a friend had pointed out:

'No repetition .. you?'

Kenneth, always alert to a situation, gave the nod to the others to allow me to finish my minute, as a sporting gesture I imagine. Mr Parsons then commented:

'Well done, John. Obviously the team didn't notice you repeat the word 'it' but nevertheless, well done.'

Afterwards, Kenneth, who I don't think was wildly enamoured of the man in the chair, touched upon the matter with me and said in those familiar deep rolling tones:

'What a ----'

I couldn't possibly comment but my career as a panellist came to an end with sighs of relief on all sides.

Penny was fast approaching a 'special' birthday date and was taking the girls to visit her sister in San Diego to celebrate there. Prior to their departure, I was again in Cologne but feeling somewhat lethargic and generally low. There were also physical presentments, which I will not go into except to say that I put it down to the German food. A year or so prior to this, I had been taken ill on a train on my way to do a voice-over. I had felt a desperate pain in my groin and back and being surrounded by fellow commuters, I tried to hide my feelings. As perspiration poured from my brow and I was forced to loosen my collar, those nearby became aware that I was not well, so immediately hid their faces in the *Financial Times* or studied closely the rolling stock passing by. Obviously, it wasn't only in French trains that passengers looked out of windows. However, there was a distinguished looking man of foreign extraction sitting opposite me who was made of stronger stuff and directly faced the problem.

'Are you unvell?' said my Deutsch fellow traveller.

'Yes, I think I am.' I responded, in typical British lack of decisiveness or was it stiff upper lippedness?

'Don't you sink you should get OUT?'

'Yes, I think I should.'

So at a station that I had failed to notice before, Earlsfield, I disembarked to find to my surprise that my German supporter and his son got out with me. By now I was in such pain that I didn't know whether to stand, sit or lie

'Do you vish fur unt ambulance?'

'Yes, I think I do.'

Leaving me in the care of his teenage son, he departed to return a short time later to tell me:

'An ambulance is on its vay. Now, do you vish me to phone your vife?'

'No,' I said, knowing my priorities, 'my Agent.'

Having given him the number he duly did my bidding. To my great regret I was not able to express my gratitude to my guardian angels before they boarded the next train and were gone.

As I lay in the Outpatients ward of St George's, Tooting, waiting to be treated, the pain disappeared. The diagnosis was that I had kidney stone problems.

'Now you know what childbirth is like' said the man in the white coat. At a later date, the stone was removed by a method that to describe would bring tears to all male members (I use the words advisedly) of mankind.

Here I was again. As Penny and the girls flew the Atlantic, I felt ill, this time on the Underground. Lying on a platform, losing consciousness and vomiting brownish red fluid, a London Transport lackey said;

'Bloody hell, that's blood ain't it?' I had no reason to call his assessment into question.

'I'll get an ambulance.'

'And would you phone my agent and explain' I called out after him, giving the number. I thought if I 'snuff' it at least Bill Mitchell will be amused, for the previous incident was his favourite 'actor' story. When the ambulance arrived, the Underground official asked where they were taking me.

'The Middlesex.'

'You can't, I've told his AGENT that he's going to St Thomas' (which happened to be near by).

'Well, he's not, he's going to the Middlesex.'

'But I've told his AGENT that it's St Thomas' he's going to.'

He spoke with authority and also as a member of the 'in' crowd. They took me to where he commanded.

I was horrified by the conditions I found in St Thomas'. I was taken to the old part of the hospital, in a ward holding around two-dozen male patients all, in the main, cancer sufferers. It felt as if we were in the Crimea at Scutari and that Florence Nightingale should be caring for us. Although I managed not to lose my two bedside companions during my stay, each night the curtains were drawn round the bed as they removed another ex-patient.

'Two of our aircraft went missing last night, John.'

Having been topped up with several blood transfusions, my internal haemorrhage eventually ceased. The doctor was not amused at my giving my own diagnosis as to what had caused the problem, but later when I saw his report, he supported my supposition that it was due to an excessive amount of aspirin having been taken over the years for migraine relief. I was instructed never to use it again. They were also concerned with my alarmingly high blood pressure. The good aspect, as pointed out to me by my Consultant cousin, was that it had been discovered in my early fifties before it was too late. What with the death toll on the ward and the appalling state of the latrines, reminding me of my school days, I could not wait to get out.

As a welcome back to the land of the living, Humphry Berkeley took his sister, Jane Russell, and me for lunch at the Cadogan Hotel in Sloane Street. Apart from the pleasure of being wined and dined and being presented with a signed copy of his book *The Life and Death of Rochester Sneath*, to go with my own heavily used version, there was the particular emotion of being with the man who was considerably responsible for liberalising our attitude towards homosexuality, in the very hotel where Oscar Wilde had been arrested.

# 51

# ON THE MOVE

After determined endeavour, Tessa made her way to Nene College in Northampton, an outpost of Leicester University. She was to take a degree in Combined Studies, which comprised History, Drama and Sociology. The saying 'Jack of all trades, master of none' is somewhat shallow, for Tessa's degree seemed to cover the complete spectrum of knowledge. When three years later she achieved a 2:1 BA, I knew she could take on any challenge.

My main concern had been Northampton. The county was known for the number of hospitals it had for those with mental disorders. At that time it became a government policy that, wherever possible, patients should be returned 'back into the community'. The philosophy being that those with these problems would be better served in an open environment rather than being incarcerated. More to the point, I suspect, it would cut down on National Health expenditure. The result was the disturbing number of citizens wandering the streets of Northampton, shouting abuse and waving knives – or perhaps that was considered normal behaviour for the inhabitants of the shoe-manufacturing town. Tessa survived and we saw her receive her degree in 1989 in the Derngate Theatre.

Louise was on the lookout for her next academic haven. We went on a quick 'recce' 'up north' taking in Manchester and York Universities. We thoroughly enjoyed the trip but she decided that she wanted a port of call nearer to home, so she chose Portsmouth. She gained her degree in psychology in 1990, which gave her a BSc. We thus had the arts and the sciences under one roof.

The chance to voyage into uncharted waters came my way when my cousin with the scalpel in Birmingham invited me to take a week's sail with him and three other 'medics' on his Moody 38, the good ship 'Eskimo Nell'. Sailing out of Lymington, as we approached The Needles, the skipper ordered me to take the helm. Having sailed the Indian Ocean a year or so previously with his brother, I felt confident at navigating around any obstacle in the English Channel. However, as we progressed under sail to Alderney, I felt the effects of mal de mer, which became so bad that I was incapable of performing my sea-going duties. I seriously considered the possibility of having to get a flight back to Blighty from Jersey. I was then asked by one of my fellow seadogs if I had taken a Stugeron. I thought this must be an important part of the boat's sailing mechanism, only to be informed that it was an anti-seasickness tablet. My cousin had never informed this old landlubber about that 'the sailor's friend' but fortunately, the crew was well provided for, and I was able to take one as I fell out of my hammock each morning. I never had a moment's qualm after that. I shall most certainly ask Charon, as he takes me across the Styx to Hades, to provide me with that 'after life' saver.

Our days were spent on sunlit waters and under sail, heading for an evening destination, to drop anchor, splice the mainbrace (not with rum but the obligatory gin and tonic), followed by our taking the harbour town by storm. We dined in St Malo, Lezardrieux, Tequier, where the behaviour of these fellows of the Royal College of Surgeons left something to be desired, but by God we laughed.

Stormy Weather, a good title for a song maybe but not when you are at the helm. We were en route for Tequier, when I observed a blackened sky some distance 'forrad'. The skipper was studying his charts below, presumably with Squire Trelawney, so I did not wish to distract him. As the ominous cloud came nearer and the seas became a little choppier, I felt I should point out my concern to the Second Mate. I said:

'Just a second mate, I am concerned about the fast approaching cloud.'

Quicker than you could say 'all hands on deck' it was all hands on deck. With that we were hit 'head on' and my attempts to hold a true course went overboard. In fact, we nearly all went overboard. If there had been an apple barrel, I would have hidden in it, but I simply remained strapped into my seat and in commune with my Maker. The skipper was of course calm, as attempts were made to lower sail, whilst we pitched and tossed out of control. Suddenly, much to my relief, peace came upon us, only to be informed (by the well informed) that we were in the centre of the storm and that mayhem would soon return, as it passed over us – which it did. Eventually, as it left us in its wake, tranquillity descended. The main damage was a torn sail, which dented our pride and the owner's bank balance, but we sailed on undaunted. I never believed that I would listen to the shipping forecast from the dear old BBC with such intense interest. Gale force 9 required a change of bell-bottoms and Gale force 3 was tedious to an experienced helmsman like myself. I got very picky.

As we returned to home waters, having now become a Master Mariner, I found myself, yet again at the helm as we passed The Needles. A member of the crew congratulated me with:

'He counted them all out and he counted them all back.'*

Mark, who was back working on some magazine, asked if he could go away with Penny and I, on our own, to our estate in the New Forest. This was unusual, as he had not shown particular interest in it and rarely went. He said he wanted to talk to us away from the home environment. We, of course, duly went. He seemed reticent about getting into this 'talk' and asked if we might know what it was he wished to discuss. I pointed out that this placed us in a difficult position, for if we made a suggestion that was incorrect he might be offended. It was a no-win situation.

However, I could see that there was no other option but to give an opening so I asked if it could be to do with his sexuality. His relief at our matter of fact and understanding attitude was tangible. My desperate concern was that we had heard about a terrible illness that was affecting many in the 'gay' community. Of course, later I was to find that this affliction called Aids, affected not only those with homosexual leanings but also heterosexuals and both genders. A couple of years later, I was doing a Drama broadcast with Ian McKellen in the cast, who had recently 'come out'. He told me that the worst part had been telling his Aunt, who had brought him up. He informed her that he had something to tell her, as Mark had done with us, and when he delivered the devastating news, she said with relief:
'Oh, I thought you were going to tell me something dreadful.'

There have been very few theatres that I have loathed working in but Derby Playhouse was one. Christopher Honer, whom I had worked with when he was Assistant Director at Birmingham, asked me to be in a new play, *The Brewery Beano*. Adapted for the stage by Rony Robinson from his book *The Beano*, it was based on the outings that were laid on for factory employees, where the boss would treat them to an annual day's holiday at his expense. It was set just prior to the World War of 1914-18. Originally written for radio, this railway outing to Scarborough was somewhat difficult to stage and required members of the cast to play numerous parts. I was the only one to have just one role, that of the overbearing factory owner, Mr Holles. The part was right up my street – a loudmouthed, lecherous, show-off. This, I fear, was the problem. It was apparent that the resident company resented my coming in and taking the plum role and thought that I identified too closely with the character. The result being that they did all they could to sideline me, whilst they went about eating their pulses and discussing their left-wing beliefs, looking upon me no doubt as a right-wing carnivore.

I had decided not to spend my entire wage on staying in a hotel and found a large, clean bed-sitting room, in a large, clean, soulless house. As we approached opening night, 'flu' hit home and I spent the entire run staying in bed during the day, attempting to clear my head, throat and general depression, to be able to perform at night. It was a shame because the part afforded great opportunities for vulgarity, mime and song. Lines at the hotel dining table to a lady guest like:

'Do you fancy some 'Spotted Dick', the wife does!' indicates the character's degree of sophistication.

Another aspect of his character was that he could perform feats of magic. He did this to illustrate his philosophy on the economic state of the Nation. It required him to pluck coins out of space and then make them vanish, thus demonstrating the way the government handled the economy by throwing our money away. I asked if they could get a conjurer to show me how I could perform this feat of prestidigitation. They did and he was hopeless. All he could say was that he could do it with bank notes but not coins. I knew I could do better than that and did. My method (which I reluctantly reveal) was to have a straw boater hat, with the inside having a small shelf to one side, so that as the coins were thrown in on the opposite side, with a slight tilt of the hat the coins would come to rest under the shelf. When the hat was turned over they did not fall out. Vanished – magic. How to produce coins from the ether? With various unseen pockets sown into the jacket of my white snazzy summer suit (to my design), and also magnetic bars sown inside the trouser legs, adjacent to the bum, to which the coins would adhere thus allowing me to grasp and seemingly pluck them out of thin air. Thus, the illusion was achieved. But, I hear you cry, coins are non-magnetic .. well spotted. I had bronze coloured metal discs made, which from the audience, *appeared* to be coins. It required dexterity and practice but worked perfectly ..... UNTIL .....

At the last performance, after the first half, I went to the dressing room to change out of the Harris Tweed suit I wore for Act 1 into the 'magic' suit for Act 2. GONE. I screamed for 'wardrobe' and enquired as to why they had removed the costume, as there was still one act to go before they packed up later after the play had finished.

'We haven't touched it,' they bridled.

It had been purloined. Was it an outside intruder or a warped fellow actor seeking some form of maligned retribution? I visualised the immaculately dressed thief in his new white suit being somewhat confused as he walked past a metal radiator, finding himself sucked into contact with it by the magnetic bars inside his trouser legs. I will never know who the villain was but what I did know was that he/she had also taken all my own personal clothes. I would have to leave the theatre naked on my departure, nevertheless, I was determined that I would go out on a magic note.

'Have you any spare magnetic bars? Do you remember where you sowed the false pockets?' I enquired of the wardrobe mistress.

'Yes and yes.'

'You have ten minutes to put them into the Harris Tweed suit.'

'Done.'

Following the extended interval, the second act curtain went up, with the irate director wondering what had caused the delay, only to see the leading man in an unchanged suit. He knew it was therefore impossible for there to be magic that night .. WRONG!

After the final curtain, I beat a hasty retreat from the Playhouse, dressed in oddments from the 'Wardrobe' Dept. Exiting through the foyer doors, I slipped up on the decaying cabbage leaves that always greeted the audience at the entrance to that vegetarian theatre. The Playhouse was seemingly set in its very own Covent Garden, giving I suppose the impression of Drury Lane. When, somewhat bruised in appearance and pride, I was asked on my arrival home, what had happened to my clothes and in particular my shirt, I simply confessed that I had lost it at the Derby.

* A reference to restricted reporting by BBC Correspondents of aircraft sorties during the Falklands War (1982).

# 52

## POP STAR

*"Now, I'm hot stuff and there's no denying, today's your lucky day"*

**Nick Ryan**

Enter Pop Star. I had been doing voice-overs on commercials for Nick Ryan of Lintas, for some time. He had made his name by suggesting that a catchy jingle for an ice-cream product might be the use of the melody of *O Sole Mio*. So, *Just One Cornetto* became the song on every errand boy's lips and did the product a considerable service. He and I hit it off, having very much a similar sense of humour and I asked him to write the songs for *Rochester Sneath*. He then asked me if I would record a 'poppish' number which he had written called *You Either Got It Or You 'Aint*. It would have fallen into the comedic zone of pop, being simply the story of the lad with delusions of adequacy, chatting up a girl in a bar and slowly through the number becoming more and more inebriated, until he finally collapses. The idea amused me but at the recording session with the band, it became apparent that I was too straight! To sing off the beat, I found virtually impossible. I might be able to render a Handel Recitative but not a Ryan Groovy. After a day in the studio it was on disc but was not, I fear, taken up. Exit Pop Star.

Nick was not 'put out' when he saw me at a surprise stag-night party that was arranged for him shortly after. Dinner with all the trimmings, plenty of booze and of course, the obligatory Stripper – they all went down well. As at a wedding, telegrams were read by a best friend, including one that stated: "Sorry that I cannot be with you tonight but all the best for the future. Tony Selby." As the festivities went on well into the early hours, I explained to our groom-to-be that it was difficult for me to get back to London, it being some distance from Leigh-on-Sea.

'Well, you can sleep with me,' he offered generously in Dexterish tones.

I didn't realise that he meant it literally, him an almost married man too. Let it be said that he was still a virgin on his wedding day, as far as I was concerned. As we lay side by side, he enquired:

'Who the hell's Tony Selby?'

It would seem that all the invitations for his surprise night's debauchery had been sent out by his bride-to-be, the beautiful Sue. She had obviously gone through Nick's address book and chosen names that caught her eye. It would appear that my bedfellow had once possibly considered Mr Selby for a commercial and had obtained his address, but never taken up the idea. As I said farewell the next morning to my soon-to-be ex-bachelor friend, the thought of Mr Selby festered in my mind.

I did not attend the wedding in Oxford but nevertheless made my presence felt. I sent a telegram, which I knew the Best Man would read at the reception. It stated:

"Wishing you both every happiness. I quite understand your feelings Sue, but I will never forget the time we were together. Love, Tony Selby."

I also phoned the hotel where the celebration was taking place and asked them to inform the Bride and Groom that:

'Mr Tony Selby has just phoned and apologises for not being with you.'

Their honeymoon was taken away from it all, in Hua Hin in Thailand. I obtained the hotel telephone number and spoke to Reception, asking them to convey a message to Mr & Mrs Ryan, that Tony Selby was due there in two days and would look them up.

I also contacted Tony's agent and asked if he could get his client to send signed photographs to my two sick children, Nick and Sue, who were his greatest fans. On their return home they both found on the doormat a warm card signed:

"Get well soon, love Tony Selby xxx."
Like Calais, his name will be forever engraved on their hearts.

--------0--------

Perhaps I had allowed a TV series that I was in to go to my head. It was called *Assert Yourself*. Produced for Channel Four by Michael Rolf, with Andrew Sachs as Presenter, it featured Anne Dickson, a well-established authority on assertiveness training, instructing woman how to be more forthright in a male-dominated world. The programme was made up of scenes illustrating lack of assertiveness and then playing the same scene but with authority. For some reason Ms Dickson thought that I confused assertion with aggression, which was not the case. The programme was a success, for I heard of it being used at seminars and 'assertiveness' classes for some years afterwards. I presume I received a 'buy-out' for I don't recall receiving any repeat fees.

A one-man show yes, but one man playing every character in a drama was something else. Eleri Jones, on attachment from BBC Wales (where else) to the BBC Schools Dept in Langham Place, on the recommendation of the writer Derek Farmer, (whom I had worked with on many occasions and who had written a great number of fine roles for me), invited me to take part – no rather, take 'all', in a series called *Radio Club*. It was a great opportunity to show off but difficult talking to oneself without taking a breath, over a quarter of an hour period. Incidentally, it was also an astute BBC ploy to cut down on actor's fees. Shortly after, Mr Farmer and Ms Jones became partners, so at least they got something out of it. Keri Shale did a similar one-performer play for adults on radio – perhaps he heard me when he was at school!

Sam Walters asked me to take part in *An Evening with Chekov* at the Orange Tree, performing the one-man piece *The Harmfulness of Smoking Tobacco*. This gave me a further taste for performing solo items and I proposed putting together a dramatisation of the life and work of Siegfried Sassoon, which he encouraged me to

155

do. Either through laziness or uncertainty, I did not do so. My main concern was having met the man, I knew I bore no resemblance to him either physically or emotionally. This was foolish because the man was to be found in what he wrote rather than in what he looked like. The fact that Peter Barkworth was unlike Sassoon did not stop him doing a successful one-man show about him. At least you could hear him, unlike that quiet poetic hero.

I found all these occasions interesting and amusing but I suppose this levity could not be expected to last. There were dark clouds on the horizon.

# 53

## DARK DAYS

Mark had been growing more withdrawn from the family. He made a trip to visit friends in America and spent some time with his aunt and cousin in San Diego. The rest of us were spending a few days in Lyme Regis and on his return I agreed to pick him up from Axminster Station, he having flown to Exeter airport. I was alarmed at his appearance. He was pale, gaunt and thin. He was very uncommunicative and seemed to have totally lost his appetite. The fact that he was cold, even though the weather was reasonably warm at the time, boded ill. We expressed our concern to him to which he did not respond well.

After a short time back at home, he disappeared and for a fortnight we had no idea where he was. The torment was terrible. With deduction and detection, we managed to find out that he was in St Mary's Hospital, Paddington. We knew that this was one of the leading hospitals in caring for those with HIV. Penny and I entered the Almroth Wright ward for the first time that September, which was to become a second home for the next three years. Within a day or so there was the Great Storm of '87, causing havoc everywhere. The following day, when we went to visit him in his private room, knowing how interested he would be in such an event, we told him that we had hardly been able to get out of the house due to the fallen trees, caused by the previous night's tempest. He simply responded:
'I thought I heard something.'

Life for us all became the here and now – the here being St Mary's in the main, the now – now. We grew to know every corner of that top floor ward and were to witness such love, such joy, such sadness, that it altered our lives for good. From this emotional roller coaster of existence, I really believe it enhanced my being. All the staff, from the Consultant, Anthony Pinching and his Junior, Barry Peters, to the Matron and the Nursing staff, became our close associates and friends. Mark had very soon been diagnosed as HIV Positive and the journey we were all to embark on had begun. It really is difficult to relate briefly and also to do those three years justice, not just because of the emotion of it but because so much took place that it was like going on a world trip and trying to recall afterwards every single stop that was made on that journey.

There was a stigma attached to the letters HIV and the word Aids. Mark asked us not mention his condition to anyone, which placed a huge burden on the family. The five of us carried this secret, having to listen to the misinformation given in the media and cope with the prejudices and bigotery that this brought out of some of one's fellow humans. It was hard to bear. It gave one the experience of what it had been like for those in Leper colonies. From those too terrified to use the same cutlery as a sufferer, to the florist delivering flowers to the ward and refusing to step over the threshold for fear of contamination. Had he done so he would have found some of the finest, most talented, dedicated and caring people it has been my privilege to meet. We listened and could say nothing.

It made me aware of the blood transfusions that I had received at St Thomas', for it was known that infected blood had been used for some patients receiving transfusions. This had a particular effect on those suffering with haemophilia. I enquired of the hospital if all the blood that I received had been screened. Mr Webb Peploe, who had been my overall consultant in St Thomas', was not able to give me total assurance. I asked my GP for an AIDS test, which he persuaded me against. The reason being that once I had taken the test, even if it were negative, I would not be able to get insurance cover ever again. I believe this policy was rescinded some years later but I found it hard to comprehend at the time.

Mark spent not only a great deal of time in St Mary's but also lengthy periods at home. He had the top floor of the house to himself, which allowed him to carry on doing things close to his heart, one of which was writing. As I attempt to do the same, it brings me very close to him, remembering the reams of text he produced at his word processor. He was an outgoing loner somewhat like his father, and I feel that I understand him more now than ever.

As the illness progressed, so his stays at St Mary's became more frequent and protracted. The number of drugs given became greater and greater and in the latter stages, they asked Mark if they could insert a Hickman Line into his chest, to facilitate easy and immediate access for drug infusion. His humour did not leave him, for he asked his Doctor who had become a friend and ally:

'Have you had much experience in performing this procedure?'
'Well, I have done it a few times' said Barry.
'Will I be able to swim with this in?'
Dr Peters carefully considered his reply.
'Yes, I believe that would be possible.'
'Oh good' replied Mark 'because I was never able to swim before.'

After three years, Mark's condition grew progressively worse. He lost the sight in one eye and was being cared for, when he was at home, by the wonderful nurses from the Princess Alice Hospice. He frequently had to be rushed into hospital and more than anything we feared for the state of his mind. Following his last journey, the day before Louise received her Degree, I felt that the number of tubes that were in his body was now getting out of hand. I spoke to Dr Peters a day or so after and asked how much did Mark have to take. Nothing was said but quicker than I anticipated, all the paraphernalia that surrounded him was removed. This is something that has disturbed me ever since and will never leave me, but it was meant with love. He seemed to slip into a semi-conscious state but I was able to speak to him and told him he was safe, that we loved him and that we knew he loved us. To each comment he gave a small sound of understanding and of approval. Two hours later, with Penny and Louise with him, he died. He was just 28 years of age. It was Louise's twenty-second birthday.

None of us get through life without grief coming to our door. The passing of someone affects those left behind in totally different ways. Perhaps the most painful bereavement that can be felt, however, is the loss of a child and for the siblings, a brother or sister. Apart from her own loss as a parent, Penny was able to share the pain Tessa and Louise felt, as twenty years before she had lost her own brother. John was born profoundly deaf, so he was labelled, in the phraseology of the day, as deaf and dumb. His early years were spent in the relative comfort of being brought up and educated by those who understood his disability. However, on leaving that security to enter the world of work, he found those round him to be less caring, even tormenting, which led ultimately to him having a complete breakdown and becoming schizophrenic. The last years of his life were spent mainly in Brookwood Hospital, where the family would visit him in what was a nightmare world. John must have found his life intolerable, for at an age not much older than Mark was when he died, he took his life.

Mark's funeral was at St Andrew's Church, Ham, where he had been christened. The Service was attended not only by the family and his friends, but also members of staff from the Almroth Wright ward. Dr Barry Peters gave the Address, which included a poem that he had written for Mark. His God Father, Jeremy Paul, gave a reading and Martin Jarvis read the Lesson. A colourful friend of mine, John Bull, sang a song that Mark enjoyed from one of his favourite films, *Harold and Maude:*

*If you want to sing out, sing out,*
*If you want to be free be free* (Cat Stevens)

*Mark*

# 54

# 'REP'ETITION

Once more unto the 'Beeb', dear friends, once more.

Why not? A weekly pay cheque again from dear old understanding 'Auntie' seemed a good idea, after all it was over twenty years since they had seen my face on a regular basis and it would give me time to re-group. It could not be at a more appropriate time, for I needed to be on the home scene and since last I held a staff number they had relaxed the regulation that you were barred from doing any outside work. I was told that as long as it did not affect their schedule, anything goes, which meant I could still do the voice-overs. Ideal. A word with Matthew Walters and it was fixed.

I met an actor who was now a member of the RDC\*, whom I had admired ever since seeing him in the first production of *Waiting for Godot* - Peter Woodthorpe. With his drawling northern tones and his colourful demeanour, he was the height of 'camp'. Each morning, at rehearsal, as I greeted the females in the company with my usual warm embrace he would say:
'You can't fool me, lovey!'
We were both in a play by Don Howarth, directed by the warm and tolerant Richard Wortley, called *Events at the Salamander Hotel*. It was a dramatisation of an event in Norfolk in the mid-nineteen thirties, where a group of men went on trial for murder. They were travelling salesmen, selling their various wares from door to door or shop to shop. They all knew each other and would meet on the Monday evening at a well-known hostelry in the town where they would be hawking their wares that week. The main item for discussion was where they would all stay for the next five days. The accepted procedure was for one of them to go to the best hotel in the town and book the largest suite they had,

then report back to his co-mates giving them the room number. During the course of the evening they would make their way individually to the Bridal Suite, knock on the door to gain admittance, and crowd in. In this way, the week's rental per capita was very reasonable. However, it could be somewhat cramped, so they would have to sleep on top of each other. This was called 'stacking'. The performers playing these characters, we were required by the wicked Mr Wortley to lie on top of each other in order to create a feeling of reality – somewhat similar to my experience with Sheila Allen several years before. The difference being this time being was that we had to cope with the wandering hand of Mr Woodthorpe. The drama relates that due to the overcrowding, one of the incumbents is suffocated and his fellow travellers are faced with having to dispose of the body. One of their number, a defrocked priest, is voted in to perform the burial service and they decide that their ex-colleague's corpse should be taken by fisherman's smack out into the North Sea so that his mortal remains could be sent to Davy Jones' locker. Their deception, however, comes to the surface and they are all hanged.[**]

--------0--------

Perhaps it was playing Owen Glendower that gave me a fascination for learning gibberish. When it came to *Love's Labour's Lost,* as Costard, the clown, I was faced with the longest word in Shakespeare and did my best to pronounce this fictitious Latin word from the pen of the Bard. Reading his daily paper in the corner of the studio, was the actor playing the role of Holofernes, who beckoned me to him and said in his glorious and compelling drawn out nasal tones:

'I've played that role and worked on that piece of Shakespearean nonsense. It is: On.. or.. if.. ee.. car.. be.. lee.. chewed.. in.. e.. tar.. ti.. bus.' (honorificabilitudinitatibus).

Who would doubt the word of Paul Scofield?

-------0-------

Bristol never lost its appeal for me. There was a multi-episodic serial on the life and times of Oliver Cromwell called *God's Revolution* written by Don Taylor, produced in the BBC studios in Clifton. It was co-directed by the recently retired Head of Radio Drama, Ronald Mason and the Bristol Head of Drama, Sean Macloughlin. There was a large and in the main, talented cast, with Bernard Hepton playing the man with the wart. I say, in the main, for after the first read-through, Mr Mason asked Mr Taylor for his comments on the actor's interpretations.

'Bernard, excellent; Tony (Jackson), very amusing; David (March), as always, superb; John (me), good; Nigel (Anthony), a long way to go, of course.'

After that, I have always referred to and introduce my talented friend as Nigel 'a long way to go' Anthony.

I felt I should help the dear boy come to terms with this singular put-down and when he offered me the opportunity to share a house with him that had been put at his disposal for his stay I, of course, accepted. We would arrive for rehearsal each day together, which caused comments from the members of the cast, assuming that we were now 'an item'. We never disillusioned them.

David March, a man of cultured tones and sophisticated manner, loathed both the production and everyone in it. He did, however, accept Nigel and myself and was never happier than when we went back to his hotel for a pre-prandial. I noted on one occasion, when he was well into his G & T's, a particular vocal nuance with one of his acid comments.

'David' I enquired 'Where do you come from?'

There was a slight pause before he said sheepishly:

'Birmingham.'

At last he'd 'come out'. Not only had I discovered that we were natives of the same city but that we had been to the same prep school. He was my senior by some years but had the audacity to

164

tell everyone thereafter that he had been my 'fag' at school – with the emphasis on 'fag'.

When not sitting with David as he moaned into his cups, Nigel and I would dine out at various Italian, Chinese or Indian restaurants. There we would discuss our life in art and our life in life. I became so used to our dinners together that I was quite shocked when he told me one evening that he was going out to visit friends in Bath. I sat alone eating a burnt pizza and then walked back to my lonely homestead. After midnight had passed, I recalled Jimmie Grout waiting for me in Norfolk. So I left a message on the bedroom doormat of 'a long way to go', which simply stated:
"Where have you been, I've been worried sick." He never left me after that.

There was tension in the air at the Christchurch Studios. Mr Mason had taken a strong disliking to the author of this lengthy work. The main reason being that the man so skilled at holding the pen never once joined the rest of us in 'The Coronation Tap' to hold a glass of ale – and most certainly did not feel inclined to buy a 'round' for anyone. This was a heinous sin and totally lacking in decorum in the eyes of the man from Northern Ireland.
'To think, at the read-through, that I acclaimed the performance of Ellen Dryden. Why didn't somebody tell me she was married to him.'
One of the skills of actors experienced in radio is their ability to improvise dialogue, in any given 'period'. This was required here particularly in battle and courtroom scenes. They would also suggest judicious 'cuts' in text if it benefited the moment. This occurred in our *Cromwell* and Mr Taylor objected. He said if there were to be 'improvised' lines he would write them and wanted to receive an extra fee. He also stated that there were to be no cuts in his text. This was all said within the confines of the Director and Engineer's soundproofed cubicle. We, on the studio floor, were aware of some tension by the steamed-up window. We were instructed to leave everything as it stood by our Belfast

born director and were informed later by insiders, that Mr Mason had then turned to Mr Taylor and said:

'And when I get this into the editing suite in a week's time, I will cut every f------ word.'

'The Coronation Tap', which was a mere ten yards from the Studio front entrance, meant that Tony Jackson could head for it if he thought there was a break in his recording requirements, in order to quench his understandable thirst. This was not always well judged. When he was shouted for, I would claim, in all honesty, that he was answering the call of nature and that I would go and get him. With that I would hasten to the 'Tap' and tell him that his presence was required, at which he would race to the 'mic' with a cry of:

'For that relief, much thanks.'

Tony was a hedonist par excellence and introduced me to many gastronomic delights and a considerable amount of alcohol. But for him I might never have sampled the delights of caviar, escargots or numerous dishes from the Indian sub-continent. An evening out with Tony required you to take a good pinch of salt with you, whilst he provided the pepper. On one 'Bristol' occasion, wishing to indulge himself, he stayed for a few days at the Avon Gorge Hotel (or 'Avon George', as it was referred to once by the disc-jockey, Tony Blackburn). Tony (Jackson, not the other one) invited me back to his suite for a nightcap after we had savoured the succulence of a Murgi Marsala Tandoori at the Delights of Delhi. As we climbed the stairway to paradise, I felt like a girl being taken back to see his etchings. Maybe I was, for as we stood in the bay window looking at the Clifton Suspension Bridge, lit not only by its own coloured illuminations but also by the shimmering night sky, he mused:

'Perhaps, we should hold hands.' So we did.

*"Oh, Gerry, don't let's ask for the Moon, we have the stars."*

I could happily have worked in that lovely city for months and whether it helped my cause by telling Mr Macloughlin, a devout Roman Catholic convert, that I was willing to take 'Instruction' I am not sure, but I found myself a frequent visitor to the BBC

Bristol, Whiteladies Road or the Christchurch studios. On one such occasion, I was thrilled to be cast as someone's son, for saying 'Dad' was a rare experience for me, the last time being thirty years before in a radio series called *Home to Roost* when I played the tearaway son of loving parents, Mollie Sugden and Deryck Guyler. My 'Dad', on this occasion, was Harry Andrews, who at the time was suffering badly from emphysema due to his having been a heavy smoker. He came armed with various pieces of apparatus, which included a breathing mask with oxygen cylinders and he would have to go regularly into the Green Room to top up. It was sad to see this fine actor that I had seen in so many films fighting the war for us, now fighting for breath. Sitting in my hotel restaurant, taking a light breakfast of egg, bacon, black pudding, mushrooms, tomatoes, sautéed potatoes and a small lamb chop, I happened to glance at the birthday anniversary column in the paper and observed that it was Harry's that day (77). I went with all convenient speed to the studio and announced the fact. Harry, it was thought, would not wish to make an event of it, to which I responded in the testicular. Later that morning, a birthday card signed by everyone involved in the production and a cake bearing a suitable number of candles was presented to him. For such a beefy man, he was quite moved. I was glad that I had insisted, for I wished to make up for a crass statement that I had made in his presence when we had worked together some years before, which he would have forgotten but that I had not.

Harry died four months later.

I took the opportunity of using the BBC Paris studio in Lower Regent Street, under the pretext of 'experimental radio' with the overall authority and support of a well-established radio producer, Glyn Dearman, of putting on and recording in front of an audience *A Night with Rochester Sneath* for charity. Humphry Berkeley, who was a professional fund-raiser at that time for the Sharon Allen Leukaemia Trust, agreed that we would divide the proceeds, a third going to his charity and the other two thirds would go to the Terrence Higgins Trust, which was my charity. Supporting me, as Fawcett Major, was another RDC member, Richard Pearce, who with his shorts, boyish good looks and acting ability, was perfect as the Head's favourite boy. His timing of changing the slides and occasionally bringing me back onto the text was excellent. There was also a backing group to lend colour to the proceedings and to accompany my songs. On piano was Brian Hatt, who I was told played by ear, who was so stooped over the keyboard that I thought he must do it literally; Nigel 'a long way to go' Anthony was on drums, whom I compared to Buddy Rich in that they both used drumsticks; and on rhythm guitar was my musical composer and MD, Nick Ryan. Following the Headmaster's oration, he (I) conducted an auction, the result being that £2000 was raised for the charities. In a virtually full house, I was touched that a group had come straight from the funeral that afternoon of Michael Richmond, founder member of the Orange Tree Theatre, as they wanted a laugh and also felt that my charity was particularly fitting for Michael. I was also delighted to observe that for some time afterwards, brave souls of both genders were seen to be wearing lapel badges that proclaimed:

I'VE SPENT A NIGHT WITH ROCHESTER SNEATH.

[*] Radio Drama Company

[**] I initially believed on reading the script that this was a dramatised documentary of an actual happening - until I saw that they were all hanged!

168

# A Night with Rochester Sneath

Devised and
Presented by
JOHN BADDELEY

Richard Tate

# 55

# EXCHANGE & MART

Martin Jarvis is always loyal and generous to his friends. Perhaps he felt he was in some way indebted to me for helping him out of the mire when he was a mere cub in Croydon. He must have suggested to Patrick Sandford, who ran the Nuffield Theatre in Southampton, that I would be ideal for the part of the sleazy house agent in Michael Frayn's translation of a play by the Russian author Yuri Trifonov, *Exchange*, which was to be premièred at that theatre.

This came at the right time for me, as it not only helped to distract me a little from Mark's deteriorating condition but with rehearsals in London and being able to commute to Southampton, made me still accessible on the domestic front. Patrick, a most perceptive and receptive director, was a joy to work with. His constant words of appreciation 'very guuwd' were always welcome. Yet again, I had complicated words to utter and hopefully not stutter. This time it was place names and locations in dear old downtown Moscow. As the agent, I was always attempting to barter one residence for another, so the names had to trip off the tongue. My coach was the redoubtable Russophile, Michael Frayn himself.

Martin's role was both as the leading protagonist and the narrator. Rosalind Ayres, Martin's wife, played his wife and others in a classy cast included Faith Brook, Zena Walker, Marcia Warren, Colin Douglas, John Hudson and Roger Hammond. Although they were all established, it was the first time I had worked with any of them apart from Marcia. Zena's career had started on a high note as Juliet in Stratford when she was 17 and had remained up there. She had a cottage in the New Forest and whenever I drive through that area and see the speed restrictions to save the lives of the celebrated ponies I think of her, for she was responsible for them being put into place. Marcia and I had worked together in Birmingham and I always admired her dedication to the 'business.' I recalled the hard work she had put in for months in order to do one 'tap' routine in Richard Harris' *Stepping Out*, at The Duke of York's Theatre. It paid off; she won an Olivier award for her part in that play.

*Exchange* was a play about Muscovites and their housing shortages and the length they would go to secure a roof over their heads, and if possible to improve their situations, even at the cost of moving one's mother into a somewhat less desirable residence so that hers would become available. 'Exchanging' could be the solution to accommodation problems even if it were a moral dilemma. The play received excellent notices and encouraged the management to take it to London where it played for a short run at the Vaudeville Theatre. There were a few cast changes in London, with the wonderful mother-earth figure of Doreen Mantle coming in to play Martin's mater. The last time I played this theatre I had my own dressing room. Now, being a somewhat large cast for a commercial production, I found myself in the Chorus room with four others – how are the mighty fallen? Roger Hammond, a man who does like to be surrounded by quality and is always to be seen at all the 'best' parties, decided to improve our surroundings by introducing a large Persian rug to cover the beer-stained, sweat-drenched and cigarette-burned carpet and he also brought in vases holding flora of all seasons for every available corner of the room. There is a tradition of never having real flowers on stage but I did not know this applied to dressing rooms. The false blooms, which Roger grew in our subterranean dungeon under Maiden Lane, were given a touch of reality by him plucking off petals to lie at the base to give the impression that they needed fresh water. These remnants, denoting the passing of time, were never removed - indeed they could be there now.

It was at this time that I became aware of the ageing process. In my anxiety to show the scurrying of the house fixer, I had suggested jumping off the stage on my exits and going out through the audience. This should not have been physically demanding for a man of my athletic prowess but I became aware that each time I did it, I felt sick. When I discussed this symptom with my dressing-room companions, who were either doing the crossword or tending the false flowers, they said unsympathetically:

'Well, don't damn well do it.' So I didn't. Another form of exit was found which was perfect – going down a sewer, like a rat.

I suppose I deserved to be arrested. I should have learned from Mr Jarvis' experience when we were in Southampton. With great generosity he had taken the company out for an 'Italian', even though we were supposed to be Russian. The restaurant was only about 150 yards from the Jarvis' hotel but as he had left the Bentley just outside, he decided to drive the short distance back to it after he settled the hefty bill. Wrong. The long arm of the law was waiting for him with breathaliser in outstretched hand. Result, one year's driving ban, which brought about a 'get you' moment from me. Not being allowed to drive he had been forced into using the services of a chauffeur-driven limousine. On one occasion, as I was recording a broadcast during the day, he offered to give me a lift from the BBC in Portland Place to Southampton. He asked me to contact him on his mobile phone to confirm that I was ready and waiting for the car under the Eric Gill carving of 'Prospero and Ariel'* above the main vestibule of Broadcasting House. I did as requested and was somewhat surprised by a stranger answering. He informed me that he was the driver, so I asked to speak to his Master to which he politely informed me that:

'Mr Jarvis is on the other phone.'

When we were settled into our London home, next to the Adelphi, as a way of showing my appreciation for his generosity of spirit, I would sometimes give *him* a lift back to his Belgravia mansion in my modest Morris Minor, usually following a few post-theatre drinks in an adjacent hostelry. On one occasion, or should I say,

172

on more than one occasion, he invited me chez Jarvis to partake of a few more, the outcome being that I would not leave until 1.30am. On the night in question, I was on my way home when I was flagged down by an earnest member of the constabulary. He had observed that a rear brake light was not functioning. He also detected an aroma of Nuits St. Georges on my breath and requested me to blow into a bag. He accused me of not exhaling from the diaphragm but of using my top register, thereby trying to hamper the cause of justice and he cast me into irons. Leaving the car by the roadside, I was taken to the Richmond Police Station and stripped. All my personal effects were removed, which could have been very painful and yet again I was requested to breathe into an apparatus, which this time appeared to be an Iron Lung. Lights flashed and dials spun. There was a pause during the proceedings in which I was told, quite rightly, that I was irresponsible and a menace to society.

'You should be ashamed of yourself, a gentleman like you.'

The temptation to look over my shoulder to see who had entered the room was resisted. As I sat in my Y-fronts, I pondered on the day. That very morning I had been photographed and interviewed by *The Richmond and Twickenham* Times for a feature in a series entitled 'Celebrities' Favourite Views'. I had chosen Richmond Bridge looking up the river. I now visualised that week's edition carrying an article and photograph bearing the headline 'Local Actor, John Baddeley's Favourite View', side by side with a column headed 'Local Actor, John Baddeley, Arrested for being Drunk and Disorderly.' As I mused over this dilemma, having turned down the services of a doctor under pressure from my Inquisitors, I was ordered to blow yet again into the machine from outer space, for the lights and dials to go into overtime. After studying the ticker tape, which the machine had spewed out, the Peeler informed me:

'Well, I don't know how, but both readings are below the figures for which you would have been charged. You are very lucky. Get dressed.'

With that I was taken back to my abandoned vehicle with a warning never to darken the house of the blue lamp again.

--------0--------

The play which was billed 'for a limited season only', ran for a shorter time than the season we were actually hoping for and the Stage Door in Maiden Lane banged behind me for the last time.

\* Leslie French, the actor, had posed for Eric Gill as the naked figure of Ariel. There were, however, complaints from the public as to the size of the 'airy Spirit's' male member, which the BBC demanded, in its sense of decorum, that Mr Gill should reduce. Thus leading perhaps to the expression: 'being cut down to size'. Mr French was furious.

# 56

## FURTHER EXCHANGES


'Boards' in the evening, 'mics' in the day. Light Entertainment still offered me the opportunity to do silly voices. For a time it was *Week Ending* on Friday, with notables like Sally Grace (a superb E II R and Maggie Thatcher), Bill Wallis, David Tate, Jon Glover and others of high rank. It was a wry look at the week and I particularly enjoyed playing the Trade Union leader, Jimmie Knapp, whose Scottish brogue was so pronounced that no words were required from the script writer, just improvised 'blarb'. Whilst Week Ending took a summer break there was a series going out in the same slot, directed by Lissa Evans, which I was also in called for. It was entitled *Little Blighty on the Down* (which sounds somewhat similar to the TV programme some years later, *Little England).* The inhabitants of Little Blighty all sounded amazingly like those we loved/loathed in high places. We did three series over the years. It was during one of these that Mark died and the sensitivity and understated compassion shown to me by everyone concerned, I will never forget. There was also a TV daily satirical programme for BSkyB called *Up Yer News*, which did the same as the aforementioned but on a daily basis and in vision. Rehearse at 2.0pm, go out live at 9.0pm. It was hard to recall what we had done the next day, let alone years later. I do, however, remember a young kid on the block, Caroline Quentin, being in the cast.

The BBC celebrated the fiftieth anniversary of the founding of the Radio Drama Company (RDC) with a 'bash' at the Theatre Museum in Covent Garden. Although working, I had not felt like socialising at this time but the invitation for this occasion was not to be turned down. It was wonderful, not only to see my old mates but to meet again some of the 'greats' from the more distant past. Having drunk the Museum and the 'Beeb's' entertainment budget dry, many of us crossed the road to see if we could do the same at the Marquess of Anglesey. At around 5.30, I remembered to phone Bryan, my agent, to show that I still cared. He asked if I would care to take over the lead part in a production called *Fool's Mate* by Pavel Kohout, at the New End Theatre, Hampstead. The actor originally cast had pulled out, pleading an inability to learn the lines. At that precise moment, I had an inability to comprehend what anyone was saying, for I was not only seeing but hearing double. I offered to meet the director the next day and lurched back to the bar. The next day, I hazily recalled that I had made a commitment the previous evening and duly found myself at the New End Theatre, being interviewed by Karis Mond. She seemed to be an enthusiastic amateur who was mounting this production out of her own pocket. She talked about her horses at Newmarket and I think must have seen me as a replacement jockey. She was desperate for anyone who could stay in the saddle and I think would really have preferred Lester Piggott for the part but was worried about the diction – him not being trained in speech and drama. The play was a three-hander, in which my character was on for the whole piece. I managed to persuade her to delay the opening and agreed to do it. I felt that it was good for me to force myself to do some work, to take me away from the black hole of post-bereavement depression, rather like a fallen rider remounting his steed to make sure that he did not lose his confidence. The two other members of the cast were Catherine Schell, (known for having featured opposite Peter Sellers in a Pink Panther film) as my wife and Donald Gee, a mysterious intruder. The theatre had at one time been a morgue and the auditorium was where students had watched bodies being dissected. It seemed the ideal setting for my work. The storyline now evades me but I do know there were Nazi/SS overtones. Having to concentrate on studying was difficult and after a short time I began to think that my resigning predecessor had got a point. It was indeed a challenge but one I was glad to have faced.

I was in for an initial shock when I discovered that the Stage Manager was none other than that intense observer of spotlight elements from the Welsh valleys thirty-five years before, Peter Theobald. I suppose it was fair enough that I should be shocked, for after all, the shock that I had inflicted on him all those years ago had nearly blinded him. Having spent the intervening years recuperating on the staff of BBC TV, he was now bespectacled, retired and back where he came in.

I became extremely irritated at the time it was taking the management to alter the posters advertising the show, from the previous intended incumbents name to mine. As I pointed out, they had a head start in that we both shared the same Christian name and also the initial letter of our surname. I asked them if they would have been happier if my name had been Bladdeley.

There was touching support from all my friends, including one particular night, in which I detected the guiding hand of Martin Jarvis, when it seemed that the entire cast of *Exchange* was out front. This was followed by a repast with them all afterwards at The First Emperor of Qin. Whereas that was a pleasure to savour, there was an occasion during the run of the play, which was not so pleasurable. It was indeed a first for me and I trust a last. At a point well into the drama, I became aware that my fellow male colleague and I were at some odds with the text. Having worked with some of the great 'stand-ups', I felt certain that we would eventually get back to base. I was also convinced that the error was not mine but suddenly to my horror, my companion-in-confusion, turned to the audience and said:
'I'm afraid we've lost the plot, Ladies and Gentlemen. Will you excuse us while we check where we are in the script?'
With that he left the stage, to return some moments later with news from the prompt corner. Although we continued from a point where he had decided to pick it up, it totally destroyed the performance. Afterwards I said :
'What was that all about?' to which he responded:
'Well, I could see you didn't know where you were, John, so I thought it best for me to sort it out.'
'What do you mean, 'John'?' said the Prompter, who had been

trying in vain to get the lines across,
'It was you Donald. You cut two pages.'
It just shows, nothing is as uncertain as certainty.

# 57

# WEDDING BELLS AGAIN

Arranging a wedding seems to be very similar to mounting a West End production – only more expensive. Louise, having graduated the year before, accepted the hand of Keir Schiltz. 'Keir' after Hardie, the first Socialist to be elected to Parliament and 'Schiltz' after …. Schiltz. The family may have been ardent left-wingers but lacked the extreme aura of my girlfriend at Drama School, having had the first Communist MP as a grandfather. The ceremony for Louise and Keir was in the same church that her parents had been married in and where her brother's funeral service had recently been held – all rather emotional. For reasons of timing and circumstances the reception was held in the Church Hall, which was decorated the night before the ceremony by the parents of the bride and groom and loyal friends. Tessa, who had graduated the year before her sister, had been studying TEFL* in Bournemouth and as a result, our house sometimes gave the impression of being the United Nations building. One particular young man, who was of Japanese stock but born and brought up in Korea, on being welcomed as he crossed our threshold, bowed deeply with hands clasped before him, as befits the extreme politeness that his race is known for. Observing our hall floral wallpaper he commented:
'Wonderful. It is like a festival!'
We had it redecorated immediately.
He did pose a question that I found myself considering with some degree of interest. On being invited to attend Louise's wedding, he asked how much it would cost to be a guest. It would appear that the custom in his home country was for a charge to be levied and that it would be considered a 'loss of face' not to accept. This was in addition to the wedding gift. I questioned him as to a rough guide on what price the tickets might go for and he said that it could vary, but that a minimum amount would be £50. I

seriously considered contacting all those who had already been invited to inform them that there would now be an entrance fee – with no concessions. When I told Shi (for he was Shi) that I did not expect him to pay, being an honourable guest, I feared he might commit hara-kiri. However, he was able to make a worthy contribution to the occasion, for he assisted with putting up the decorations in the Church Hall in which he appeared to be able to climb up the walls to hang the garlands, without apparently needing the services of a ladder. Inscrutable, those sons of the Rising Sun.

The wedding ceremony went swimmingly under the guiding hand of the Curate, the Rev. Don Markwell (who in fact was older than the Vicar, being a somewhat late entry to the Cloth) and the reception in the church hall went even more swimmingly, in that a large barrel of Young's Best Bitter burst it's bung and flowed freely in the bar and across the dancing area. Fortunately, replacement casks were close at hand and Shi did the mopping up. The food was provided by an actor who had branched out into catering and ultimately branched out even further by leaving his wife and family to settle with the man of his choice – nothing like the real thing.

Fortunately, like St Joan, I still kept doing the 'voices', which I needed to in order to pay for the nuptials. There came a surprise request, unrelated to the 'while stocks last' aspect of my career, from the English National Opera Company to audition for a role in *Die Fledermaus* by Johann Strauss. I was amazed that they had called for me and assumed it to be for the part of the non-singing, Frosch, the drunken Jailor – a comedy role. But no, it was for the small but 'straight' singing character of Dr Blind, an Advocat (it must have gone to his head). I was asked to study the number that he was involved with and present myself in good vocal nick for an audition. I asked my agent how he had come to put me up for it.

'Nothing to do with me,' said Bryan 'they just asked to see you.'
I could only assume that someone at The Coliseum had heard me singing on the radio.
The score was delivered to me and I hastened to my old friend, David King, asking him to work on the piece with me. With his musical expertise (a Cambridge music scholar), we licked it into reasonable shape. I also tested him to see if he had remembered how to bowl a googly orange. As instructed, I presented myself in the foyer of the Coliseum and was asked to take the lift to the Balcony rehearsal room. As I reached its zenith, suffering somewhat from a lack of oxygen, I looked down to observe ants sweeping the stage. Above the Stalls, there is the Dress Circle, the Upper Circle and then the Balcony and as I stood at the back of Row K of the latter, I recalled the words of Paul Smythe thirty-five years before, assuring me that my voice was strong enough to fill the Coliseum – perhaps he meant the Coliseum, Oldham. I could detect where the rehearsal room was, as I heard powerful baritone tones issuing forth. I waited at the door and as the previous prisoner was released, he took one look at me and said:
'Well, if you are up for it, I needn't have wasted my time.'
Who the hell he was I had no idea.
I was greeted by the Repetiteur and presented to a table behind which sat at least a dozen eager beavers. I didn't recognise any of them, so decided to disarm them by simply saying:
'I've brought you all here today ....' and went into some foolhardy stand-up patter. They were charming and simply requested me to sing. It went surprisingly well and when the man in the centre (could he be the Maestro) said:
'Would you please sing bar forty three with a crescendo on the C,' I felt pretty sure he was.
'Where the hell is that?' I pleaded with my friend at the keyboard. He pointed to where x marked the spot and we let fly, only for me to realise that the man with the stick had spotted my one weak point. Give him credit. They thanked me, and my ivory-tinkler escorted me to the door, saying:
'You should be part of this Company, we could do with someone like you.' What that meant, I wasn't quite sure.

On reaching home I received a phone-call from Bryan Drew.
'They liked you and want to coach you for a week and then hear you again.'
The problem was that we were visiting our friends Christine and her husband Finn the Dane, on their home soil the next day for a week. To have cancelled at that stage would have caused upset and also the loss of the non-refundable flights, so I offered the Opera House the day that I returned, which was when I was to be re-auditioned, for an operatic instruction session. I fear it was an error, for the time spent with my friend, the 'coach on the keys', was too short and although I learned a good deal about operatic technique in that brief time, I would have benefited so much more if I had had the days that had been offered. When it came to singing on stage to my Inquisitors in the Stalls (somewhat far back), I felt a degree overwhelmed seeing how far back the Balcony was to which I would have to project the voice. I'm sorry Mr Smythe but you were wrong. I received a most charming letter from the Management (does anybody display that kind of courtesy now), saying that they had decided to go with a singer that could act rather than an actor who could sing – you never know, they might also have been disappointed with the acting!

The Nuffield Theatre, Southampton and its Director, Patrick Sandford, obviously had a penchant for plays of a European origin. Martin Jarvis introduced them to a play that had been introduced to him by his friend, actor and flower-arranger, Roger Hammond. Written by the French playwright, Leopold Le Bien-Aimé and translated by Anne Queensbury, it was called *Leo in Love*. This was a story of love going out of the window due to a letter not being delivered through the letterbox. The postal service of La République-Française could be as unreliable as the GPO. I was offered the part of the employé de la poste, responsible for the debacle, a Monsieur Pince. We were obviously supposed to be very 'Français' but suspect we were rather more 'Anglais', except for the slightly 'off the wall' Angela Pleasance, who had a touch of the Hulots. I wondered how Jacques Tati would have handled the piece.

My main requirement for the role and also main concern was the ability to ride a bike. I had no fear of being on two wheels, indeed, I found it as easy as falling off a log but my problem was the area of the 'set' allowing me to get up steam. Apart from playing at the Nuffield we went on tour to Bath, Swindon, Brighton, Oxford, Richmond and Poole. Each Monday, on arrival, I would nervously examine the launching area back stage to see if I could give the impression to the audience of nonchalantly peddling along the highway. I frequently found myself in the standing position in the stirrups, being launched forward by a nervous stagehand. The countdown was even tenser than at Cape Canaveral and on occasions I sped across the stage with such velocity, that to the amazement not only of the audience but my fellow artistes, I would disappear off the opposite side and would have to return in a sheepish fashion to deliver not only the post but the dialogue. I knew of the appeal of the Tour de France but this was ridiculous.

Our tour de South England was a combination of the joy of playing to full houses in Bath, to the misery of the 'vacuum' in Swindon, from the 'campness' of Brighton to the 'erudition' of Oxford and finally from the 'convenience' of Richmond to the 'harbouring misgivings' in Poole. Speaking of Poole, a group of us visited the Blue Pool, near Wareham. The weather had been overcast with intermittent showers during our visit, so in fact it was more of a Grey Pool. In my anxiety to study more closely the marine life that inhabited this feature of nature, I lost my footing and slid twenty feet down its greasy grassy bank and into the muddy waters. My companions found this hilarious but I commanded them to cut the levity and return me to my hotel post-haste, as I had now taken on the appearance of a Dorset Apple Cake. Removing only my caked trousers, I stepped fully clothed into a hot bath, washing not only myself but laundering my underwear at the same time. Finding a nearby Dry Cleaners, I enquired if they cleaned trousers to which, with a look of some

incredulity, they assured me they did. To their mortification, however, I then drew out from a paper bag what appeared to be a large clod of earth with the daunting request:
'Well, clean these!'

Those that witnessed my dowsing had been Christopher Godwin, Debra Beaumont and Ms Pleasance. Martin had stayed at the Hotel pondering over what eight voice-overs he would do the next day and Sarah Badel, who was unavailable for outings that afternoon, was most upset not to have witnessed the event, so I promised to take her with me, à deux, for a sea voyage the following day. Afterwards, she assured me that she had thoroughly enjoyed the five-minute cruise that I had taken her on from Mudeford Harbour to Hengitsbury Head. I suspect she felt that it was quite long enough to be alone in a boat with me. Her father had been that powerful actor Alan, and I always noted the emphasis on their surname being Ba*del* and indeed, I considered calling myself Ba*ddeley* .

Speaking of the supernatural, if we were, our leading man told me that when we were playing the Theatre Royal, Brighton, as he sat at his dressing table putting on his eye shadow, he felt not only a cold sensation in the room but a firm tap on his shoulder. Looking immediately behind him he found nobody there. On questioning his dresser he was told, without any surprise, that it was probably the spirit of the Grey Lady, better known as Mrs Nyechart, the first woman manager of the Theatre Royal. I also gather from the present manager, John Baldock, that if not her, then it could have been that of a Nun, who had been murdered in an alleyway over which the dressing rooms had later been built, or one of two children to have suffered a similar fate. My opinion is that it was the former making sure the 'Leading Man' was not 'off'.

On a similar matter of things spiritual, actor Kenneth Dight told me that when he was a student at the Bristol Old Vic Theatre

School and was helping with the 'get-in' for a new production at the Theatre Royal, at about 2.30am, he found himself, alone, sweeping the stage. It was then that he noticed a woman walking round the back of the Balcony but that she appeared to be slightly higher than would be normal, so he felt she must be exceedingly tall. He mentioned this to Bert/Alf/George, whoever the Stage Door keeper was, who said:

'Oh, that's Sarah, I've seen her plenty of times.'

He was, of course, referring to the great Sarah Siddons who, apart from her successes at Drury Lane, was a star in both Bristol and Bath. The reason that she appeared elevated it would seem, was that the original Balcony was slightly higher than in its present redesigned position.

Sleep well.

* TEFL = Teaching English as a Foreign Language.

# 58

## JUST ONE MORE TIME

I had heard there were rumblings at BH and that the REP might soon be RIP. I asked to finish off my last stint, which had been interrupted due to the domestic trauma that we had been going through and was welcomed back. Ms Wilmshurst, the supremo of the Rep, said there was no point in interviewing me as part of the usual welcome pack, as she felt I knew the routine as well as she did. So there I was back on my first day with *As You Like It*, which was just as I liked it. It was directed by the popular, Gordon House, who at that time was the Head of Drama for the World Service, and later became Head of BBC Radio Drama. I was never quite sure if he really took to me, which was not surprising as I was never quite sure who he was. One year I had been in Edinburgh for the Festival and saw, standing outside the Assembly Rooms, a BBC Radio Producer I had enjoyed working with in Glasgow in the Sixties. I remembered that as well as directing plays he was also a poet. I introduced my wife to him with enthusiasm:

'Penny, this is Stewart Conn.'

'Gordon House' replied the disconsolate man.

'Just checking, Gordon,' which did not go down that well – it never does.

Shortly after I had started back on the regular payroll, there was a BBC party celebrating something (not my return). I heard that day the sad news that the 'Beeb', in its financial, and my old soccer-playing opponent Michael Checkland's wisdom, was closing down the 'state of the art' radio studio in Christchurch, Bristol. There, with a glass of the BBC Club's Chardonnay in his hand, was the Head of BBC Bristol's Drama Dept. I swept straight up to Sean Macloughlin, pumped his hand, kissed his cheek (in an RC kind of way) and told him how appalled I was at the closure. He seemed slightly nonplussed but agreed with my sentiment. I talked of the wonderful work done there and hoped that there was a future for him to look forward to. At this point a new actor member to the Company joined us and as always, ever willing to be helpful, I enquired:

'Do you know each other?'

'No' they replied.

With my hand on the shoulder of the brave, studio-less director, I said to the young greenhorn:

'This Julian, is the *wonderful* Sean Macloughlin.'

'Gordon House' said the man with a quivering lip.

I can see now why he may not have taken to me.

It went from bad to worse, for I then espied an actress I greatly admired and introduced her to the young man.

'And *this* is Marjorie Westbury'.

'Mary Wimbush' she responded in a manner bordering on apoplexy.

'Just checking the MW's' I desperately pleaded. There is a strong probability that Ms Westbury was at that time dead. I feared if I went on like this I could be too.


A few months before my return to the BBC Radio Drama Company Matthew Walters had asked me to read a long 'short story' on Radio 4 by an author unknown to me, Stacy Aumonier. He had died in 1927 at an early age, following ongoing TB, presumably contracted during the First World War. The story had been passed on to Matthew for him to produce by the Head of Short Stories, Duncan Minshull, (the BBC had Heads for everything – there might even have been a Head of Long Stories for all I knew), called *The Landlord of The Love-A-Duck*. In his short literary life, Aumonier was considered, if not in the Guy de Maupassant league, well up there with the best. John Galsworthy was convinced that he was the master short story writer of his time. Matthew, a master at editing a short story to bring it to the right length for the broadcasting 'slot', could not reduce this particular one to a fifteen-minute reading, so it was agreed that it would be a story in two episodes, the second part going out the night after the first. The tale was of a competition, set up by the landlord of *The Love-A-Duck* public house, in which bets were placed on two young children who were able to recite mammoth lengths of poetry, to see who could remember the most. The youngest, a nephew of the landlord, Mr Seldon Wright (obviously called Seldom Right by the regulars of the pub) was five, the other boy more than twice his age. Needless to say, the former was able to recite twice as much as his opponent. It left both children mentally and physically distressed. To understand the nuances of the story it has to be read, or failing that you should make a request to the BBC for it to be repeated.

I became interested in finding more of Aumonier's short stories as I thought there might be an opportunity to re-establish the author and more to the point provide me with some future employment. Not having access to the World Wide Web at that time, I trailed round bookshops enquiring after the author. None had heard of him. I felt that my last hope was to go to the celebrated bookshop at the foot of Richmond Hill, Balder Books, owned by the wonderfully eccentric Eric Barton. On stepping into the dimly lit, Dickensian atmosphere of the shop, I saw, just visible at the far end, stooped over a high desk, Bob Cratchit-like with quill in hand, the bookseller himself. I asked if he had heard of Aumonier to which he responded:
'Of course.'
Somewhat taken aback, I enquired as to whether he had anything by him. Shaking the cobwebs from his right arm, he indicated a distant corner of the shop saying:
'If you get the ladder and go to the far end of that top right-hand shelf, you will find that the fourth book along is entitled *Modern English Short Stories* last impression 1934, in which there is one story by Aumonier called *Where was Wych Street*?- £1.'
Perilously ascending the decaying ladder, I espied in the gloom the book referred to and blowing off the dust, I opened it to find the story mentioned. Although there was only one, it was a start. As I descended and made way to remunerate Mr Memory Man, I observed the vague outline of an elderly female figure.

'I saw one of his plays on television the other week,' she said. Suddenly, not having found anyone who had heard of him, I now had two within the space of five minutes. I could see my hopes of cashing-in on my research were fast disappearing, for she had seen an adaptation on the dreaded gogglebox.

'Really?' I said, in a disappointed fashion.

'Yes' she said and continued 'I thought it was rather cruel making that poor child remember all that poetry.'

'Was it good?' I ventured to ask.

'Oh yes, the setting in particular was wonderful but I just thought it a little harsh making such a young one recite all those poems.'

'I'm so glad you enjoyed it' I said, making no further comment. Perhaps it was the best critique I ever had – she had 'seen' my radio reading.

Eventually, through various book searchers, I obtained three collections of his short stories and Matthew adapted about a dozen of them for me to read on the radio. Of course, you will always find that there is someone who will say that they have been a 'fan' for years, of whoever it was that you could find nobody had heard of. One such was the writer Martin Worth, who presented Mr Walters with dramatisations of some of the stories, as half hour plays. These were duly recorded and I, because of my by now close association, was the Narrator. After one of the recordings, the adaptor introduced me to his son, Mark Wigglesworth, an up-and-coming conductor. Obviously, our writer had decided to cut out the 'wiggles'.

A rider to this interlude was that Matthew, my director and editor, received a request from a Mr Andrew Aumonier of East Twickenham, saying that he was a descendant of the mystery author and as the broadcasts had brought him considerable kudos in the workplace and he wondered if it were possible to have some recordings of the stories that we had done. It so happened that Matthew lived within half a mile of the man who, it also so happened, dwelt only five houses from what had been my first marital home. Contact was made and Matthew suggested he might like to meet the reader of his forebear's work (what a thrill). So it was that we found ourselves being offered drinks, as we gave him tapes of the stories. His gratitude knew no bounds and glass after glass was consumed. He requested his wife to put on dinner for the four of us, to which she acquiesced in a courteous, if slightly disgruntled manner. The radio twins finally departed Cresswell Road at 1.30am, with your writer half carrying his employer home – that man needed more rehearsal.

If I were asked which of the Aumonier stories that I read was closest to my own emotions, it would be *The Match,* which ranks alongside the famous chapter in A. G. Macdonnell's *England, Their England* for describing a village cricket match. The latter's writing was based on his experience of playing for the celebrated Invalids Cricket Club (so well captured in Jeremy Paul's *Sing Willow).* The similarity between the two stories is striking and as Aumonier died six years before *England, Their England* was first published, I wonder if Macdonnell might have been influenced by that lovely short story in which the narrator recalls a match that he had played in some time before, when he revisits the ground where it had taken place. Now it was un-mown, without the lines of a crease to be seen and the Pavilion had been turned into a workshop. The story concludes:

"Decades have passed, and I have to press the spring of my memory to bring these things back; but when they come they are very dear to me.

I know that in the wind that blows above Gallipoli you will find the whispers of the great faith that Bunty died for. Eric Ganton, young Booth, and Jimmy Guilsworth, where are they? In vain the soil of Flanders strives to clog the free spirit of my friends.

"Good noight, sir. Good luck to 'ee!"

Again I see the old man's face as I gaze across the field where the long grass grows, and I see the red ball tossed hither and thither, with its story still unfinished, and I hear the sound of Jimmy's voice:

"Oh, well hit, sir!" as he encourages an opponent.

The times have changed since then, but you cannot destroy these things. Manners have changed, customs have changed, even the faces of men have changed; and yet this calendar on my knee is trying to tell me that this all happened *two years ago to-day*! And overhead the garrulous rooks seem strangely flustered."

In an attempt to further my education, I decided to go to Night School. The Central School of Speech and Drama were doing evening courses in Advanced Human Communication and I felt it might do me the world of good. I suspect that I did not take it as seriously as I should, which would not have surprised my schooldays teachers. I was the only one of the dozen students that came from the world of thespian pursuits. I did not do my homework – I was too busy delivering radio communication during the day. When an essay was required I tended to hand in something that I had already done which was in print. I adopted a similar ploy of using material previously used when we were asked to deliver a lecture on a subject that we had 'researched'. For my personal amusement, and to see how far I could go with the ludicrous, I chose 'cross-dressing'. I explained that my wife and I, one weekend in four, would exchange robes and roles so that we were constantly aware of the others problems and feelings. To prove the point I showed photographs of myself in 'drag' that I had used in *'A Night with Rochester Sneath'*. I am uncertain what they made of me in a Matron's outfit but they believed my fantasy and found the idea of the monthly charade riveting. Perhaps I'd hit on something and that it should be compulsory for all married couples!

There was one woman I could not abide who gave us relaxation and voice exercises. One evening during her class I felt, apart from my usual irritation, extreme chest pains. It was so noticeable that she asked if I should take some fresh air, the suggestion of which I accepted gratefully. However, the pains did not diminish, which resulted in my being rushed to the Royal Free Hospital, where they were of the opinion that I had had a minor heart attack. I was placed in the 'at risk' ward, where everyone seemed to be wired for sound. I was horrified to see men of all ages having to carry life support equipment with them wherever they went. There followed two or three days of x-rays, sonic booms, hill climbing on ramps and finally an optic fibre camera being sent from my groin, up an artery, into my heart (cardiac catheterisation). I was able to watch this procedure on a monitor, but my request for them to turn over to another channel was considered puerile. It was found that I had not had a cardiac arrest and that my arteries were as clean as a whistle. All good news but when the consultant asked me what I thought might have caused the problem and I honestly stated:

'Over-acting,' he left me without a smile.

The fact is that during the day of my evening collapse, I had been recording a play called *'The Battle of San Remo'* by Royce Ryton, for the wonderful Enyd Williams, in which I played the father of the Kaiser. This was a play based on historical fact and at that moment in history my 'character' was suffering from cancer of the larynx. In fact he had lost the use of his voice, making it complicated to portray on radio. I therefore created a stressed voice from the top of my chest register, which was painful to hear and to do. I believe that this ultimately set up a form of cramp, which I was to continue to feel occasionally for years after. Fortunately for the production, I had recorded all my scenes, bar one, on that first day. As I was in hospital for the rest of the week a way had to be found to convey my dialogue for the remaining scene. This was done brilliantly, in that another actor grunted where I should have spoken and my wife, played by Anna Massey (whom I had last worked with when she played Ophelia in Birmingham), would declare:

'I know what you're trying to say, darling ...' and then translate the strangulated noises for the sake of the other characters and the audience. I'm only sorry that I wasn't there to witness it.

I gained very little from the Course except for an illuminated address that I was presented with. Sadly, I cannot credit the author as I never knew who it was but I committed it to memory.

*I know that you believe you understand*
*What you think I said*
*But*
*I'm not sure you realise*
*That what you heard*
*Is not what*
*I meant*

--------0--------

It was at this time that I discovered the true meaning of being in a supporting role. I had known Harold Innocent for a few years and always found him a delight. We were in a play directed by that passionate Welshman, Martin Jenkins, called *To Strangle a Parrot*. At the read-through I was fascinated by Harold's unusual approach to his part and thought that it was either a piece of sheer brilliance that I could not appreciate or that he was 'barking'. In his first scene with me, when we came to the recording, I realised that Harold did not know what he was doing. He looked concerned and I suggested a way he might say a line. He expressed gratitude and asked me to do the same for each of his lines, which he would then record parrot-fashion – I feared I might take the title of the play literally. It was difficult for me to concentrate on my own part but our Director encouraged me to carry on. Eventually, it was agreed that the whole procedure was taking too long and it was decided that the production would be 'postponed' until a later date. Harold died a fortnight later from a brain tumour.

I cannot let there be only a sad reference to Harold. He was a great friend of an actor with blue blood in his veins, James Villiers (pronounced 'Villers'). When they were on tour together, James would make for the theatre to see that they both had 'good' dressing rooms, whilst Harold went to sort out the 'digs'. Having selected a room for Mr Villiers and a room for himself, he would then report to his friend that all was satisfactory. On one such occasion in Leeds, he mentioned to the landlady that his friend was very deaf but that he tried to hide the fact, so he requested her to speak loudly and clearly to him.

'I quite understand the situation, Mr Innocent.'

He also passed on to James the news that the Landlady was very deaf and that he would have to project somewhat.

'Quite understood, old boy.'

For the next week the residents of Shakespeare Street found the decibel volume unbearably high.

Harold, not so innocent.

It was unusual for the Light Entertainment Dept. to present a non-comedy programme, so the serial adaptation of Susan Hill's novel *Gentleman and Ladies* was somewhat of a one-off. The director was Lissa Evans, whom I had worked with *on Little Blighty on the Down* and she cast me to play the male lead (there being only one man in it). A gentle story of a group of woman of mature years, brought together out of their solitude. It opens with a funeral of one of their number and they observe a stranger on the periphery, holding a bunch of snowdrops. This gentleman affects the balance of the close-knit ensemble and it brings out emotions and tensions that they had kept, up to then, hidden beneath the surface. Ultimately, he marries one of their coterie. I was blessed with having a distinguished cast of female actors to play 'my ladies'. On the wall beside me as I write, there is a Radio Times photograph of myself surrounded, James Bond fashion, by my lovely women; Sian Phillips, Jill Graham, Gwen Watford, Stephanie Cole, Pauline Letts, Patricia Hayes and Anna Cropper, who ultimately became my 'wife'. I look like the cat that got the cream ... and I do mean 'the cream'. Sadly, a dozen years later, of that octet, only Sian, Stephanie and I are still here. We all received a delightful letter from the Head of Light Entertainment, Jonathan James Moore, expressing his appreciation for such a prestigious cast being in a production going out under their banner.

Susan Hill said of *Gentleman and Ladies* that it was her favourite novel, as far as her own work was concerned.

In the opening paragraph of the story there is the line:

"Hubert Gaily liked churchyards, they gave him a sense of well-being." This reminded me of Harold in that delightful film, *Harold and Maude*, which was one of Mark's favourites. Eighty year-old Maude's philosophical advice to teenage Harold is worth consideration:

"Go team, go! Give it an 'L', give it an 'I', give it a 'V', give it an 'E'...LIVE, otherwise, what have you got to talk about in the locker-room?"

--------0--------

It was at this time that I celebrated my forty years of broadcasting – I'm not sure whether others did! When asked by the Head of Religious broadcasting to take part in a Christmas Day Service, broadcast 'live' at 9.0am, it seemed as good a way as any, for a one-time possible man-of-the-cloth, to say thanks. *Crisis at Christmas* is a charity that provides accommodation and sustenance during the Christmas week, for those who live and sleep in cardboard boxes under the arches or in the doorways of the Capital throughout the year. The service was broadcast live from a warehouse in Stepney, which housed them for the week in that particular year. The Bishop of Southwark, Roy Williamson (well known for his TV broadcasts with children), led the service. Our 'church' was a vast hanger-like building, full of tins of baked beans, tomatoes, corned beef, sides of bacon, thousands of boxes of eggs and vast quantities of 'Mother's Pride' (white sliced). A veritable cornucopia of gastronomic delight for the City's homeless.

The service was held in freezing conditions with those officiating all wearing overcoats – you could just glimpse the Bishop's purple stock. With the congregation, some sitting, others wandering around, it became a true place of worship. I read two lessons and with one slightly disturbed worshipper wandering up and studying my features only an arm's length away, found it somewhat challenging knowing that our listening audience might be visualising the tranquillity of a church setting with the congregation all seated in respectful silence. The fact that he looked as if he might 'put one on me' if he disapproved of my delivery, gave an added spiritual dimension to the occasion. After the warehouse service, I made my way to St Andrew's Church, Ham, for their Christmas Morn celebration. By the time I arrived, the service was well under way but I had arranged for a space to be kept for me at the end of a pew in the centre aisle. Sitting next to Penny and the family and directly behind Princess Alexandra and her husband, Angus Ogilvy, I found the whole ambience disturbing. Having just worshipped with some of life's most disadvantaged members, and then so soon after to find myself sitting in this comfortable, middle class, well bred, well fed and well protected atmosphere, seemed more than surreal. I know which felt the most real to me.

Happy Christmas.

# 59

## AL FRESCO

Performing a play in the open is only occasional and in a radio drama, hardly ever. I am not sure if it was done due to lack of studio availability, but it was certainly a most atmospheric location for *The Night of the Hunter* directed by Andy Jordan in BBC Bristol radio production. This adaptation of the 1955 Cinema Noir classic, originally featuring Robert Mitchum as the sadistic psychopathic preacher, was recorded in an off-the-beaten-track, ruined old farmhouse. Outside there was a stream, which was used for the pursuit of the children by the villain. The evil one was played by the compelling Struan Rodger, and I had the pleasure of playing the children's father, with the opportunity of giving my 'deep south' tones.

The power of the production was so strong that it terrified people even before it was broadcast. On arriving for my 'call' one morning, I came across a young couple exploring the area. On hearing cries and shouts in the distance, they asked me what was happening 'up there.' I warned them that there were strange 'goings-on' and when the sound of gunshots echoed round the valley, they departed quicker than an MP caught with his trousers down. For the record, the production won a Sony Award.

The great risk with anything 'shot' or recorded outside, is the weather. It can prove a director's nightmare particularly if working to a tight budget. Matthew Walters took that risk with a play set on a golf course called *Straight Down the Middle* by actor/writer Robert East. There is no doubt that however well an outdoor acoustic is achieved in the studio, it is not as realistic as reality. Using the BBC's sports ground at Motspur Park, gave exactly the acoustic required for a golf course. The story followed three couples, two male and one female. The female couple comprised Liz Crowther and Cherith Mellor (the author's wife); the males were a boxer, played by the young and virile Mark Straker, with myself as his manager/trainer; and the author himself playing with Dinsdale Landen. It was not a complex storyline, simply a comedy of bad manners, where the trio became involved with each other. Dinsdale and I were both members of the Stage Golfing Society, although the opportunity to play at that time was somewhat limited for both of us. We were asked to bring along our golf clubs to achieve the right effect of balls being struck. During a break in recording, with someone idly throwing a golf ball in the air, it happened to fall into Dinsdale's golf bag and vanish. Removing the clubs he upturned the bag to obtain the ball and with arm stretched inside, his expression changed.

'Good God' he profaned, 'I can't believe it.'

He pulled out a dank, mildewed wallet containing £20, a few address cards and a diamond ring.

'I put that there twelve years ago when we were going on holiday, thinking that the bag was as safe as a safe. When I got back, I had forgotten my canny ploy and thought it must have been stolen and claimed off the insurance.'

I heard him relate this story several times over the next few years and on each occasion the value of the contents grew:

'There was £2000 in notes and a diamond ring worth ten grand.'

Sometime later I went to see him give his Sir Toby in *Twelfth Night* in a Peter Hall production at the Playhouse Theatre. I sent a card round to Mr Landen stating:

"I am attending the performance tonight and would like to see you afterwards.

I. N. Clink, Norwich Union, Fraud Dept."

He was nowhere to be seen in the bar afterwards, even though his Agent was there and Sir Andrew Aquecheek (my old mate, Martin Jarvis) was left to do 'the honours' for Dinsdale.

Mark Straker's character of a young East End boxing talent, who was forced to carry his Manager's clubs as a way of keeping him fit, was constantly pleading:

"Let's 'ave a whack, Boss."

The Manager eventually grants his request, the result being somewhat impressive. Mark hit the ball, giving the audible effect of it being struck off the tee and I (as myself) watched its flight. The text required there to be a slight pause before the manager says:

"Very good son, you just need to straighten your grip a little." There was indeed a pause, somewhat longer than would be natural for a radio drama, for I was watching the ball sail at least a hundred and fifty yards, making directly for a greenhouse in an adjacent garden, just outside the boundary fence of Motspur Park. I had the vision of there being a direct hit and the whole glass structure collapsing in a million pieces. I am sure Mr Walters was white at the prospect of an additional budget having to be called for. In fact, the ball struck the base plate of the hothouse, for it to ricochet back onto the playing area.

"Very good son, you just need to straighten your grip a little."

It's good to play to a full Castle.

"There is no such thing as a small part, only small actors." I felt, therefore, that playing the part of the Pedant *in 'The Taming of the Shrew'* at the Ludlow Festival within the Castle grounds, could be a pleasant and not humiliating diversion. Rehearsing in London under the direction of Val May, was relaxing for me if not for all. Petruchio was played by Michael Simkins and Katherina by Prunella Gee (could she have been related to the helpful Donald). I had been offered the use of a very smart house in Ludlow, which was either the second, third or fourth residence of actor Gary Watson. The pubs were perfect, in particular The Blue Boar which was frequented on a twenty-four hour basis by Simkins, Vincent Brimble (Tranio) et moi. Apart from David Gooderson (Baptista), who always had to return to his 'digs' straight after the show to phone his wife, the rest of the cast were new to me and it was a pleasure to lead them astray. The Inner Bailey made an ideal auditorium and the dressing-rooms back-

keep were like the tents at Harfleur. The preview night, which was our final dress-rehearsal, was presented to the local shopkeepers who had advertised our coming in their windows, and who had warned the citizens to lock up their daughters as the time approached for the actors to arrive. It poured with rain for the entire performance and for the drenched actors, hardly able to keep their feet on the slippery, sloping boards, it was misery. The audience remained undaunted and sat under umbrellas with raindrops seeping under their collars. If this were a foretaste of how the 'run' was going to be, then Hades would be a welcome haven. Fortunately, all was changed the next day by glorious sunshine welcoming the First Night audience, as they sat in the Outer Bailey prior to the performance attired in their dinner jackets and décolleté dresses, armed with hampers of caviar, smoked salmon and numerous jeroboams of 'bubbly', determined to make this a Shropshire 'Glyndebourne'. For the rest of the 'run' there was never a cloud in sight – it was perfect.

It cannot be said that my performance was perfect but then was it ever the case, and there were one or two 'wrist-slapping' moments. After the Pedant's first entrance, being alone he decides to urinate behind an up-stage pillar, only to be almost caught in the act by Tranio, so he has to adjust his dress, hiding his embarrassment behind his bowler-hat, whilst delivering the dialogue. Mr Brimble was used to my response to his line:
"First tell me, have you been to Pisa?" to which the Pedant indicated that he had just had one behind the pillar, but he found it impossible to cope when before replacing his headgear the little man gave a couple of flicks of his 'bowler' to shake off any droplet left on the brim. It is true that when this action was first performed, the loyal Vincent Brimble had not been informed that it would occur and was therefore somewhat unprepared. The audience found the moment hilarious, the trouble was so did the actors – pure amateur theatricals. Regrettably, that was not the only piece of extemporised 'business' to be inserted from the would-be Charles Chaplin, causing his fellow artistes to find themselves illogically amused and having to face upstage, but of

that, "enough, no more ........"

I had three or four away-day trips to keep the heart racing. A quick visit to see the town of my birth. I did not see the place of my birth (I feared that they might not have got the blue plaque up in time), but I did see the Bank where my father was nearly Manager.

I was invited to lunch by a resident of Ludlow whom I had last seen when we worked together in Morecambe. Carol Snape always had a forthright nature but I was somewhat surprised when on my arrival she took me immediately to the verandah at the back of the house and threw herself in a brazen fashion on her back. I pointed out that this was hardly the moment as we could be seen from Ludlow's theatrical castle across the meadows, and it was possible that the Company Manager might be watching through binoculars. It was then she pointed out that the deckchair she had just sat in had collapsed under her – a likely story.

One non-matinée day, I took Tranio to Edgbaston in Birmingham to watch Warwickshire play. Be warned, those who might consider a similar outing, that the journey from the metropolis of the Midlands to the cultural centre of Shropshire is further than you think. We nearly missed the show, which would not have been cricket – but it was.

I was blessed in that our leading man was of the Buddhist faith and although 'his' Sussex had been beaten by 'my' Warwickshire with the last ball of the Final of the previous year's Nat West Trophy, he bore me only a little ill will. My Accountant wished to see me most urgently regarding some claims I was making to the Inland Revenue. It so happened that he had recently moved from one of the Chalfonts to North Wales. There was no escaping it, I would have to drive up there to see him. As I departed, Mr Simkins, sensing my concern, said that he would 'chant' for me, and so, to the sound of a tinkling bell and indistinct incantations, I set off. It worked. Mr Gair was satisfied with my explanations and it was with a light heart that I made my way back to Ludlow, scattering sheep in all directions, whilst considering the power of prayer (Buddhist style).

Although asked to return for the following year's festival, I declined, not wishing to take away the pleasurable memory or the excitement that I had found in visiting the county of my birth for the first time since the actual event.


## 60

## BADDELEY'S THE NAME


'Of course, we are related to the Cake, you know.'

Although my Grandfather may have worked on the pâtisserie counter for a time, I was unable to understand how I could be related to a Battenberg or a Pavlova. Robert Baddeley (1733 – 1794), as a young man, had for a time been gentleman's gentleman and pastry cook to the actor/theatre manager Samuel Foote. Being able to observe closely the workings of his master's profession, he felt that he could do it, as many do and usually can't. On asking if he could have a part in a forthcoming production, his celebrated employer ordered him back into the kitchen. On the strength of that rebuttal, Baddeley left the service of Mr Foote and gained employment of a similar kind with a Gentleman going on the Grand Tour. This allowed him to study several European languages and accents and on his return he went to see Garrick, a close rival of Foote's, and persuaded him to take him into the company at Drury Lane. For the rest of his life he worked as an actor, mainly at the 'Lane' and gained a reputation for playing character parts, with a particular talent for "foreigners and Jews".

He had fallen for a 'stunner' in the shape of Sophia Snow, whose father was Valentine Snow, sergeant-trumpeter to George II. Baddeley introduced her to Garrick and she too joined the Company and became a ravishing success. Although married to 'Sniffer' (Baddeley's nickname), she was wont to 'put herself about' somewhat and had quite a reputation with the young 'bucks' in Town and also with members of the Company.

*"There was a young actress called Sophia,*
*Who was had by a distinguished young Peer,*
*There was Sheridan, Bannister, Kelly and King,*
*Spranger Barry and Macklin, the licentious old thing,*
*There was Garrick himself, which was quite a boon*
*And also the Band of the Royal Scots Dragoon."*

Apart from appearing at the 'Lane' she would go post-show, post haste, post-chaise, to Ranalagh Gardens to sing and to seduce those she considered 'celebs'. Baddeley challenged Garrick's brother, George, to a dual over their relationship and George went to his brother to ask what he should do, to which his famous brother stated that as he'd got himself into it he would have to get himself out of it. Baddeley chose pistols and the two met at dawn in Hyde Park. Baddeley fired the first shot and missed (perhaps he had lined-up on the man standing next to him – a family weakness) which left him at George's mercy, but La Baddeley (as she was called) stepped out from behind a tree and pleaded with GG to desist, to which he concurred. This incident was reported in the leading daily newspaper the following morning. No life was lost but the Baddeleys' marriage was, and Sophia was to die at the age of 38 of consumption, a pauper.

'Sniffer's' career, however, went from strength to strength and he became David's shadow. If the Boss wanted something doing, Baddeley would offer his services before he knew what was required. With Garrick's inspiration he helped in the formation of the first actor's charity, The Drury Lane Theatrical Fund, instigated to help those that had worked at the 'Lane' and who had fallen on hard times. When Garrick purchased his house at

Hampton, Baddeley bought one in Molesey – not to be too far from him. When Garrick died, Baddeley helped found the Garrick School of Acting (in a way, the first drama school). He obviously adored his boss and everything to do with the theatre. Those working at Drury Lane were allowed, under Royal patronage, to wear a special uniform to indicate that they were a "King's Comedian". Most of the actors found that walking down The Strand wearing this outlandish garb was somewhat OTT but Mr Baddeley wore it to his dying day. He was the last to do so, apart from the flunkeys that still do, at the foot of the Theatre Royal foyer staircase, on First Nights.

I obtained from an American source a breakdown of Robert's performances night by night and realise how many of the same parts we have both played – obviously in the genes (which he would never have worn), and also how many ways our surname could be misspelt – and still is! The part that he was most wellknown for was Moses in Sheridan's *The School for Scandal*. He not only created the role but hardly missed a performance of it for the rest of his life. *The Times* of Friday, November 21 1794 states:
"Yesterday morning died, at his house in Store Street, Bedford-square, Mr. Baddeley, comedian, of Drury-lane Theatre. He was seized with a fit, on the stage, on Wednesday evening, in performing the character of <u>Moses,</u> in the School for Scandal, and was taken home and expired between twelve and one o'clock in the morning."
He had obviously made a bob or two, for in his will he left "£100 in 3% Consolidated Bank annuities to produce £3 to be applied and expended in the purchase of a twelfth cake* and wine or punch… for the Ladies and Gentlemen performers of Drury Lane Theatre … will do me the favour (of celebrating) on twelfth-night in every year in the Green Room." In what must be one of the oldest of theatrical traditions, it has been held every 6th January for over 200 years and I've been fortunate to be at a few. This privilege for me was brought about through research I was doing at the 'Lane' with their celebrated manager and later the theatre's

archivist, George Hoar and Jennie Walton, who for many years was all things 'Baddeley Cake'.

He also left his house in Molesey to be used for "the care of indigent actors" – I suppose the first 'Home' for elderly thespians. At the turn of the millennium the house was still there – sadly, no actors.

He was buried at the Actors' Church, St Paul's, Covent Garden, "attended by most of the principal Performers in both theatres" *(The Times* Sat. November 29th). He obviously had a reputation for imbibing as it is marked by there being a 'Baddeley Bar' in The Opera Tavern, opposite the Theatre Royal, to this day. I approve and envy.

The story of Robert Baddeley and Sophia and their life at Drury Lane is so colourful, perhaps I might try and ……

---

* The Twelfth Cake, marking the end of the Christmas festivities, was celebrated and consumed by everyone until late into the nineteenth century, whence it was moved forward into December and thus became the Christmas Cake.

# 61

## ENCORE

The new Orange Tree Theatre, which is directly opposite the pub, opened its doors for the first time in 1991. It took Sam Walters several years before he plucked up the courage to ask me to perform there. He decided to repeat the success he had had in that small upper room eighteen years before, with *The Memorandum* by Václav Havel. He asked me to recreate the role of Mark Lear, the lecturer and the fact that I had aged by a similar number of years was not a disadvantage – indeed, if he were to repeat it again after a further similar interlude, my performance might by then be fully matured. As part of the package another play, *Portrait of a Woman* by Michel Vinaver, was included. Sam had a passion for Mr Vinaver's work, which was beyond my simple mind's comprehension, as one speech did not appear to follow another. I knew of non-sequiturs but this to me was nonsensical. The story was centred round a young French female student who was tried for the murder of her lover. It was a one-act drama lasting an hour and a half, set in a courtroom – I was the Presiding Judge. Mr Vinaver was enthralled with the case, having found details of it in an old newspaper in his loft. He felt he had made a discovery and was somewhat irritated when I said:

'Oh, you mean the Pauline Dubuisson case in 1953.'

One of my interests has been criminology, particularly if it involved a decent murder. I felt that there was good dramatic material in the actual case that was missed in the play. It appears the author's response to that was that the British Press exaggerated everything – to which there was no answer. The best aspect of the play from my point of view was that I sat omnipotent throughout the piece and as it lasted only an hour and a half with no interval, we all got to the bar in record time. There was an occasion when I was totally lost as to where we were in the text. One word of improvisation caused every member of the courtroom to turn a whiter shade of pale and there was the strong possibility of the play stumbling on into the early hours. I looked directly at the accused and stated:

'I don't know what you are talking about' (never was a truer word spoken). The confident actress playing the role, Lucy Tregear, without hesitation, repetition or deviation, stuck her neck out, as Mlle Dubuisson very nearly had to do, and continued seamlessly. She had saved the day, whilst I had been tempted to adjourn the case to a later hearing.

I felt much relief when we followed that play with our old favourite. Václav Havel, the bold, outspoken Czech playwright, who spent most of his time in prison when we last performed *The Memorandum* was now its country's President – so I suppose it was all rather respectable. This production benefited from the larger acting area of the new theatre, in which the audience surrounded you. My role of the preposterous preaching pedant was appreciated, if anything, even more than the first time and I enjoyed reading the notices – several times.

The opportunity was there again to say words even longer than Shakespeare's Latin tongue twister. Teaching the synthetic language of Ptydepe was challenging and rewarding in having to learn words of such complexity. Whereas Mr Vinaver's play was comprised of speeches seemingly thrown in at random, Ptydepe appeared to be made up of words created by throwing a handful of consonants in the air, and on impact reading what lay on the floor – not dissimilar to the author's native tongue. When I saw Jamie Callum, the young Jazz performer, being interviewed about the legendary Ella Fitzgerald, the Interviewer said:

'I suppose singing 'scat' is great if you forget your words.' The courteous young man said little but did imply that although his inquisitor had a point, he knew little of what he was talking about. When it was said to me that I could talk gobble-de-gook and it would not matter, having spent hours learning the astonishing 'lingo', I felt as Mr Cullum did. It was a pleasure to say for example, the Ptydepe word for 'hurrah':

'franygkojefrdabuxaltepdysavarubgoztexeres' thus beating Shakespeare by 13 letters.* The audience listened to these scenes with a mixture of hilarity and fear. As with the previous production there was the dread thought that because of their close proximity to the actors they might be asked questions as well as the characters in the play. It was all too much for a woman on the front row one night. With tears running down her face laughing hysterically with amusement, she pleaded:
'Stop, oh please stop' – at least I think she was amused.

There was also another woman who appeared to be giggling but she was on-stage and masked, as were all Mr Lear's students, conveying a blank expression to show their lack of comprehension. It was a young actress playing in her first professional theatre production after Drama School, in the role of the Secretary at the Translation Centre. I told Victoria Hamilton at the first-night party that I was interested in her future career and that if I could be of help in any way, to contact me. She then introduced me to her father, who had employed me in a Commercial – so that sorted that out. Peter Hall also spotted her talent but surprisingly overlooked me.

It seemed worthwhile trying to resurrect dear old Rochester Sneath. I suggested to BBC Light Entertainment that there might possibly be a series to be had out of it. They agreed and decided to do a pilot. Whereas it had been my idea to do several ten minute solo items as R. Sneath addressing the nation, regarding his educational philosophy and the success of his school, they wanted a comedy series, which seemed to me rather like a rehash of Jimmy Edwards' *Whacko*. On the day of the pilot recording, opening my paper on the way to the studio, I was horrified to read of the death of Humphry Berkeley. He had been looking forward to this venture and his passing certainly put a dampener on the proceedings. The programme did not get over the next hurdle, so it was not only the death of Humphry but also of Rochester

Sneath for me.

I was approaching my sixtieth birthday and fortieth anniversary as a thespian. A garden party was arranged, mainly for my co-mates from the 'Beeb'. Tessa, who had seemingly given great support to the League of Nations, had brought into the family circle at around this time a young monosyllabic Italian called Rudi. She had spent a period in Livorno teaching English to eager 'Eyeties', one of whom was a cake-shop-owning Pasticciere. It seemed he wanted to have his cake and make it in London – I feared he might have heard of the Baddeley Cake. He stayed with us briefly, with Tessa translating his every Tuscany word. I greeted him each day with the conventional 'Good morning' to which he responded with:

'Good ….' the rest being a step too far. On the day of my double celebration, he produced a cake the size of a dining table, having been instructed to do so by my daughter. I felt somewhat guilty, however, when she 'ditched' him the following day. Women can be like that. He went on to become Head Pasticciere at the Hyde Park Hotel and, it appears, speaking reasonable inglese. His cake was a great success.

'I'm going to see if I can join the Twickenham Amateur Operatic Society' said Tessa, going out of the front door. She wanted to get involved with a musical drama group and had heard good reports of them. She was accepted and it was to lead to dramatic changes in her life. It was obviously a sociable Society, for a few weeks later she brought home a young man for the evening.

'This is John from TAOS.'

Having met several former male friends of hers from various parts of the world, I assumed that he might come from a country lying adjacent to Laos and Cambodia. So, speaking slowly and clearly, I said:

'Do … come … in' gesturing for him to step across the threshold. He made no reference to our recently decorated hall and so I indicated with elaborate mime for him to go into the sitting-room. 'Please..... do ..... go ...... through.'

Pointing to the sofa:

'Do .... sit.... down,' bending my knees to a crouched position, in a Marcel Marceau fashion.

The man looked at me as if I were demented. The fact that he bore no Oriental features and had been born and brought up in Hanworth, had not been explained to me. He may have been disconcerted at his first encounter with me but the family was delighted to meet this charming and talented Englishman.

This confused meeting ultimately led to Tessa and John moving-in together and after a period of three years they decided to set the wedding bells ringing at St Andrew's Church, Ham. We had 'been here' before but the reception this time was mid-Thames in Surbiton on Ravens Ait. I liked the process of groups being ferried from the shore to the island, which allowed time for the Reception Party to meet everyone in comfort. Also, as the Bookings Dept., had erroneously almost caused the date to be cancelled and then hastily reinstated it, provided us, as a token of apology, the arrival drinks gratis – perfect.

The celebrations lasted hours, firstly with the Wedding Breakfast (why is it called that when it's at lunchtime?), followed by further guests arriving in the evening for the now compulsory 'Disco', which proved slightly tiring for those over ninety.

As the Bride and Groom sailed away down the Thames at the end of these festivities, reclining in a silken-lined open barge, with the moon reflecting on the water, to their honeymoon destination, they seemed like Anthony and Cleopatra going up the Nile.

---

* In 2008 Penny and I were invited to a gala performance of Havel's *Leaving* at The Orange Tree Theatre, in the presence of the author. I was pleased to mention to him that in *The Memorandum* he had given me the longest word that I had ever had to learn, which he then quoted. It didn't sound anything like the way I pronounced it - but then he's Czech!

# 62

# COMIC CUTS

Having 'dubbled' with *Urmel* in Cologne and the Skeksis in *The Dark Crystal,* I knew there was money to be made from doing things peculiar – some were of the opinion that my career was about little else. I had been used to recording stories for children, using odd voices in such masterpieces as *The Fantastic Mr Fox, Jungle Book, The Snowman, Winnie-the-Pooh, The Famous Five* and of course, *My Family and My Zoo.* There was also a TV series called *Tugs* in which I played a leading tug, but I really felt that I was turning into a cartoon when interviewed by Tony Collingwood, who was an up-and-coming creative artist in that genre. I was asked to 'come up' with possible voices for a series they were making of *Dennis the Menace.* I generally showed off, which seemed to impress them and after a time they gave me a thirteen part series called *Oscar's Orchestra*, which didn't sound like *Dennis the Menace* to me. It was a stunning concept of introducing kids to great orchestral works, with the adventures of the instruments from an orchestra being pursued by an evil tyrant wishing to do away with music.

One of the voices I had offered at my original interview had been Field Marshal Bernard Montgomery. This had been liked so much that the character of the Violin that I 'voiced' was named Monty. In the first series Dudley More was the voice of Oscar the Piano but as he was not in good health at the time, all his lines were recorded separately or 'wild' being the technical expression. So, although I worked with Dudley, I never met him. As we recorded the script before the cartoonists got to work, it allowed a great deal of freedom and creativity from the 'voices'. With a most talented bunch at work, it was a happy and hilarious time. Soon after we'd completed the first series of *Oscar, Dennis*, took off, in which I gave my bemused and confused 'Dad' " dowwww...."

and also a character not in the comics, The Colonel. He was so successful, that he was introduced into that celebrated journal and became a regular feature in *The Beano* – now that is fame. Of course, all of us taking part gave the voices to the many other characters that appeared, not just our main roles. Ten years later Dennis could still be heard going out on some kid's TV channel virtually every Saturday morning – pity is, we were 'bought out', so no repeat fees .... "dowwwwww".

I look back with great delight on all those who took part in the two different series, which, apart from the regulars comprising: David Holt (who took over from Dudley), Colin McFarlane, Elly Fairman, Michael Kilgarriff, Murray Melvin, David de Keyser, Eric Meyers, Steven Lander, Sean Barrett, Eve Karpf, Richard Pearce (Dennis) Kerry Shale (Gnasher), Jill Lidstone, Gary Martin and Judy Bennett, there were also guest appearances from lauded ones of our profession like (in order of appearance): Ruby Wax, Robert Lindsay, Josie Lawrence, Sally Grace, Richard E. Grant, Rik Mayall, Edward Fox, Denis Quilley, Hugh Laurie, Billy Connolly, Leslie Phillips, Tim Brooke Taylor, Willie Rushton, Derek Nimmo, Greg Proops, Mollie Sugden, Ken Dodd, Prunella Scales, Patrick Fyffe & George Logan (Hinge and Bracket), Bernard Cribbins, Simon Callow and Brian Blessed – now come on, that is some line-up and name-dropping par excellence. You will obviously be keen to know who did the art work – that was the Su Zhou Hung Ying Animated Cartoon Co. The only problem they seemed to have was drawing 'round' eyes but then I knew of that from my own Chinese experience.

The creative fun in the studio and the drinks session afterwards in the Bricklayers Arms, next to Saunders and Gordon was pure undiluted pleasure – which was how we liked it.

--------0--------

I'd always been fascinated by illusion and ventriloquism. Doing funny voices for a living was all part of it. Having been given a box of conjuring tricks dating back to the early part of the century by my estranged grandfather, performing magic was second nature to me!

WAIT..... it occurs to me that I did not explain, as promised, the vanishing pony dollops in *Cinderella* at Wednesbury all those years ago – forgive me. When the crystal coach, drawn by the four magnificent white Shetland ponies came on, my knockabout companion, Buttons and I carried on a carpet heaped with dung, masked from the audience's view by Cinder's glittering conveyance to the Ball and we placed it to the rear of the animals. When the coach departed and the monstrous sight came into view, the Fairy Godmother was called for assistance by Baron Hardup's idiot servants. Attached to the carpet was a sisal string so that with the wave of her magic wand and the powerful utterance 'Vanish', worthy stage hands in the wings, bribed only by a pint of Guinness, yanked on the string so that the offending pile disappeared instantly. The audience was amazed. Magic.

Wandering down Church Street in Notting Hill Gate, I glanced in a window and saw a young man staring at me. I had experienced this situation often before but his stare was so unblinking and unrelenting that I entered the dimly lit shop and enquired as to who he was. The owner of this somewhat macabre establishment, with bodies hanging from the ceiling and decapitated heads on shelves, brought him to me. With one glance he observed:

'You have bonded. He's yours for £200.'

And so Terry (Woodcock) entered my life.

Trafficking in human kind, up to this point, had been anathema to me, but my attitude changed with Terry, for I felt he would be useful around the house and would also be an amusing companion at dinner functions. The fact that his first words to me were:

'Gottle o' geer,' meant that we had a future together.

To help support him in the manner that I felt he would wish to grow accustomed, I had to take all the opportunities I could for financial remuneration. The BBC World Service at Bush House in the Aldwych, must have heard of my work as a Tug, for I was offered a role in a series called *Lifeboat*. This dealt with the life and loves of those intrepid men who go down to the sea in boats, to rescue others from the briny deep. Following on from this I was offered a contract with English Radio, previously known as English by Radio, also at Bush House. This had virtually nothing to do with acting, so I was ideal. To a vast listening audience of something like 150,000,000, the World Service would teach English to people in virtually every country around the Globe. My role was to speak the English whilst sitting opposite the teacher from whatever country he or she was a native of. Of course, most of the time we 'translators' had no idea what our companion the other side of the 'mic' was saying and would wait to say our piece when given a hand gesture from the lecturer. After a short time however, one seemed to develop a sixth sense of what was being said, so that the hand gesture became redundant. I found this short period of eighteen months fascinating, informative and more to the point it taught me of the relationship we should all have with each other. I learnt more about political, religious and social differences and to respect them, than anything prior to. The value of the BBC World Service worldwide was immeasurable and yet one heard that it might be cut. It was not only a job that gave me huge pleasure and insight but more importantly, allowed me to use the restaurant at Bush House, which provided fare for so many people of different ethnic backgrounds, making it the best canteen at the 'Beeb'.

# 63

## FANCY A FOURSOME?

You might like the idea but try arranging it. Although I had hung onto the skirts of *The Stage Golfing Society* for many years, I had involved myself very little in the cut and thrust of the fairways. I had done as my mentor, Billy Tasker, had bid me and joined that band of thespian high and low handicappers, but whilst I loyally paid my annual subscription, I was hardly ever on the golf course. Perhaps it was the 'Cake' that drew me back and furthermore some exercise would not go amiss. As my forebear had gained theatrical notoriety with a cake, perhaps I could use the same ploy with golf. With the 200th anniversary in 1996 of *the* Baddeley Cake ceremony having recently been held at Drury Lane, I bribed the Committee of the SGS with a silver cake, for an annual competition, which would be played for but not consumed. They accepted and in many ways this led to my returning to their golfing fold and becoming heavily involved with all aspects of that Society of adorable ne'er-do-wells. I was invited onto the Committee, for they suspected perhaps that I might have more silver to throw their way. One of the oldest Golfing Societies in existence, it shortly afterwards reached its Centenary and as a man who knew a great deal about antiquity, I was invited to be it's Captain in that prestigious year. Perhaps, along with the Colonel in *The Beano,* it was the greatest accolade to come my way.

The President of the Society in 'my' year was Garfield Morgan, but the most important man for me at that time was the Secretary, John Hine. Dragged out of the alcoholic world of advertising, he was to care for those strolling golfers with tact, courtesy and understanding for seventeen years. He certainly cared for and supported me and being a Master Mariner, guided me through any troubled waters that occurred during my time at the helm or was it before the mast? Dealing with sensitive artistes, particularly about their golf, requires supreme diplomacy and I only regret I did not have the experience that that year gave me earlier, as I could have entered No.10 without any problem. My main joy was socialising with such an entertaining group, (like the actor and the Society's 'Golfer of the Century', Terence Longdon, or Terence Frisby and Richard Harris the playwrights, Tom Courtenay, an all round fine actor and dresser, Tony Verner, an all round fine farceur and director, Roy Holder, an all round imbiber who saw himself as a second Olivier and of course, the redoubtable and indestructible Eric Sykes. There were those that I had known for years outside the world of 'niblicks' either on the boards or before the 'mic' such as: Trevor Bannister, James Bolam, Gordon Clyde, John Hollis, Stephen Greif, Jeremy Kemp, Mark Kingston, Dinsdale Landen, Robin Parkinson, Benjamin Whitrow, Robert Young. Then there were the new(ish) kids on the block to me, like Ian Ashpitel, Philip Glenister, Scott Gorham, John Hannah, Sion Tudor Owen, John Peters, Robert Pugh, Dougray Scott, Paul Thornley, also their seniors who were also new to me, such as Boyd Catling (Hon.Treasurer), Ronnie Laughlin, David Belcher, Ian Pearson and Barry Palin. There were also those slightly removed from treading 'the Green' but qualified for membership as artistes nonetheless, such as David Coleman (Conductor) and Stan McMurtry (Cartoonist), and Danny Thorpe, actor/theatre manager but most importantly wine and food connoisseur and generous distributor of both. They all made a veritable cornucopia of talent and seemed like a family – happily including a few black sheep.

One of the most interesting aspects of being a Captain of such a group is taking teams to various Clubs for matches, some of which would return to play on our own Richmond sward. The delights of Sandy Lodge; of weekends spent in an alcoholic haze and being thrashed at the beautiful John O'Gaunt Club with it's two playing courses and even more courses at dinner; of excursions to Frinton, seemingly stepping back into the thirties, playing their splendid North Sea lashed course, followed by barbecues and booze. Limpsfield Chart, (under the guiding hand of Bob Dexter), giving a lunch of poussin and fine wine after playing the first nine holes, enabling them to wipe out whatever lead we had built up in the morning and soundly thrash us over the second nine. Coming into our orbit around the time that I was Captain was the heather-covered West Hill Golf Club in Surrey, which through the initiative of one of their Committee, Maurice Hazzard (later to be their Chairman), links were made again between us after a seventy-year gap. This was to lead to our becoming affiliated to that superb Club with its daunting and beautiful course – a bit of rough is one thing but try getting out of heather – bless her. The first time I went into the bar at West Hill, I thought I was seeing double and that was before a glass had touched my lips. I was introduced to this unusual image, whose face I knew and whose bowling action I knew even better – it was of course the Bedser twins, Alec and Eric. Penny and I were invited to a dinner given in their honour and it was fascinating to see at their table so many of my cricketing heroes and also to sit opposite Lord Weatherill, former Speaker of the House and President of West Hill. It was sad when both he and Eric passed away within a short time of each other but I was delighted that the Club made Sir Alec their President in Lord Weatherill's place.

My sporting achievements have been few and that most certainly includes golf. However, I did have one moment of glory when winning the prestigious Gold Cup in 2000. How I did it I will never know but my name is on the board, so that is that. I felt it was a nod towards Billy Tasker who had persuaded me to take up the game and who had himself won the same trophy just over half a century before.

It is perhaps the most social of all sports and what I like is that etiquette, honesty, sportsmanship and good manners are paramount to playing the game, also coping not only with winning but losing with good humour. If you find that difficult, take up something else.

"If you can meet with triumph and….." all that.

# Stage Golfing Society

# Centenary Day Celebration

## The Richmond Golf Club
## 4th December 2003

Eric Sykes
Guest Speaker

Garfield Morgan
President

Boyd Catling
Hon. Treasurer

John Hine
Secretary

John Baddeley
Captain

YEARS

mac

# 64

## NOTTS & BOWLS

Calls to return to my home patch seemed to have ceased but Nottingham came briefly onto my circuit as the town of the best looking girls in England (so they claim) beckoned. Paul Spencer, with whom I had worked on 'steam-radio' was now Head of Drama for ATV in Nottingham and invited me up for several TV comedies. The most memorable for me was in a series featuring Paul Merton. This was a re-hash of several of Tony Hancock's pieces, my episode being *The Lift*. Without doubt Paul was one of the wittiest and sharpest of performers and although I felt that I could respond quickly to a given situation or comment – compared to Merton, I was stuck in a siding at Clapham Junction. I did feel that re-doing something as well known as any of the sketches performed by that former resident of The Railway Sidings, East Cheam, was a risky gamble to take. I am sure I was right. Nevertheless it turned out to be a nice little earner but not in a manner that might be expected. There was a television programme presented by Denis Norden of 'out-takes' called shown *It will be All right on the Night*. This was an ongoing series showing 'bloopers' made during the recording of programmes, which of course were cut out before transmission. One of those shown frequently was out of *The Lift*. Whilst always grateful for 'repeat' fees, I was not necessarily sure about exposing one's incompetence. I never watched it.

There was something I did watch, however, with alarm. A group of us fellow performers went out one evening for an 'Indian' – there being quite a few in Nottingham. As a 'starter' I ordered a green salad, and although I enjoy escargots I was not drawn to slugs, particularly having to watch it crawling over my lettuce. I had given up consuming live creatures since my Hong Kong days, so using the knowledge I had assimilated in the assertiveness training programmes I called the turbaned waiter across. I suggested that this was unacceptable, even by Nottingham standards and that the local food officer might feel that this particular chef's offering would be enough to have the 'Taj Mahal' closed down. He pleaded with me:

'Goodness gracious, very sorry. Please to accept another fresh green salad.'

I informed him that I never wished to see a fresh green salad ever again and asked to be brought my main course of lamb Jalfrezi with Peshwari naan, immediately. I then suggested that to overcome the discomfort that we had all felt, he should provide, on the house, our alcoholic drinks for the rest of the evening, with an assurance that all living and deceased slugs, caterpillars and beetles would be removed from their future menus. He concurred in all respects.

--------0--------

'Bowls.'

Being of a sporting bent I was up for anything. A. J. Quinn asked me to play an old 'buffer', Wilf Dixon, who played Sir Francis Drake's game in an episode of *Noah's Ark* for Carlton TV, starring Anton Rodgers and Angela Thorne. The plot now evades me but I know it was 'shot' on location in Hadley Heath, near Droitwich, in Worcestershire. The 'local' had it's own bowling green, so that both exteriors and interiors were in most convivial surroundings. However, the title of the episode proved to be an omen, for we filmed a considerable amount of *Stormy Weather* in the pouring rain. As we were all wearing our immaculate white suits and straw boaters, ostensibly perspiring from the warmth of the summer sun, it proved challenging. My closest compatriot, as we played 'ball on the jack', was Edward Kelsey, whom I had worked with on many occasions, dating back to the Jurassic period. His character was called Walter and seeing that he played Walter Gabriel in *The Archers* it made me wonder at the depths considered when casting. As I had never played anyone called Wilf (except perhaps Lawson), I wondered how I'd got the part.

We spent most days in the caravan that we shared listening to the rain attacking the roof *almost* making it impossible for us to dwell in our anecdotage. Of course, we had food brought to us from the unit canteen and became annoyed when being interrupted, as they occasionally attempted to 'shoot' a scene. One of our cast members, playing the local vicar, was Duncan Preston whom I knew from the Stage Golfing mob. Although, he too might not have approved of having to attempt recording a scene in the rain, it didn't stop him, once we had been given the 'rap', going to the Droitwich Golf & Country Club to play in it over eighteen holes. An aspect that he did approve of was my character's appearance. I wanted to make sure that I was wearing suitable neck attire and attempted to wear my MCC egg and tomato tie, which I felt was right for 'Wilf' but our director, the mighty Quinn, said it was too distracting. I presented another tie to him, which he innocently found acceptable – it was the white, yellow and green of the Stage Golfing Society. I felt in good company, for one of the Society's most established and respected members, playing the role of a school master in a film some years before, wore that same tie throughout. Duncan was delighted with my tribute to Sir John Mills and the SGS.

Somehow, we completed our game of bowls, which had taken so long to play that even Sir Francis himself would have been concerned. I was fascinated that the weeping heavens and the spray following the bowls journey across the green to the jack was not apparent on transmission. Could Wimbledon learn a lesson?

# END

# 65

# CHURCHILL

Was this to be my finest hour?

George Roubicek asked me if I could do a 'Churchill' voice for one line in a film I was working on for him. I had done it in *Saved* for the Birmingham Rep, so I could do it again. This was to lead me into doing him again and again. I was assured from a reliable source that the family of the great man were pleased with what I did.

Bryan Drew arranged a voice test for me with TransWorld International for four, one-hour-long programmes, called *Churchill*. I was the last one to be heard that day and having read several extracts of his writings, I finished with a letter that he had written to Clemmie, expressing his love for her. Following my offerings I went into the Control Room, to find not a dry eye in the cubicle. I got the job. It was a privilege and a pleasure to be entrusted with his words. I also had the chance to do my 'Monty' and appreciated the old man's remark about him: "Indomitable in retreat; invincible in advance; insufferable in victory."
As well as *Churchill*, there was: *In the Footsteps of Churchill, D-Day in Colour, 10 Days to D-Day, Japan at War, War Lords* and *Allies at War.*

His voice would always come to my aid with an audience well into their cups at 'after-dinners', making sure that they were on my side.

--------0--------

As more and more of my friends and producers at the Beeb and elsewhere faded away, so I felt that I was slowly doing so myself.

Actors, unlike real people, rarely retire but they have their four stages:

'Who's John Baddeley?'

'Get me John Baddeley.'

'Get me a young John Baddeley.'

'Whatever happened to John Baddeley?'

Before she stepped out of the main spotlight at Broadcasting House, I was employed by dear Enyd Williams, on many occasions. All the productions with her were joyous and when the BBC Club became less attractive to the creative and the eccentric, she would see that we went to the St George's Hotel, just across the road from the main portico of BH in Portland Place, for our libations. Sitting in the top floor bar looking out over the rooftops of London, the cast would sit listening to more anecdotes than speeches in the play from those 'seniors' taking part. Ms Williams said she thought that she had made a serious error of judgement by casting in one episode of *Poirot,* not only John Moffatt, (playing the Belgian detective) but Donald Sinden and myself for she feared there would be no time left over after the 'stories' for recording the play. A similar situation occurred in a *Miss Marple,* with the quite wonderful, both in temperament and talent, June Whitfield in the title role, and also featuring Richard Todd. He would relate to us a history of theatre and film, always wearing his 'paratroopers' tie. On all these occasions I played the well-meaning but somewhat dim-witted detective from the House of the Blue Lamp. The plays were adapted for radio by Michael Bakewell, whom I had known from my early days of broadcasting and more recently when directing me on film dubbing for World Wide Films.

For me it has been the 'personalities' that I have worked with that stick in my mind rather than the dramas themselves. They were there in abundance with Enyd, as in an 'Agatha', suitably entitled *Appointment with Death*, when the feisty Miriam Karlin arrived one morning to announce with pride that she had just been made a life member of the Euthanasia Society, which I found such an extraordinary contradiction in terms that I had to apologise for my overt mirth.

Another of Enyd's little masterpieces was a play by Nan Woodhouse, *Now or Never* set in a home for the elderly, made up entirely of women, with one man – which, of course, was me. Having been in *Gentleman and Ladies* I felt I must be cornering the market in playing the extremely mature James Bond to the older woman. My girl friends this time were, Thelma Barlow, Ann Beach, Kathleen Helme and Katherine Parr. Sadly, the hoped-for series never materialised – perhaps it was felt that I might not have the stamina.

I was anxious to do a broadcast after 13<sup>th</sup> May 2004, which was the 50th anniversary of my first broadcast and I feared it might not happen. However, a call came from Tim Dee at the BBC in Bristol to be in a play to be recorded in a day. We spent eight sunny hours on location at Blaise Castle, on a play whose title sums up what it was about, *Making of the English Landscape*. During breaks in the recording, urgent mobile phone calls were being made to find out how England were faring against the Australians – it was all so very English.

I had been booked into the Avon Gorge Hotel by the 'Beeb' but was disappointed to find that I had been given a room with no view and although it was 6pm, it had not been made up. I complained 'assertively' and they apologised, saying that they would move me to another room immediately. I was to find myself back in the Bridal Suite where I had held hands with Tony Jackson fifteen years before – fate works in odd ways.

I had mentioned to the cast that this broadcast celebrated my 50th year before the 'mic' and following my emotional reunion with 'our' room, I went with them to have dinner at an Italian restaurant in Clifton. These were actors that I had not met before – indeed, most of them had not been born when I played Rocky Harris in *Sulky Annie*. They raised their glasses to me and to the fortitude of the BBC. I was very touched.

# 66

## AMATEUR WAYS

Working for nothing does not go down well with any professional. Charity, however, is another matter. Matthew Walters who had retired from the BBC aged about 20, went on to work for *Listening Books,* who recorded books on tape for those with disabilities. He asked me to read the autobiography of the celebrated cricket umpire 'Dickie' Bird. Although a lover of the great game, I did find this work somewhat long and drawn-out. Indeed, it took me so long to record it that my producer also appeared to look somewhat long and drawn-out. An interesting experiment that he tried was to gather a group of established actors used to the requirements of 'steam radio' and to record a couple of plays 'cold' without any rehearsal whatsoever. These were: *Journey's End* by R. C. Sheriff and J. B. Priestley's *An Inspector Calls.* Both were so successful that there was a fear that if this became generally known, rehearsals might become totally redundant. It reminded me that in the '60s the BBC had brought in a high-powered Time and Motion team from America to look at their efficiency. One question they posed was what the time between the initial read-through and the recording was used for. They obviously had a point, for Matthew not only cut out the rehearsals but the read-through as well – and to think the 'Beeb' gave that boy early retirement.

--------0--------

'Why don't you pass on some of your hard earned knowledge to the local amateurs, rather than sitting there watching constant re-runs of Warwickshire's victory over Sussex in the 1993 Nat West Final?' suggested my long-suffering wife, wanting space.

Since my Drama School days, I had never been interested in, or even seen, an amateur production, apart from the girls at their school and Tessa in productions for the Twickenham Operatic Society (which had reaped a fine husband). The idea of being involved with one seemed like asking a doctor to join a First Aid class.

'The Teddington Theatre Club is looking for somebody to help with voice work.'

I pointed out that I was no Cicely Berry or Patsy Rodenburg[*] and that I was not qualified as a voice coach.

'After 50 years making your living from it – you're qualified,' Penny exclaimed.

I presented myself to John Buckingham, an academic, who was directing a production of Arthur Miller's *The Crucible*. He welcomed me warmly and I didn't even need a recall. I knew I would have to approach this with a different mind-set from my usual professional experience and I also felt that there might well be resentment from some of the actors. The learning curve was, in many ways, greater for me than for them. As with all amateur companies it was made up of enthusiastic lovers of the drama, who worked all day earning a living and spent the evening indulging their pastime. One or two were 'ex-pro's' who had had to seek other areas of employment – not being able to get away with it as I had. It was certainly different. Some had talent and some were devoid of it. Rather like a golf 'pro' who knows what kind of golfer you are before you've hit a shot, simply by the way you take a club out of the bag, I knew the moment they came through the door, those that had 'done it' in the past. What was important was that they all enjoyed it, and as one enthusiastic member unfortunately put it:

'We do it for love, you do it for money.'

He was not able to comprehend that professionals have so much love for it that they put their very existence on the line. Try doing it ...... no, don't.

The main problem was the understandable lack of rehearsal time, for apart from their work, their domestic needs took preference, such as school concerts, holidays, wedding anniversaries, dinner parties and shopping at Waitrose. Their lives were so busy that learning the lines took some time to come to fruition. What the Theatre Club certainly did have was the Hampton Hill Playhouse, an excellent facility cared for by loyal members who protected their kingdom and corner of it tenaciously.

The cast was made up of schoolteachers, bank cashiers, BBC staff, accountants and personnel managers, as well as a bevy of young beauties (mainly students) playing the witches of Salem. We warmed to each other and they loyally listened to my modest words of advice and more importantly to my anecdotes! I saw myself more as an encourager than an instructor. It so happened that a few days before the first night Arthur Miller died, so it was a fortuitous tribute to him and was perhaps the first of his works to be performed anywhere, following his death. I thought that everyone gained a great deal from the production – I know I did.

Obviously undaunted by the experience, the same director asked me to repeat my previous efforts on another production. This either meant he felt that I might get it right the second time – or that I had become a mascot. Thomas Middleton's *The Revenger's Tragedy* was certainly a challenge to take on and I thought, better him than me. The complex plot was difficult to follow and it was not made easy by some actors having to 'double' parts with no discernible difference in their characterisation. A woman audience member buttonholed me in an Interval saying:
'Could you tell me – who is it that's dead?'
It was, however, an admirable effort, regrettably seen by very few – the members preferring to see an 'Ayckbourn' I suspect. Nick Young (an 'ex-pro'), gave a most committed performance as Vindici and I determined that if I should direct a play there, I would see that he was in it.

The opportunity presented itself when I was asked if I would like to do a production in The Studio Theatre. I felt I should play to my strength and do a comedy. Patrick (Sherpa) Blackwell was over on his annual trip from Oz and remembered a one act play that he had seen, featuring Frank Finlay, as part of a double-bill that he'd been involved with many moons before. It was a Theatre of the Absurd play, *Alas, Poor Fred* by James Saunders.[**] I eventually tracked down a copy and loved it. It is a two-hander and I knew that I wanted Nick to play the man, the other part being that of his wife. I needed a second play and chose a straightforward 'slap and tickle' comedy with six characters by an old friend, Terence Frisby,[**] called *Seaside Postcard.* It was a case of going from the absurd to ridiculous. I gave the overall title for the two plays: *Double Take.*

Joining Nick for *Fred,* as his wife, I cast a lady from the Bank, Merlyn Lowther. To attempt to describe the plot with characters as confused as the 'Pringles', is challenging – and really not the point. Suffice it to say that they are a married couple of many years and that he "can't get over poor Fred" – who is dead. Whilst she is clear as to what has happened, he cannot come to terms with the fact that he is responsible for Fred's death. It evolves that she was married to Fred and that she had an affair with our confused hero and that Fred nearly caught them in flagrante delicto. Lover boy hid in a wardrobe stark naked, only to be discovered by Fred, whereupon the man in the nude cut Fred in half. The point of the piece is not in the logic of the story but the lack of logic in the mind of the axe-wielding present husband. I was asked to give a breakdown of the scenario to a man I hardly knew and he said:
'The same thing happened to me.'
I recoiled in horror.
'What, you cut someone in half?'
He chose to ignore my understandable concern and explained that he too had nearly been discovered in a similar situation and that he had hidden naked in a wardrobe within me ladies chamber until he could make good his escape via window, roof, garden and fence, donning his attire as he went. Life imitating art.

I was told by an audience member (as I had been many times before), that she preferred a play that had 'a beginning, a middle

and an end'[***] and asked what it all meant. I answered with a line of our licentious hero:
"It's a mystery."

The title of the second play, *Seaside Postcard*, says all that is needed to describe the plot – Mum, Dad, daughter, boy friend, a couple of married friends, sea, sun, sand, sex and sandwiches. The high moment of excitement of the drama for the audience in the cramped studio, was watching at close proximity the characters changing into swimming costumes (some very brief) to a musical accompaniment. It could have brought back the Lord Chamberlain and censorship.

The cast, stage management, technical team and the committee, gave me enthusiastic support, but I suspect that the Theatre felt they dare not invite me back again for fear of losing their license and reputation for clean living. So I had to give up my hard-won amateur status and settle for simply being a professional.

[*] Celebrated voice coaches to The Royal Shakespeare Company and the National Theatre Company.

[**] Perhaps, James' best-known play is *Next Time I'll Sing to You* and Terence's *A Girl in my Soup*.

[***] I have tried to fulfill that requirement in this book.

# 67

## JUST CRICKET

I appreciate that the mention of that seven-letter word is offensive to some. Sensitive to those feelings, I have saved this item towards the close of play so that they can 'skip' it.

My first chance to see first class cricket came in 1946. The war having ended in '45, it was the season of '46 before County cricket got into its stride again and being desperate to see Warwickshire play at Edgbaston, my mother would take me there as often as possible in that summer holiday. The touring side, that first post-war season, was All India, as it was called. It is possible that this was the first match I saw 'The Bears' play, with a side that included their dashing pre and post war Captain, Peter Cranmer, and H.E. (Tom) Dollery who later became the first professional to be Captain of a county side (and very successful too). There was Tom Pritchard, an import from NZ, as one of the fast bowlers, the legendary leg-break bowler Eric Hollies and a young Oxford undergraduate, Richard Sale, who scored 157 in Warwickshire's first innings. India included V. M. Merchant (Capt), Mushtaq Ali, A. S. Hazare and Vinoo Mankad. The Captain for the tour was The Nawab of Pataudi, who did not play in this game. The match was drawn.

1947 saw 'the same procedure as last year'. The touring side was South Africa under the Captaincy of Alan Melville (who did not go on to write West End revues). In their match against them, Warwickshire achieved an overwhelming defeat, although their cravatted Captain, Cranmer, scored a century in the first innings and made 38 in the second innings total of 76 – obviously the only one of his side playing. During this encounter a gentleman slipped into the seat beside my mother and myself saying:

'I thought I'd find you here.'

It was my Uncle Percy (PG), my godfather and brother of my late father. Always anxious to keep my father's (and his) enthusiasm for the great game alive in me, he had driven up from Cheam to see if this was the case. PG had a 'big personality' – indeed, I'm surprised that his entrance into the ground did not stop play. After sitting with us for a time, he excused himself, to return half an hour later with the announcement:

'John, you are now a member of the Warwickshire County Cricket Club.'

He had been to see the Secretary, the much respected Leslie Deakins, who signed me up for the 1948 season and this being August he gave complimentary admission to myself and my mother for the remaining matches of the '47 season. I have remained a member ever since and would suggest, that as I pen these words, being my sixtieth year of paying their annual 'sub', that I must be one of their longest serving kids on the block.

In 1948, my first full year of membership, I saw the first Australian side to visit these shores since the cessation of the 39-45 hostilities. You devotees of the game will wonder if I saw 'The Don', who was on his last tour of England – of course I did. In their first innings of 254 against Warwick, he made 31 and was bowled by W. E. Hollies (an omen perhaps), in which Eric took 8 for 107. Requiring 41 to win in their second innings, they lost only one wicket, of course, to Eric. Bradman was not out on 13 and it was said that the Warwickshire Vice-Captain, 'Tom' Dollery, told Eric not to show 'The Don' his 'googly' – the reason being that he had been selected to play for England the following week at The Oval in the final 'Test' against the deadly foe. He felt that Eric should keep his secret weapon up his sleeve. When the great man came to the wicket for his last Test innings, requiring just four runs to give him a Test Match batting average of 100 per innings, Eric, with his second ball, bowled him for a 'duck' with his 'googly'. Bradman's test match average at the end of his career was therefore a mere 99.94 – pathetic!

To recall most of the matches I have seen would be tedious even to me, so I will be selective. There was the thrill of watching Warwickshire play the all-conquering West Indies in 1950 and of seeing every ball bowled on the 9th, 10th and 11th of that glorious August. I witnessed 'the minnows', through sheer crowd power, overcome a side unbeaten that season, crawling across the line in just getting the 95 needed, with three wickets to spare.

The following year was 'Festival of Britain' year, also my last year at school. A group of boys were brought from the school to experience this occasion on London's South Bank and to see the new Festival Hall, the Queen Elizabeth Hall and the Skylon, an odd cigar shaped celebratory construction. We were instructed that should we become detached from the party, we must gather at 5.30 under the said phallic symbol, in order for us to get the coach to return us to school. Christopher Benjamin and I were aware that the 'The Gentlemen' (amateurs) were playing 'The Players' (professionals) at Lord's. The temptation to go to the home of cricket was too tempting, so we decided to 'disappear' and we made our way to St John's Wood (our first but not our last visit). Compton made 150 for the Players and Peter May, a Cambridge undergrad, 119 for the 'Gents', the Players ultimately winning by 21 runs. (The last time this fixture was played was in 1962). We hastened back to the South Bank to be at the appointed place on time, to face the ire and concern of our jailor.
'Where have you been?' he demanded.
'We've been looking for you *everywhere*, sir,' protested the innocents.

This was not the first time the two cricketing-loving, would be thespians had gone AWOL in order to see those more skilled at the game than they. The previous year, a group of non-cherubic choristers from the school had been taken on a ten-day camping holiday to Heacham in Norfolk, so that they could join with other members of the Royal School of Church Music to sing in places where they sing. We two castratos decided to take the day off and hitchhike to Norwich, to see The Minor Counties play the West

235

# THE
# 2d. WARWICKSHIRE 2d.
## COUNTY CRICKET CLUB

**The Bowler at Pavilion end is indicated on big board by figure on right.**
DISCS: White at 55 overs.   Yellow at 60 overs.   White & Yellow at 65 overs, New Ball due.
HOURS OF PLAY—First two days 11-30—7-0 p.m. Third day 11-0—4-30 p.m. with extra half-hour on third day if demanded.   LUNCH 1-30—2-10   TEA INTERVAL—20 minutes.
**You spoil the enjoyment of others, and indicate a lack of understanding of the Game on your own part, if you move about behind the Bowler's Arm.**

| WEST INDIES | 1st Innings | | 2nd Innings | |
|---|---|---|---|---|
| *1 J. B. Stollmeyer | c Spooner b Grove | 17 | lbw b Grove | 29 |
| 2 A. F. Rae | c Spooner b Grove | 1 | c Kardar b Fritchard | 28 |
| 3 F. M. Worrell | b Grove | 29 | c Dollery b Pritchard | 46 |
| 4 R. Marshall | c & b Grove | 33 | c Pritchard b Hollies | 9 |
| †5 C. L. Walcott | c Dollery b Grove | 14 | lbw b Hollies | 41 |
| 6 K. B. Trestrail | b Grove | 0 | b Hollies | 28 |
| 7 R. J. Christiani | c Hollies b Pritchard | 4 | st Spooner b Hollies | 18 |
| 8 C. B. Williams | c Don Taylor b Kardar | 21 | lbw b Hollies | 0 |
| 9 P. E. Jones | lbw b Grove | 20 | not out | 0 |
| 10 A. L. Valentine | b Grove | 5 | lbw b Fritchard | 1 |
| 11 L. R. Pierre | not out | 0 | b Hollies | 0 |
| Umpires | Extras | 12 | | 22 |
| H. Parks & A. Skelding | | | | |
| West Indies won the toss | Total | 156 | | 222 |

1 wkt. for   3   2– 42   3– 61   4– 97   5– 97   6–102   7–104   8–139   9–152   10–156
1 wkt. for   63   2– 66   3– 94   4–113   5–174   6–214   7–214   8–219   9–220   10–222

| Bowling Analysis: | O | M | R | W | Nb | Wd | O | M | R | W | Nb | Wd |
|---|---|---|---|---|---|---|---|---|---|---|---|---|
| Fritchard | 23 | 6 | 55 | 1 | 1 | – | 19 | 5 | 57 | 3 | 2 | – |
| Grove | 26–4 | 8 | 38 | 8 | – | – | 35 | 6 | 69 | 1 | – | – |
| Hollies | 14 | 3 | 39 | – | – | – | 29–3 | 12 | 57 | 6 | – | – |
| Kardar | 10 | 3 | 12 | 1 | – | – | 3 | – | 14 | – | – | – |
| Don Taylor | | | | | | | 1 | – | 3 | – | – | – |

| WARWICKSHIRE | 1st Innings | | 2nd Innings | |
|---|---|---|---|---|
| 1 F. C. Gardner | c Worrell b Fierre | 8 | hit wkt b Valentine | 13 |
| 2 J. R. Thompson | c Stollmeyer b Jones | 26 | c Worrell b Jones | 16 |
| 3 Don Taylor | c Rae b Worrell | 24 | not out | 36 |
| 4 J. S. Ord | c Trestrail b Jones | 7 | lbw b Pierre | 1 |
| *5 H. E. Dollery | lbw b Valentine | 3 | c Jones b Valentine | 0 |
| 6 A. V. Wolton | b Fierre | 89 | b Fierre | 5 |
| †7 R. T. Spooner | not out | 66 | c Walcott b Valentine | 3 |
| 8 A. H. Kardar | b Jones | 5 | b Valentine | 8 |
| 9 T. L. Pritchard | c Christiani b Valentine | 15 | not out | 4 |
| 10 C. W. Grove | b Valentine | 11 | | |
| 11 W. E. Hollies | c Marshall b Valentine | 6 | | |
| Scorers: | Extras | 24 | | 10 |
| G. C. Austin & W. Ferguson | | | | |
| * Capt. † Wicketkeeper | Total | 284 | | 96 |

1 wkt. for   12   2– 44   3– 55   4– 63   5– 87   6–210   7–230   8–259   9–276   10–284
1 wkt. for   34   2– 34   3– 43   4– 47   5– 62   6– 72   7– 51   8–   9–   10–

| Bowling Analysis: | O | M | R | W | Nb | Wd | O | M | R | W | Nb | Wd |
|---|---|---|---|---|---|---|---|---|---|---|---|---|
| Fierre | 15 | – | 57 | 2 | 1 | – | 5 | 1 | 17 | 2 | – | – |
| Worrell | 23 | 6 | 51 | 1 | – | – | | | | | | |
| Jones | 31 | 10 | 66 | 3 | – | – | 21–4 | 12 | 33 | 1 | – | – |
| Valentine | 23 | 5 | 57 | 4 | – | – | 26 | 13 | 36 | 4 | – | 1 |
| Williams | 4 | – | 29 | – | – | – | | | | | | |

Advertising rights acquired by the Property Publishing Company, 46, Watford Way, London, N.W.4, and printed by C. W. Towers & Son, Ltd., Stechford, B'ham, 9.

236

Indies. It was considerably further than we imagined but we did manage to see the celebrated Ramadhin (his partner Valentine had been excused boots for that particular match) take seven wickets. The problem was getting back to camp. Nobody seemed anxious to stop and pick up the two choristers – perhaps wearing a cassock and surplice had not been a great idea. Eventually, a burly, grease-covered admirer of choirboys, pulled up in his lorry and proffered succour. Of course, in retrospect it could have been the two absconders that were the suckers but in fact his interest was purely of a philanthropic nature, unlike some clergy I've met. We sat huddled in the back of the open truck, all the way from the home of Coleman's Mustard to the site of the jolly campers. Mr Ferns, our music and choir master, who had taken me through the intricacies of *Comfort Ye My People*, having been driven demented with concern as to our well-being, might well have proffered no comfort whatsoever, but seeing that we were in the latter stages of hypothermia, relented.

'I trust you have learnt your lesson. However, as it was to see the West Indies, you are forgiven.'

*"Many waters cannot quench love, neither can the seas drown it."*

A month later I went to the Oval, where England were playing South Africa and saw a rare dismissal. In a not particularly memorable match, Len Hutton having hit a ball somewhat vertically, in trying to defend his wicket (he said) from it being hit by the descending object, attempted to strike it a second time. In so doing nearly took the South African wicketkeeper's head off his shoulders, impeding his chance of catching him. Endean was indeed, nearly endead. Mr Hutton was given out 'obstructing the field' – he should have been given three months.

The August of 1968 saw me at the Oval again in relaxed mood as I had been offered another 'stint' on the BBC Drama Rep. Company. With Louise, our third child, having been born a month earlier and with a new, larger mortgage to pay, I felt that I might be looking at another couple of year's security. On the last day

Australia were struggling to stave off defeat and at lunch on a glorious sunny day, they were 85 for 5, needing another 267 to win and England, just 5 wickets. Victory over the old 'foe' seemed assured. However, as the players made their way to the Pavilion for a light repast, the heavens opened and within fifteen minutes the entire ground was flooded. It seemed inconceivable that there could be more play, thereby denying England the chance of levelling the series. Ted Warn, the Head Groundsman, had other ideas. By 2.15 the sun had reappeared and calling for volunteers from the spectators, a vast army set about clearing the ground of water, using brooms, blankets and other assorted implements. Such assistance would not be allowed in later years – indeed, would the customers have worked so diligently if the Aussies had a chance of winning? By 4.45 play was possible, leaving seventy five minutes for their objective to be achieved and on a drying pitch, Underwood became almost impossible to play and England won with ten minutes to spare and the series was tied.

Another 'I was there' occasion was the Nat West Trophy final at Lord's in 1993 between Sussex and Warwickshire. Accompanied by Matthew Walters, cricket-loving BBC Producer and Andrew Ball, a charming young neighbour, we witnessed an extraordinary end to the match. Warwickshire may have regretted putting Sussex in to bat, for after the first hour they were 85 for 1 and the 'Brew XI' men could be facing a mammoth total. They managed, through Dermot Reeve's astute captaincy, to hold them to a mere 321 for 6 after their 60 overs. Warwickshire's innings crept steadily nearer the seemingly impossible target, with a century from Asif Din (his career's crowning moment) and the resolute Dermot with 80 not out. The final over required them to score 15 runs to win. With 4,2,2,4,1 (all from the Captain's bat), Roger Twose was left to score 2 off the last ball (the only one he had to face), which he sliced away and the target was achieved. Extraordinary.

Having seen Brian Lara play several times for Warwickshire in

1994, seemingly scoring a century every time he went to the crease, I witnessed him hit a mighty blow at Lord's, in a match against Middlesex. In an innings of 140, he hit a 6, which struck the south turret of the Pavilion. If it had been a couple of feet to the right, the ball would have easily cleared that celebrated building and have been only the second time in the history of the 'Home of Cricket' for that feat to have been achieved – sigh of relief from the spirit of Albert Trott.

I have to state, unlike 500,000 others who claim the honour, I was *not* there to see Brian Lara make the highest score in the history of first class cricket: 501 not out, in Warwickshire's match against Durham in August 1994. The story was reported of a Birmingham businessman, who hearing on the radio that BL was nearing this momentous landmark, sped through the streets of his native city at 100 mph in his BMW, pursued by the Police with siren wailing, to get to the County Ground. Both cars screamed into the car park at Edgbaston, where they attempted to arrest him.
'Later, you idiots,' he declared.
He then rushed them into the Pavilion, where he and the boys in blue witnessed the great moment. He was let off with a caution.

An off the field and in the studio cricketing memory comes through my taking part in a TV programme in Birmingham. The format was sketches and songs related to the great game, interspersed with conversation between several well-known cricketers, in front of an audience. My involvement was in a sketch, concerning an interviewee and his interviewer. I played the former, as the man seeking employment and hoping to be given a management position, whilst the latter, the boss and man of authority (a sort of Alan Sugar), was taken by David King, whom I knew well from our musical callaboration in the past. During the scene the two protagonists recalled being at school together. The old-school-tie syndrome came into play and the job was virtually mine. The matter of a House Match crept into the conversation and I recalled having hit him for a six, which he hotly disputed. We then re-enacted the scene using his desk as the wicket, a spoon for my bat and an orange as the ball. The 'bowler' was required to bowl a 'googly', of which I had considerable experience! David, however, had never played the game in his life. Knowing him to be a skilled pianist with dexterity at his finger tips, I described how he should grip the orange and deliver it down the desk from the back of his hand. This he did with great success when the scene was performed. How adept I was with the spoon I refuse to remember. The morale of the story was: never challenge a superior. I was 'fired' before I got the job.

The Director of the progamme, knowing of my interest in and knowledge of cricket, invited me to join the panel of distinguished Midland cricketers. These included, Eric Hollies, 'Roly' Jenkins (two great spin bowlers), Peter Cranmer and David Steele. David was celebrated for being brought out of obscurity from his county of Northamptonshire in 1975, to play for his country and face the bombardment of the terrifying Australian fast bowlers in the Test Match at the Home of Cricket. When the time came for this doughty man of steel to face the onslaught, he made his way from the England dressing-room and descended the flights of stairs of that celebrated pavilion. Becoming somewhat confused, instead of walking through the Long Room to go out onto the hallowed turf, he found himself taking 'guard' in the Gent's lavatory in the basement. He was escorted back by a member of the MCC, through the sleeping fellow cardholders, shown the way down the Pavilion steps and through the wicket gate, so that he could face his tormentors. He became the hero of the day, nay year, for he showed true dogged grit and withstood the assault of the Australian bowlers for a considerable period of time, which would ultimately save the match for England, making 50 in the 1$^{st}$ innings and 45 in the 2nd. It was rumoured that the considerate guide with the egg and tomato striped tie was not amused when it was pointed out that his flies were undone.

I was sitting next to this celebrated cricket stalwart in one of the recording breaks and he commented on how much he had enjoyed the sketch I had taken part in.

'When did you start learning it?' he enquired.

'Last night,' I informed him, to which he seemed somewhat impressed. He then asked who my partner in the sketch was and I duly gave him my supporting artiste's name.

'He's a good actor,' responded Mr Steele, with far too much emphasis on the 'he' for my liking. Showing my charming qualities, however, I forbore to make any wry or bitter comment but instead expressed my admiration for the way Mr King had delivered his 'googly' orange.

'He knows nothing about cricket, I had to demonstrate what to do,' I preeningly informed the steely-haired Mr Steele.

'Didn't he do it well?' I said with pride.

There was the slightest pause and without a trace of sarcasm, England's cricketing hero from Lord's said:

'I think his little finger should have been further round the seam.'

What ------- seam? It was an orange. They should have locked him in that urinal.

A cutting kept from the good old *Guardian,* unrelated to the above, may be of interest to you.

".... an uneventful day. MCC took their score from 33 for four at the start of play to 447 for seven at luncheon, whereupon they declared. Boycott by then was 193 not out." I do so hate slow play!

# 68

## POETS CORNER

At the end of Gilbert White's *The Natural History of Selborne* there is a section entitled 'Poems', which I assume to be his own. Although I could not manage that, I admire the skill of the poet perhaps more than any other literary form and wanted to include a few poems that have meant something to me.

Firstly, two by Siegfried Sassoon.

### *ALONE*

*"When I'm alone"* – the words tripped off his tongue
As though to be alone were nothing strange.
*"When I was young,"* he said; *"when I was young ...."*

I thought of age, and loneliness, and change.
I thought how strange we grow when we're alone,
And how unlike the selves that meet and talk,
And blow the candles out, and say good night.
*Alone* .... The word is life endured and known.
It is the stillness where our spirits walk
And all but inmost faith is overthrown.

### *EVERY ONE SANG*

Every one suddenly burst out singing;
And I was filled with such delight
As prisoned birds must find in freedom
Winging wildly across the white
Orchards and dark green fields; on; on;

and out of sight.
Every one's voice was suddenly lifted,
And beauty came like the setting sun.
My heart was shaken with tears, and horror
Drifted away ..... O, but everyone
Was a bird; and the song was wordless; the
    singing will never be done.

The next by Cecil Day Lewis reflects on parting.

## *WALKING AWAY*
### for Sean

It is eighteen years ago, almost to the day –
A sunny day with the leaves just turning,
The touch-lines new-ruled – since I watched you play
Your first game of football, then, like a satellite
Wrenched from its orbit, go drifting away

Behind a scatter of boys. I can see
You walking away from me towards the school
With the pathos of a half-fledged thing set free
Into a wilderness, the gait of one
Who finds no path where the path should be.

That hesitant figure, eddying away
Like a winged seed loosened from its parent stem,
Has something I never quite grasp to convey
About nature's give-and-take – the small, the scorching
Ordeals which fire one's irresolute clay.

I have had worse partings, but none that so
Gnaws at my mind still. Perhaps it is roughly
Saying what God alone could perfectly show –
How selfhood begins with a walking away,
And love is proved in the letting go.

Here, Philip Larkin examines loss:

## *HOME IS SO SAD*

Home is so sad. It stays as it was left,
Shaped to the comfort of the last to go
As if to win them back. Instead, bereft
Of anyone to please, it withers so,
Having no heart to put aside the theft

And turn again to what it started as,
A joyous shot of how things ought to be,
Long fallen wide. You can see how it was:
Look at the pictures and the cutlery.
The music in the piano stool. That vase.

I have always loved animals, cats in particular. Whereas a dog needs a master, a cat requires staff. They are exceeding wise. So, of course, T. S. Eliot's:

## *THE NAMING OF CATS*

The Naming of Cats is a difficult matter,
  It isn't just one of your holiday games;
You may think at first I'm as mad as a hatter
When I tell you, a cat must have THREE DIFFERENT NAMES
First of all, there's the name that the family use daily,
  Such as Peter, Augustus, Alonzo or James,
Such as Victor or Jonathan, George or Bill Bailey –
  All of them sensible everyday names.
There are fancier names if you think they sound sweeter,
  Some for the gentlemen, some for the dames:
Such as Plato, Admetus, Electra, Demeter –

But all of them sensible everyday names.
But I tell you a cat needs a name that's particular,
  A name that's peculiar, and more dignified,
Else how can he keep up his tail perpendicular,
  Or spread out his whiskers, or cherish his pride?
Of names of this kind, I can give you a quorum,
  Such as Munkustrap, Quaxo or Coricopat,
Such as Bombalurina, or else Jellylorum –
  Names that never belong to more than one cat.
But above and beyond there's still one name left over,
  And that is the name that you never will guess;
The name that no human research can discover –
  But THE CAT HIMSELF KNOWS, and will never confess.
When you notice a cat in profound meditation,
  The reason, I tell you is always the same:
His mind is engaged in a rapt contemplation
  Of the thought, of the thought, of the thought of his name:
    His ineffable effable
    Effinineffable
Deep and inscrutable singular name.

What to choose of Shakespeare? One of the most wonderful of verse speakers was Robert Donat and every Christmas Day, when I was a child, it was he that linked us by radio to the far corners of the earth, prior to the Monarch's 3 pm speech.
'Come in, Hong Kong….'
I know it has been said that the problem with Shakespeare is that he used too many quotations (like too many notes for Mozart) but a most heart-warming comment passed on by Donat, was that of a Manchester woman who said to him:
'He's such a comfort, is our Will.'

245

## *SONNET*

Shall I compare thee to a summer's day?
Thou art more lovely and more temperate:
Rough winds do shake the darling buds of May,
And summer's lease hath all too short a date:
Sometimes too hot the eye of heaven shines,
And often is his gold complexion dimm'd;
And every fair from fair sometime declines,
By chance, or nature's changing course untrimm'd;
But thy eternal summer shall not fade,
Nor lose possession of that fair thou ow'st,
Nor shall death brag thou wander'st in his shade,
When in eternal lines to time thou grow'st;
So long as men can breathe, or eyes can see,
So long lives this, and this gives life to thee.


Finally, words of wisdom from our Will close to my heart:

Frame your mind to mirth and merriment,
Which bears a thousand hurts and lengthens life.

# 69

## ALL THAT JAZZ

Whilst I frittered away my talent, the rest of the family had applied themselves more assiduously to the important things of life. Tessa was a Drama and English teacher in various Secondary schools, both in the public and private sector, whilst at the same time bringing up Toby and Sophia alongside her husband John. She also managed to pursue her AmDram interests, as did her husband. The family was blessed with having John, an international man of mystery, in its ranks. Louise worked as a Mental Health Officer, then ran a Community Counselling partnership before going on to be a Student Mental Health Advisor at Brunel University. Her team won a prestigous award for their work from The Times Higher Education Supplement, against worthy opposition, at a glittering ceremony held at the Grosvenor House Hotel in October 2008. This recognition for Outstanding Support for Disabled Studunts gave considerable kudos to Brunel University. As Tessa pointed out, the family had at last won an Oscar! On the domestic side, Louise's marriage to Keir foundered and they went their separate ways. However, as totally caring and loving parents they shared the upbringing of their children with a 50/50 care arrangement. This worked well and Brontë and Cory came through this difficult period as happy and balanced individuals – quite an achievement. All of the grandchildren were delightful and talented in their different ways – but then I would say that.

It was understandable that Penny, who could never rest unless she was on some course or another, with the constraints of work no longer there, wished to polish up her singing. Having appeared in musicals when we first met, she had not 'trilled' for more years than is reasonable to mention. She joined various choral societies but wanted more than anything to study Jazz. It so happened that in Richmond there was one of the leading Jazz schools in the country and she was accepted onto the course. First of all it was the Intermediate and then the Master class. Through the College she performed with many young up and coming divas at clubs like the Ram Jam Jazz Club in Kingston and the Bull's Head in Barnes such as Helen Baden, and Zena James, who also became good friends. We also saw and heard many of the Jazz 'greats' like the brilliant Americans, Scott Hamilton (Sax) and Kenny Devern (clarinet). The enthusiasm and interest engendered by those involved in jazz towards each other seemed to me to be far more generous than usually found amongst my fellow thespians. Jazz musicians like to listen and learn from each other, whilst actors often seem to feel threatened by those they suspect may be more talented than they. For me, it was the improvisation of the jazz performer that fascinated me. That's making Jazz!

At the same time Penny had offered her services as a volunteer counsellor to the Mulberry Centre at the West Middlesex Hospital, a delightful facility set up for those with, or affected by, cancer. She also became involved with the quite wonderful Shooting Star Hospice for Children. Therapists in various fields, ranging from Aromatherapy to Reflexology, would give their spare time for these causes. Apart from her counselling, Penny, with Michele Ingham, did several 'gigs' at the Ram Jam Club in aid of the Mulberry Centre and raised a four-figure sum. As with laughter, singing is a great therapy.

--------0--------

*Paul Baden*

Penny jazzing at the Ram Jam

Sisterly Love!
Tessa and Louise

*Tony Chick*

Talented
Grandchildren!

Toby, Cory, Sophia
and Brontë

*Tony Chick*

250

'Have you retired?'

A question never asked by one actor to another, for in the main actor's never retire – they just don't get the work. However, one of the joys of growing older is that if you have managed to save enough acorns for one's winter, you don't need to kow-tow. If you're not asked for or if you don't like what's on offer – so what! Sir Alec Guinness, when in his eighties, was asked by an enthusiastic interviewer if he would like to return to the stage, he said:

'Oh, no, I wouldn't be tempted back into the theatre now, however SMALL the part.'

There are those, of course, who feel differently. An actor well-known for his roles of dominant characters in dozens of major films, especially 'Biblical' blockbusters, such as *Quo Vadis* and *Solomon and Sheba*, was approached to play in yet another epic of a religious nature. Being in his nineties, his agent pointed out to him that as it was only two days work and that he would have fly to Hollywood to do it, so he felt bound to advise him to decline.

'No, no, I'll do it,' said Finlay Currie 'you never know what it might lead to.'

What should one do with time on one's hands? Write the old memoirs, sit on some committees? What about my alma mater, which in 2007 was celebrating its tercentenary? I had done all that with Selhurst in *A Night with Rochester Sneath* but now it was the real thing with Warminster. On offer were various celebratory events but I felt that summer balls and athletic events were perhaps a little beyond the capabilities of the seventy-year olds. I wanted to see how some of my contemporaries looked – could they be as youthful as me (surely not)? I contacted the few that I had kept in touch with: a Doctor, a Headmaster, an Accountant (who seemed to keep a close account of all his contemporaries) and my fellow Thespian. Apart from us two actor laddies, all were now retired. With the cooperation of another, long-time-no-see old alumna, ex-Town Clerk, Julian Macdonald (son of 'our' Headmaster), we contacted and built up a motley collection who were able to attend a Service of Thanksgiving for the school in Salisbury Cathedral led by the Bishop, after which the 'Macdonald' boys made their way for lunch at the Rose & Crown in Harnham, to ruminate and reminisce, whilst looking out over the 'Constable' view. It was a pleasure to have as guests the incumbent Headmaster and his wife, Martin and Alison Priestley, in what must have seemed to them like a theatrical reunion, for there was a plethora of those who had been involved in *Twelfth Night* fifty-six years before. Apart from actors, Christopher Benjamin (Sir Toby) and myself (Feste), there was Roger Seckington, the headmaster (Sir Andrew) and Andrew White, the accountant (Malvolio). There was Howard Burgess, solicitor (Sea Captain), Duncan Straughan, engineer (Sebastian) and on the production side, Andrew Ajdukiewicz, the doctor (Electrician), and Philip Terry, schoolmaster (Scenic Design). Present also was the widow of Allen Ferns, the musical director, added to which there was physician, George Misiewicz, who had played Charles I in a previous production.

"Is all our company here?"

--------0--------

And so we move on.

In fact, we had already moved on from our Teddington home of over thirty years to the delights of Hampton. As employment started to take its natural decline, I become concerned as to how I might be able to afford to cover over the cracks. I also felt that whilst Teddington was going up in the 'yuppy' stakes, it was going down from an environmental aspect. There were good reasons for staying but it seemed sensible to 'down-size'. Having the birth-sign of the crab, there was a need to be near water. In finding our house on the Thames we achieved this and in many ways felt it was an upgrade. The river could be seen from every room and from the back there was a three quarter of a mile aspect down to Hampton Court Palace. The fact that we were adjacent to Garrick's Villa and his Temple to Shakespeare made it almost essential – I'm sure their spirits must have been delighted that I was so near by! We had moved into the house four weeks prior to the entrance of the new millennium and invited a small group of friends to celebrate that moment. Armed with champagne, winding our way through the packing cases, we stood on the balconies at the back and watched a fifty minute pyrotechnic display erupt from the Palace and the surrounding area, with the chimes of midnight striking from St Mary's Church, Hampton. It was, in the vernacular, awesome. Could anyone in London have seen a fairer sight?

I was a riparian at last.

"I beg your pardon,' said the Mole, pulling himself together with an effort. 'You must think me very rude; but all this is so new to me. So – this – is – a – River!'
'The River,' corrected the Rat.
'And you really live by the river? What a jolly life!'
'By it and with it and on it and in it,' said the Rat. 'It's brother and sister to me, and aunts, and company, and food and drink, and (naturally) washing. It's my world, and I don't want any other. What it hasn't got is not worth having, and what it doesn't know is not worth knowing."

*The Wind in the Willows*, by Kenneth Grahame

# AFTERTHOUGHT

*"That that is, is* : for what is that but that? and is but is?"

Feste, *Twelfth Night*

Most 'only' children, particularly those brought up essentially in a single-parent situation, know solitude. In fact, I didn't, but I did feel shy and lacking in confidence, and truth to tell have remained so. Some who know me may scoff at the suggestion, however, that is how it is. My somewhat loud (so I'm told) and outgoing manner is only a shallow mask to cover reality. It's a case of the extrovert fighting to get in. I realized at the age of eleven that being shy was a recipe for leading a dull existence and having sand kicked in one's face, so I decided on an 'out front' performance. Whilst this hid my true self and was not particularly subtle, I managed to become 'popular'. Life is what you make it and not necessarily its reality. However, my hidden fears were to hold me back in really 'going for it' – "the fault, dear Brutus, is not in our stars ……" That having been said, I have relished my sojourn here and even the sadnesses that came on the journey, whilst painful to bear, have enriched my soul. If life were to be looked upon as a party, then I have felt rather like a wallflower – albeit not blushing. I'm glad I was invited.

I enjoy crossword puzzles (Quick rather than Cryptic), so I offer you an anagram that sums up my modus operandi perfectly. Although an Aston Villa supporter, I should really have followed:

Plymouth Argyle (8,2,4)

For like many other insecure ones, that is how it was.

--------0--------

Criticism and 'put-downs' are very much a part of an actor's life.

254

We crave good notices or the indulgent praises of our audience but it is the witty, bitchy, cruel and ludicrous comments that sear into the memory, as captured so well in Diana Rigg's anthology *No Turn Unstoned.*

An actor, well known for not hiding his light under a bushel, was taking part in a radio play set in South Africa. The cast was made up entirely of actors born and brought up in the Rainbow country – except for our man. He had a modest reputation for doing various dialects and accents but it was not that earth-shattering. At the coffee break after the first read-through, wherein he had displayed his talent for the speech patterns of the Transvaal, he declared, unashamedly, to the rest of the cast:
'I can do thirty-six dialects and accents.'
To which Hilda Kriseman, a daughter of the Veldt, responded instantly:
'Thirty-five!' What silver-daggered brevity.

Perhaps the most cutting personal put-down that I have received came during the production of Exchange at the Nuffield Theatre, Southampton. The translator and adaptor of Yuri Trifinov's work, the brilliant Michael Frayn, invited the company for a post-performance supper at a local restaurant. I found myself sitting opposite Michael and next to that powerful actress, Faith Brook. As is my wont I was attempting "to set the table on a roar" which Michael, who has more humorous lines in his little finger, Horatio, than are dreamt of in my repertoire, seemed to enjoy thoroughly. The next day I saw Ms Brook, prior to the show and expressed my appreciation of the generosity shown by our benefactor the previous night.
'What a splendid occasion that was' I commented.
'Ye-es' she replied.
I detected a hint of uncertainty, due to her final downward inflection.
'Didn't you enjoy it?' I enquired in amazement.
'Well ..' she replied 'I suppose, I would have preferred .......

a little more of Michael … and a little less of you.'

Point taken!

## LATE EXTRA

As with most works of an autobiographical nature the pronoun 'I' does seem to proliferate these pages. However, as it is a word that is rarely off the lips of any actor, I make no apology. This is not a diary having never kept one. It is a recall from the depths of my memory and although roughly in chronological order, like Eric Morecambe in his celebrated sketch with André Previn, I have played the right notes but not necessarily in the right order. Memory is selective. It chooses to remember; it chooses to forget. It exaggerates; it underplays. But hopefully it relates a heartfelt truth, be it spoken or unspoken.

Writing this has given me the chance to bring together family and old friends and remember those times that we shared. However, ……

*If we shadows have offended,*
*Think but this, and all is mended,*
*That you have but slumber'd here*
*While these visions did appear.*
*And this weak and idle theme,*
*No more yielding but a dream*

The Bard of Stratford-on-Avon

# GOOD TIME JOHNNY

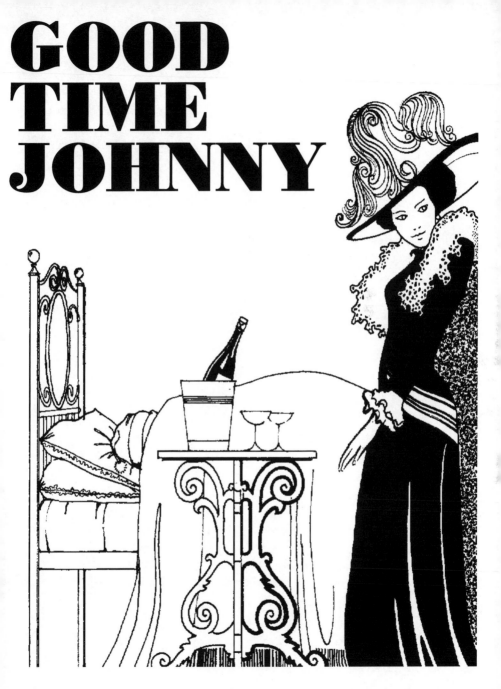

*Dream on*

# CURTAIN

# Dramatis Personae
(not in order of appearance)

Ajdukiewicz, Andrew
Aldridge, Michael
Alexander, Terence
Ali, Mustaq
Allan, Ronald
Allen, Patrick
Allen, Sheila
Andrews, Harry
Anthony, Nigel
Appel, Anita
Arden, Eve
Armriding, Elsie & Joe
Armstrong, Alun
Armstrong, Gareth
Armstrong, Sue
Asante, Christopher
Ashcroft, Peggy
Ashford, Daisy
Ashpitel, Ian
Ashton, Marcia
Askey, Arthur
Atkins, Eileen
Atkins, Robert
Atkinson, Barbara
Aumonier, Andrew
Aumonier, Stacy
Ayckbourn, Alan
Ayres, Rosalind
Bacon, Peggy
Baddeley, Annie
Baddeley, Edward (Bompa)
Baddeley, Gill
Baddeley, Louise
Baddeley, Mark
Baddeley, Michael
Baddeley, Penny
Baddeley, Percy (PG)

Baddeley, Peter
Baddeley, Robert
Baddeley, Sidney
Baddeley, Sybil
Baddeley/Davies, Tessa
Baddeley/Price, Gladys
Baddiley, Ronald
Badel, Alan
Badel, Sarah
Baden, Helen
Badley, John
Bailey, Bryan
Bailey, Trevor
Bakewell, Joan
Bakewell, Michael
Baldock, John
Baldwin, Peter
Ball, Andrew
Ball, Helga
Ballard, Edward
Banks (Mr)
Bannister, Trevor
Barbirolli, John
Barker, Alfred
Barker, 'Dickie'
Barker, Eric
Barker, G.G.
Barker, Ronnie
Barkworth, Peter
Barlow, H.J.
Barlow, Thelma
Barrett, Sean
Barron, Keith
Barry, Morris
Barton, Eric
Bates, Michael
Bateson, Timothy

Baxter, Ronnie
Baylis, Lilian
Beach, Ann
Beaumont, Debra
Beckett, Henry
Beckinsale, Richard
Bedser, Alec & Eric
Belcher, David
Bellamy, David
Benjamin, Christopher
Bennett, Arnold
Bennett, Judy
Bennett, Richard Rodney
Bennett, Tony
Bergman, Ingrid
Berkeley, Humphry
Berry, Cicely
Billington, Michael
Bird, 'Dickie'
Blackburn, Tony
Blackwell, Patrick
Blessed, Brian
Blick, Newton
Bloom, Claire
Bluthal, John
Boddey, Martin
Bolam, James
Bolt, Ben
Bolt, Robert
Bond, Edward
Bosenquet, Reginald
Boult, Adrian
Bowan, John
Bowles, Peter
Boycott, Geoffrey
Bradman, Donald

Brett, Jeremy
Brewster, Daniel
Bridgeland, Maurice
Bridges, Alan
Bridie, James
Briers, Richard
Brimble, Vincent
Bristow, Geoff
Britten, Benjamin
Brook, Faith
Brook, Lyndon
Brooks, Ray
Browne, Angela
Buchanan, Jack
Buckingham, John
Bull, John
Bull, Peter
Burden, Hugh
Burdon, Albert
Burgess, Guy
Burgess, Howard
Burman, Nancy
Burton, Richard
Bush, George
Cairncross, James,
Callaway, Cab
Callier, June
Callow, Simon
Callum, Jamie
Cameron, Audrey
Campbell, Alastair
Canaway, Bill
Cannan, Denis
Carson, John
Cartland, Barbara
Cartland, Robert

Case, Geoffrey
Casson, Lewis
Catling, Boyd
Cecil, Henry
Challis, John
Chamberlain, Neville
Chapman, Paul
Chatt, Barrie
Checkland, Michael
Chetwyn, Robert
Christie, Agatha
Christie, Julie
Christie, Madelaine
Churchill, Winston Spencer
Clarke, Jacqueline
Clarke, John
Clements, John
Clitheroe, Jimmy
Clyde, Gordon
Cochrane, Michael
Cole, Nat King
Cole, Nigel
Cole, Stephanie
Coleman, David
Collingwood, Charles
Collingwood, Tony
Compton, Denis
Conn, Stewart
Connolly, Billy
Conns, Emma
Cook, Peter
Corbett, Ronnie
Courtenay, Margaret
Courtenay, Tom
Coward, Noël

Cowdrey, Colin
Cox, Brian
Cranmer, Peter
Craven, Gemma
Cregan, David
Cribbons, Bernard
Cropper, Anna
Cross, Gerald
Crowther, Liz
Cruikshank, Andrew
Cummings, Ian
Currie, Finlay
Curtis, Ronnie
Curzon, Clifford
Dale, James
Dali, Salvador
Darrieux, Danielle
Davies, John
Davies, Sophia
Davies, Toby
Dawson, Anna
de Balzac, Honoré
de Keyser, David
Deakins, Leslie
Dearman, Glyn
Dee, Tim
Deller, Alfred
Dellor, Julie
Denham, Maurice
Dennis, Sandy
Derbyshire, Eileen
Devern, Kenny
Dews, Peter
Dexter, Bob
Dexter, Colin

Dexter, John
Dickson, Anne
Dight, Kenneth
Dimbleby, David
Din, Asif
Dobie, Alan
Dodd, Ken
Doel, Peter
Doepel, William Glen
Dollery, H.E. (Tom)
Donald, James
Donat, Robert
Donnellan, Phillip
Donnelly, Elaine
Donovan & Hayes
Dormer, Richard
Dotrice, Michele
Douglas, Colin
Dowbiggin, Kenneth
Drake, Francis
Drew, Bryan
Drinkwater, John
Drury, Gill
Dryden, Ellen
Dubuisson, Pauline
Dwyer, Hilary
Edgar, David
Edwards, Jimmy
Elgar, Edward
Eliot, T.S.
Elliot, Denholm
Ellison, Cary
Elman, Louis
Emery, Dick
Emery, Herbert
Esslin, Martin

Evans, Edith
Evans, James Roose
Evans, Lavinia
Evans, Lissa
Fairbanks Jnr, Douglas
Farmer, Derek
Farquhar, Malcolm
Farrow, Don
Feilbert, Ed
Ferns, Allen
Ferrier, Kathleen
Feydeau, Georges
Ffrangcon-Davies, Gwen
Finlay, Frank
Finney, Albert
Fisher-Dieskau, Dietrich
Fitzgerald, Ella
Fletcher, Jill
Fletcher, Ronald
Foote, Samuel
Ford Davies, Oliver
Fortesque, Frank H.
Foss, Freddie
Foster, Paul Hartley
Fox, Edward
Fox, William
Frame, Grazina
Francis, Dick
Frank, Anne
Fraser, Bill
Frayn, Michael
Freeman, Jane
French, Leslie
French, Stanley
Friebe, Mrs
Frisby, Terence

Fry, Christopher
Fyffe, Patrick
Gair, Bryan
Galie, Antonio
Galsworthy, John
Galton, Ray
Gambon, Michael
Gardner, Barrie
Garland, Judy
Garner, Rex
Garrick, David
Garrick, George
Garwood/Paul, Patricia
Gatti, Jack
Gatting, Mike
Gauld, Graham
Gaunt, Valerie
Gaunt, William
Gay, Canon George
Gee, Donald
Gee, Prunella
George, Ann
Gielgud, John
Gielgud, Val
Gilbert, James
Gill, Eric
Gill, John
Gilmore, Peter
Glanville, Brian
Glenister, Philip
Glover, David
Glover, Jon
Glover, Julian
Godwin, John
Godwin, Christopher
Gooderson, David

Gordon, Noelle
Gorham, Scott
Goudge, Elizabeth
Grace, Sally
Graham, Jill
Graham, John
Grant, Cary
Grant, Richard E.
Green, Mawby
Greenslade, Arthur
Greenwood, John
Greif, Stephen
Griffiths, Derek
Griffiths, Hugh
Grimaldi, Marion
Grimond, Jo
Grout, James
Grout, Philip
Guard, Philip
Guinness, Alec
Guy, Barry
Guyler, Derek
Haft, Lionel
Haggard, Stephen
Hale, Binnie
Hall, Anthony
Hall, David
Hall, Peter
Hall, Willis
Halliwell, Leslie
Hamilton, Scott
Hamilton, Victoria
Hammond, J.A.H.
Hammond, Kay
Hammond, Roger
Hampshire, Susan

Hancock, Tony
Hannah, John
Hannen, Nicholas
Hannington, Mr
Hanson, Harry
Hanson, John
Hardiman, Terrence
Hardwicke, Edward
Hardy, Laurence
Harper, Gerald
Harris, Mary
Harris, Richard
Harris, Vernon
Hartley, Robert
Harvey, Grizelda
Hassall, Christopher
Hassall, Eve
Hassall, Imogen
Hatt, Brian
Havel, Václav
Hawkins, Jack
Hawkins, Peter
Hayes, Patricia
Hazare, V.S.
Hazzard, Maurice
Heal, Joan
Healy, David
Heath, Victor
Helme, Kathleen
Hemer, Marjan
Henley, Drew
Henry, Paul
Henson, Jim
Henson, Leslie
Henson, Nicky
Hepton, Bernard

Her Majesty the Queen
Herlie, Eileen
Hill, Susan
Hine, John
Hird, Thora
Hitchcock, Alfred
Hitler, Adolf
Hoar, George
Hobbs, Carleton
Hoffman, Dustin
Hoffman, Mrs
Holboll, Christine & Finn
Holder, Roy
Hollies, Eric
Hollis, John
Holloway, Laurie
Holt, David
Honer, Christopher
Hooper, Ewan
Horne, Kenneth
Horst, Bernd
House, Gordon
Houseman, A.E.
Howard, Trevor
Howarth, Don
Howarth, Elgar
Howell, Mr & Mrs
Howell, Peter
Howerd, Frankie
HRH Duke of Edinburgh
HRH Princess Alexandra
HRH Princess Margaret
HRH the Queen Mother
Hudson, John
Hudson, Rock
Hudson, Tim

Layton, George
Le Bien-Aimé, Leopold
Le Carré, John
Lee, Peggy
Leesley, Geoffrey
Lefeaux, Charles
Leighton, Margaret
Lennon, John
Letts, Pauline
Levin, Bernard
Levy, Mervyn
Lewis, C.Day
Lewis, Rhoda
Lewis, Saunders
Liberace
Lidstone, Jill
Lindsay, Robert
Linney, Romulus
Livesey, Roger
Livings, Henry
Livingstone, Ken
Loach, Ken
Lockwood, Preston
Lockyer, Albert
Lockyer, Percy
Logan, George
Logue, Christopher
Longdon, Terence
Lowe, Arthur
Lowe, Erna
Lowther, Merlyn
Luckham, Cyril
Luke, Peter
Lumsdaine, David
Lund, Alan
Lynch, Joe

Lynn, Jonathan
MacArthur, Edith
Macdonald, Ian
Macdonald, Julian
Macdonald, Maxence
Macdonald, Stephen
Macdonell, A.G.
Mackay, Angus
Mackay, Mrs
Maclean, Donald
Macloughlin, Sean
Macnamara, Desmond
Maddison, Ronald
Maddock, Mrs
Maddock, Hayden
Madoc, Ruth
Mady, 'Joe'
Mahler, Gustave
Maloney, David
Maloney, Edwina
Mankad, Vinoo
Manning Wilson, Jo
Manning, Elizabeth
Mantle, Doreen
Marceau, Marcel
March, David
Margolyes, Miriam
Marinker, Peter
Marks, Alfred
Markwell, Rev. Don
Marshall, Anna Calder
Martell, Gillian
Martell, Philip
Martin, Gary
Martin, Tina
Martin, Vivienne

Martinus, Derek
Mason, Ronald
Massey, Anna
Matthews, Francis
Matthews, Geoffrey
Matthews, Jessie
Matthews, Stanley
Maxwell, Charles
May, Jack
May, Peter
May, Val
Mayall, Rik
McBain, Robert
McCowan, Alec
McEwan, Ian
McFarlane, Colin
McGoohan, Patrick
McGough, Roger
McKechnie, James
McKellen, Ian
McKern, Leo
McMurtry, Stan
McParland, Peter
Mellor, Cherith
Melly, Andree
Melly, George
Melville, Alan
Melvin, Murray
Menzies, Victor
Merchant, V.M.
Merton, Paul
Meyers, Eric
Michael (Fitt), Patricia
Middleton, Thomas
Midgely, Robin
Miles, Sally
Miller, Arthur

Miller, Jonathan
Miller, Mary
Miller, Max
Mills, John
Mills, Michael
Milner, Roger
Milton, Ernest
Minshull, Duncan
Misiewicz, George
Miss B
Mitchell, Bill
Mitchell, Norman
Mitchum, Robert
Moffatt, John
Mond, Karis
Montgomery, General Berna
Montgomery, Marion
Moore, Jonathan James
Moorey, Frank
Moray, Stella
More, Dudley
More, Julian
Morecambe & Wise
Moreton-Pritchard, Mrs
Morgan, Garfield
Morley, John
Morris, Capt. R.A.
Mortimer, John
Mouskouri, Nana
Mozart, Pere
Mozart, Wolfgang Amadeus
Muller, Robert
Muloch, D.M.
Murray, Ruby
Neill, A.S.
Neville, John
Newman, Sydney

Newsome, S.H.
Newton, Rev. Barrie
Nimmo, Derek
Nixon, President Richard
Noakes, John
Noel, Wendy
Norden, Dennis
Norman the Fan
Norman, Monty
O'Brien, Maureen
Ogilvy, Hon. Angus
O'Leary, Ursula
Olivier, Laurence
Orton, Joe
Osborne, John
Ost, Geoffrey
Oswald, Lee Harvey
O'Toole, Peter
Owen, Alun
Owen, Sion Tudor
Oz, Frank
Palin, Barry
Pape, Cecil
Parker, Charles
Parkinson, Robin
Parr, Kathleen
Parsons, Nicholas
Partington, Frank
Pasco, Richard
Pataudi, Nawab of
Pattinson, Alan
Paul, Jeremy
Pearce, Edith
Pearce, Richard
Pears, Peter
Pearson, Ian
Pendlebury, Frank

Perkins, Anthony
Perry, Clive
Perry, Morris
Pertwee, Jon
Peters, Barry
Peters, John
Peterson, Wolfgang
Pettingal, Frank
Philby, Kim
Phillips, Sian
Phoenix, Pat
Piaf, Edith
Pickles, Mabel
Pickles, Wilfred
Piffard, Frederic
Piggott, Lester
Pinching, Anthony
Pleasance, Angela
Powell, Ellis
Powell, Peter
Pratt, Mike
Pratt, Peter
Previn, André
Price, Jack
Prince, Hal
Pritchard, Tom
Proops, Greg
Prowse, Juliet
Pugh, David
Pugh, Robert
Punt, Norman
Quayle, Anthony
Queen Victoria
Queensbury, Anne
Quentin, Caroline
Quilley, Denis
Quitak, Oscar

Ramadin, Sonny  
Rantzen, Esther  
Rattle, Simon  
Ray, Ted  
Rees, John  
Reeve, Dermot  
Reindeer, Eddie  
Remick, Lee  
Reynolds, Dorothy  
Richards, Mary  
Richardson, Ian  
Richardson, Ralph  
Richins, Aubrey  
Rigby, Terence  
Rigg, Diana  
Rix, Brian  
Robeson, Paul  
Robinson, Geoffrey  
Robinson, Rony  
Rodenburg, Patsy  
Rodger, Struan  
Rodgers, Anton  
Rogers, Ginger  
Rolf, Michael  
Rosa, Carl  
Ross, Carmel  
Ross, Hector  
Rossiter, Len  
Rothnie, Alan  
Roubicek, George  
Routledge, Patricia  
Royale, Gillian  
Ruby, Thelma  
Rushton, Willie  
Russell, Craig  
Russell, Jane  
Russell, Ronald  

Ruxton, Buck  
Ryan, Nick  
Rye, John  
Ryton, Royce  
Sachs, Andrew  
Saklatvala, Wendy  
Salberg, Derek  
Sale, Richard  
Sandford, Patrick  
Sands, Leslie  
Sassoon, Siegfried  
Saunders & Gordon  
Saunders, James  
Scales, Prunella  
Schaffer, Peter  
Schell, Catherine  
Schiltz, Brontë  
Schiltz, Cory  
Schiltz, Keir  
Schlesinger, John  
Scofield, Paul  
Scott-Gilbert, Clement  
Scott Johnston, Alastair  
Scott, Dougray  
Scott, George C.  
Scott, Giles Gilbert  
Scott, Norman  
Seale, Nigel  
Seckington, Roger  
Selby, Tony  
Seyler, Athene  
Shakespeare, William  
Shale, Keri  
Shankley, Jeffrey  
Shaw, Miss  
Shaw, George Bernard  
Shaw, June

Shaw, Run Run
Shelley, Norman
Sheridan, Richard Brinsley
Shi
Shryane, Tony
Sickert, Walter
Siddons, Sarah
Sighele, Mietta
Sikorski, General
Silvera, Carmen
Simkins, Michael
Simpson, Alan
Simpson, Bill
Simpson, Michael
Simpson, Sonia
Sims, Joan
Sinatra, Frank
Sinden, Donald
Sircom, Malcolm
Slade, Julian
Slade, Peter
Smee, Derek
Smethurst, William
Smith, Maggie
Smith, R D
Smith, 'Tiger'
Smythe, Paul
Snow, Sophia
Snowdon, Canon George
Sobers, Garfield
Solomon
Solomon, Professor
Southwark, Bishop Roy
Spencer, Paul
Squire, William
Stalin, Joseph
Stanton, Barry

Starkey, Colin
Steele, David
Stephens (Fitzgerald), Sylvia
Stephens, Jane
Stephens, Penny
Stephens, Robert
Stephenson, Robert Louis
Stewart, James
Stilgoe, Richard
Stockwood, Bishop Mervyn
Stoll, David
Stone, Fred
Stoppard, Tom
Storey, David
Straker, Mark
Straughen, Duncan
Strauss, Johann
Streisand, Barbra
Sugden, Mollie
Sullivan, Hugh
Summers, Ann
Sykes, Eric
Sylvaine, Vernon
Symington, Alison
Talbot, Claude
Tamm, Mary
Tanner, Tony
Tasker, Billy
Tate, David
Tate, Richard
Tati, Jacques
Taylor, Don
Taylor, Edward
Taylor, Tim Brooke
Terry, Philip
Theobald, Peter
Thompson, Josiah

Thorndike, Sybil
Thorne, Angela
Thorne, Norman
Thornley, Paul
Thorpe, Danny
Thorpe, Jeremy
Tittensor, Elsie
Tobin, June
Todd, Richard
Tonge, Roger
Totellier, Paul
Totten, Malcolm
Treager, Lucy
Trifinov, Yuri
Trott, Albert
Troughton, Patrick
Trueman, Freddie
Tufts, Mr & Mrs
Turner, Bunty
Turner, David
Twose, Roger
Tynan, Kenneth
Valentine, Alf
Valla, David
Vallefo, Alfonso
Van, Stan
Vanelli, Luigi
Vaughan, Frankie
Verner, Tony
Vernon, Richard
Victor, Charles
Villiers, James
Vinivar, Michael
Volpis, Giovanni
Wakefield, Bishop Roger
Walbrook, Anton
Walker, Zena

Wall, Max
Wallace, Hazel Vincent
Wallis, Bill
Walters, Matthew
Walters, Sam
Walton, Jennie
Ward, Dorothy
Ward, Paddy
Warn, Ted
Warne, Jo
Warne, Shane
Warren, Marcia
Washbrook, Cyril
Watford, Gwen
Watson, Gary
Watson-Watt, Robert
Waugh, Evelyn
Wax, Ruby
Weatherill, Lord Bernard
Webb, Esmond
Webb-Peploe, Dr
Webster, Martyn C.
Wedgewood Benn, Anthony
Wedgewood Benn, Caroline
Weisner, Bill
Weldon, Fay
Wenham, Jane
Wesker, Arnold
West, Sam
West, Timothy
Westbury, Marjorie
Wetherall, Eric
White, Andrew
White, Carol
White, Rev. Gilbert
White, Tony
White, Willard

Whitefield, June
Whitehouse, Mary
Whitrow, Benjamin
Whitelock, Trafford
Wigglesworth, Mark
Wilde, Oscar
Williams, Alan Vaughan
Williams, Enyd
Williams, Kenneth
Willings, Neville
Wilmshurst, Rebecca
Wilson, John Fawcett
Wimbush, Mary
Wisdom, Norman
Wodehouse, P.G.
Wolfenden, Lord
Wolfit, Donald
Wood, John
Wood, Peggy Ann
Wood, Ray
Wood, Wee Georgie
Woodcock, Terry
Woodthorpe, Peter
Woodward, Edward
Woolley, 'Cotton'
Workman, Charles
Worth, Harry
Worth, Martin
Wortley, Richard
Wreford, Edgar
Wyatt, Peter
Wyldeck, Martin
Wynne, Ken
Wynne, Norman
Yorke, Erica
Young, Nick
Young, Robert